CHARLES BR

THE FREETHINKER'S

TEXT-BOOK

PART I.

MAN: WHENCE AND HOW?

RELIGION: WHAT AND WHY?

Elibron Classics
www.elibron.com

Elibron Classics series.

ISBN 1-4021-7191-9 (paperback)
ISBN 1-4021-2048-6 (hardcover)

This Elibron Classics Replica Edition is an unabridged facsimile of the edition published in 1893 by A. and H. Bradlaugh Bonner, London.

THE FREETHINKER'S TEXT-BOOK.

PART I.

MAN: WHENCE AND HOW?
RELIGION: WHAT AND WHY?

BY

CHARLES BRADLAUGH.

LONDON:
A. AND H. BRADLAUGH BONNER,
63 FLEET STREET, E.C.
1893.

PRICE 2s. 6d.

THE FREETHINKER'S TEXT-BOOK.

PART I.

MAN: WHENCE AND HOW?

OR,

REVEALED AND REAL SCIENCE IN CONFLICT.

BY CHARLES BRADLAUGH.

Is it true, as alleged by the Hebrew chronology, that about 6,000 years back from the present date one man (Adam) and one woman (Eve) were created, and that these were the first of the human family on earth, and that from them were descended the entire human race? The answer to this question touches the very root of the Christian religion. If Adam and Eve were not the first parents of the whole human race, then the gospel of Christianity is a false pretence. If Adam was not the first man, then his fall, by disobedience, in Eden's Garden, did not bring death and sin as heritage for all human kind. To re-quote the words of the pious and erudite Sir William Jones: "Either the first eleven chapters of Genesis, all due allowances being made for a figurative Eastern style, are true, or the whole fabric of our national religion is false." (Essay on the Gods of Greece, Italy, and India; "Asiatic Researches," vol. i., p. 225.) The task in these pages shall be to show that no portion of the Genesaic story of man's creation, fall, and disparsion on the earth can be regarded as historis

As it is sometimes disputed—by clergymen, Scripture-readers, and other persons unacquainted with the contents of the Bible—that any such limitation as 6,000 years is made to man's existence on earth, I shall first present the exact proof, by chapter and verse, of this allegation. In the orthodox chronologies used in the English schools and colleges the date of the creation of the world itself was fixed at about 4,004 years before the Christian era. First, I direct attention to the Bible account of man, as given in the Hebrew, Septuagint, and, so far as the Pentateuch is concerned, Samaritan versions. The credibility of these versions will be dealt with, after examining their several testimonies, before presenting the evidence offered by History, Ethnology, Anthropology, and Geology against the Bible.

Luke Burke, in the *Ethnological Journal*, page 17, prepared a "chronological arrangement of the Patriarchal ages, from the creation to the birth of Abraham, according to the Hebrew, Samaritan, and Septuagint versions of the Old Testament." To this are now added the chapters and verses from the ordinary orthodox version, to make the evidence complete at a glance:—

	Before Generation.			After Generation.			Total Ages.		
	Heb.	Sam.	Sep.	Heb.	Sam.	Sep.	Heb.	Sam.	Sep.
Adam (Gen. v. 3, 4, 5)	130	130	230	800	800	700	930	930	930
Seth (6, 7, 8)	105	105	205	807	807	707	912	912	912
Enos (9, 10, 11)	90	90	190	815	815	715	905	905	905
Cainan (12, 13, 14)	70	70	170	840	840	740	910	910	910
Mahalaleel (15, 16, 17)	65	65	165	830	830	730	895	895	895
Jared (18, 19, 20)	162	62	162	800	785	800	962	847	962
Enoch (21, 22, 23)	65	65	165	300	300	200	365	365	365
Methuselah (25, 26, 27)	187	67	167	782	653	802	969	720	969
Lamech (28, 30, 31)	182	53	188	595	600	565	777	653	753
Noah (32)	500	500	500						
Added century to Deluge (vii. 11)	100	100	100						
Date of Deluge ...	1656	1307	2242						

These totals show the exact period of the Noachian Deluge after the creation of Adam, and are exactly agreed with by Samuel Sharpe, in his "Translation of the Hebrew Scriptures," page 8. The generations after the Deluge are:—

	Before Generation.			After Generation.			Total Ages.		
	Heb.	Sam.	Sep.	Heb.	Sam.	Sep.	Heb.	Sam.	Sep.
Shem (Gen. xi. 10, 11)	2	2	2	500	500	500	600	600	600
Arphaxad (12, 13)	35	135	135	403	303	400	438	438	535
Cainan (omitted in the orthodox Genesis, but inserted in Luke iii. 36)			130			330			460
Salah (14, 15)	30	130	130	403	303	330	433	433	460
Eber (16, 17)	34	134	134	430	270	270	464	404	404
Peleg (18, 19)	30	130	130	209	109	209	239	239	339
Reu (20, 21)	32	132	132	207	107	207	239	239	339
Serug (22, 23)	30	130	130	200	100	200	230	230	330
Nahor (24, 25)	29	79	179	119	69	125	148	148	304
Terah (26, 32)	70	70	70	135	75	135	205	145	205
From alleged date of Deluge to birth of Abraham ...	292	942	1172						

Making, from the creation of Adam to the birth of Abraham, 1,948 years according to the authorised orthodox English version which follows the Hebrew, according to the Samaritan 2,249, and according to the Septuagint 3,414. That these versions contradict one another is no help to the defender of the Bible. They are his witnesses. Nor is it honest to teach the first version to children as truth, and then to fly for help, against grown men, to the longer chronologies in the Samaritan and Septuagint, when the falsity of the shorter chronology has been demonstrated. Yet this is precisely what has been done by many of the clergy, and notably by the Rev. Canon Rawlinson, Professor of Ancient History at Oxford, when, as mouthpiece of the Christian Evidence Society, he sought, in stumbling words, to explain away the chronological difficulties of Genesis. The learned and reverend professor says, on pages 8 and 9 of his lecture, delivered under the auspices of the Christian Evidence Society: "We possess the Pentateuch in three very ancient forms—in Hebrew, in the Greek version known as the Septuagint, and in Samaritan. Our English numbers represent those of the Hebrew text. The numbers of the Septuagint and the Samaritan version are different. Those of the Samaritan version extend the period between the Deluge and the birth of Abraham from the 292 years of the Hebrew text to 942 years—an addition of six centuries and a half—while those of the Septuagint, according to some copies, give 1,072 years as the interval, according to others 1,172 years, thus increasing the period between the Deluge and Abraham by a space of nearly eight, or nearly nine, centuries. Now, if the Greek, or even if the Samaritan, numbers are the right ones; if they represent, that is, the original text, it may be questioned whether anything more is wanted. It may be questioned whether a term of from six to eight centuries is not enough for the production of that state of things which we find existing in Babylonia and in Egypt when the light of history first dawns upon them, whether within that space might not have been produced such a state of civilisation, so much progress in art, such differences of physical type, and such diversities of language as appear to have existed at that period......If, however, the ultimate verdict of calm reason, and rigid scientific inquiry, should be against this view; if more time seem to be absolutely wanted for the development of settled government, of art, science, language, ethnical diversities, varieties of physical type, and the like, than even the enlarged chronology of the Septuagint allows, then I should not be afraid to grant that the original record of Scripture on this point may have been lost, and that, as it is certain that we cannot possess the actual chronological scheme of Moses in more than one of the three extant versions of his words which have come to us with almost equal authority, so it is quite possible that we may not possess his real scheme in any. Nothing in ancient MSS. is so liable to corruption from the mistakes of copyists as the numbers; the original mode of writing them appears, in all countries of which we have any knowledge, to have been by signs not very different from one another; the absence of any context determining in favour of one number rather than another, where the copy is blotted or faded, increases the chance of error; and thus it happens that in almost all ancient works the numbers are found to be deserving of very little reliance. Where they to any extent check one another, they are generally self-contradictory; where they do not, they are frequently in the highest degree improbable." That is, Professor Rawlinson really abandons the whole of the Bible chronologies, but lacks the candour to put his abandonment into plain language. If the reader thinks this impeachment of the Rev. Professor's candour harsh, he is referred to another controversial essay from the Professor's pen, entitled "Historical Illustrations of the Old Testament."

Dr. Kalisch, who rejects the Septuagint and Samaritan as "intentionally corrupt," gives the following chronological table on page 8 of his introduction to "Genesis :"—

A.M.	B.C.	Events and their computation according to years of the world.
	4160	Adam created.
130	4030	Seth born (Genesis v. 3).
235	3925	Enos born (v. 6 ; 130+105=235).
325	3835	Cainan born (v. 9 ; 235+90—325).
395	3765	Mahalaleel born (v. 12 ; 325+70=395).
460	3700	Jared born (v. 15 ; 395+65=460).
622	3538	Enoch born (v. 18 ; 460+162=622).
687	3473	Methuselah born (v. 21 ; 622+65=687).
874	3286	Lamech born (v. 25 ; 687+187=874).
1056	3104	Noah born (v. 28 ; 874+182=1056).
1556	2604	Shem born (v. 32 ; 1056+500=1556).
1656	2504	The Deluge began (vii. 11 ; 1056+600=1656).
1657	2503	The Deluge ceased (viii. 14).
1659	2501	Arphaxad born (xi. 10 ; two years after the Flood).
1694	2466	Salah born (xi. 12 ; 1659+35=1694).
1724	2436	Eber born (xi. 14 ; 1694+30=1724).
1758	2402	Peleg born (xi. 16 ; 1724+34=1758).
1788	2372	Reu born (xi. 18 ; 1758+30=1788).
1820	2340	Serug born (xi. 20 ; 1788+32=1820).
1850	2310	Nahor born (xi. 22 ; 1820+30=1850).
1879	2281	Terah born (xi. 24 ; 1850+29=1879).
1949	2211	Abraham born (xi. 26 ; 1879+70=1949).
1959	2201	Sarah born (xvii. 17 ; 1949+10=1959).
2024	2136	Abraham emigrated from Haran (xii. 4 ; 1949+75=2024).
2035	2125	Ishmael born (xvi. 16 ; 1949+86=2035).
2048	2112	Covenant and Circumcision of Abraham and Ishmael (xvii. 24 ; 1949+99=2048).
2049	2111	Isaac born (xxi. 5 ; 1949+100=2049).
2084	2076	Terah died (xi. 32 ; 1879+205=2084).
2086	2074	Sarah died (xxiii. 1 ; 1959+127=2086).
2089	2071	Isaac married Rebekah (xxv. 20 ; 2049+40=2089).
2109	2051	Jacob and Esau born (xxv. 26 ; 2049+60=2109).
2124	2036	Abraham died (xxv. 7 ; 1949+175=2124).
2149	2011	Esau married (xxvi. 34 ; 2109+40=2149).
2172	1988	Ishmael died (xxv. 17 ; 2035+137=2172).
2193	1966	Jacob married Leah and Rachel (2109+84=2193).
2200	1960	Joseph born (xxx. 25 ; 2193+7=2200).
2217	1943	Joseph sold into Egypt (xxxvii. 2 ; 2200+17=2217).
2229	1931	Isaac died (xxxv. 28 ; 2049+180=2229).
2230	1930	Joseph appt. Viceroy of Egypt (xli. 46 ; 2200+30=2230).
2239	1921	Jacob & family settled in Egypt (xlvii. 9 ; 2109+130=2239).
2256	1904	Jacob died (xlvii. 28 ; 2239+17=2256).
2310	1850	Joseph died (l. 22, 26 ; 2256+54=2310).
2669	1491	Exodus of the Israelites from Egypt (Exodus xii. 40 ; 2239+430=2669).

This statement shows practically the same date to the birth

of Abraham, and gives us 2,669 years from the creation of Adam to the Exodus. This takes the stay of the Israelites in Egypt at 430 years.

Bishop Colenso ("Pentateuch," part i., page 92) urges that, according to Exodus vi. 16—20, no more than 350 years, on the most extravagant supposition, can be accorded for the sojourn of the Israelites in Egypt from Jacob to the Exodus. He says:—

"Now, supposing that Kohath was only an *infant* when brought down by his father to Egypt with Jacob (Genesis xlvi. 11), and that he begat Amram at the very end of his life, when 133 years old, and that Amram, in like manner, begat Moses when he was 137 years old, still these two numbers added to 80 years, the age of Moses at the time of the Exodus (Exodus vii. 7), would only amount to 350 years, instead of 430.

"It is stated that 'Amram took him Jochebed, his father's sister'—Kohath's sister, and, therefore, Levi's daughter—'to wife.' And we read, Numbers xxvi. 59: 'The name of Amram's wife was Jochebed, *the daughter of Levi, whom (her mother) bare to him in Egypt.*'

"Now, Levi was one year older than Judah, and was, therefore, 43 years old when he went down with Jacob into Egypt, and he was 137 years old when he died.

"Joseph was 30 years old when he 'stood before Pharaoh,' as governor of the land of Egypt (Genesis xli. 46), and from that time nine years elapsed (seven of plenty, and two of famine) before Jacob came down to Egypt. At that time, therefore, Joseph was 39 years old. But Judah was about three years older than Joseph; for Judah was born in the *fourth* year of Jacob's marriage (Genesis xxix. 35), and Joseph in the *seventh* (Genesis xxx. 24—26, xxxi. 41). Hence Judah was 42 years old when Jacob went down to Egypt.

"Levi, therefore, must have lived, according to the story, 94 years in Egypt. Making here again the extreme supposition of his begetting Jochebed in the last year of his life, she may have been an infant 94 years after the migration of Jacob and his sons into Egypt. Hence it follows that, if the sojourn in Egypt was 430 years, Moses, who was 80 years old at the time of the Exodus, must have been born 350 years after the migration into Egypt, when his mother, even on the above extravagant supposition, must have been at the very least 256 years old."

If the arguments of Bishop Colenso are accepted as valid, the effect will be to still further abridge the Biblical Chronology.

If the twentieth verse of Acts xiii. be true, the period of the Judges was 450 years, to which must be added 40 years for the wilderness wandering, making, in all, 490 years, to the time of Samuel. It is evident, however, that if 1 Kings vi. 1 be accurate, that then Paul or the author of the Acts blundered, as 476 years from the Exodus are precisely fixed to the date of Solomon's accession to the throne, which would then be 3,145 years from the date of the creation of Adam. From Solomon to the Captivity is as follows:—

1.	Solomon	(1 Kings	xi. 42)	reigned	40	years.
2.	Rehoboam	,,	xiv. 21	,,	17	,,
3.	Abijam	,,	xv. 2	,,	3	,,
4.	Asa	,,	xv. 10	,,	41	,,
5.	Jehoshaphat	,,	xxii. 42	,,	25	,,
6.	Jehoram	(2 Kings	viii. 17)	,,	8	,,
7.	Ahaziah	,,	viii. 26	,,	1	,,
8.	Athaliah	,,	xi. 3	,,	6	,,
9.	Jehoash	,,	xii. 1	,,	40	,,
10.	Amaziah	,,	xiv. 2	,,	29	,,
11.	Azarrah or Uzziah.	,,	xv. 2		52	,,
12.	Jotham	,,	xv. 33	,,	16	,,
13.	Ahaz	,,	xvi. 2	,,	16	,,
14.	Hezekiah	,,	xviii. 2	,,	29	,,
15.	Manasseh	,,	xxi. 1	,,	55	,,
16.	Amon	,,	xxi. 19	,,	2	,,
17.	Josiah	,,	xxii. 1	,,	31	,,
18.	Jehoahaz	,,	xxiii. 31	,,	3	months.
19.	Jehoiakim	,,	xxiii. 36	,,	11	years.
20.	Jehoiakin	,,	xxiv. 8	,,	3	months.
21.	Zedekiah	,,	xxiv. 18	,,	11	years.

Making, from Solomon to the Babylonian Captivity, 433 years, 6 months, or 3,578 years and 6 months, from the creation of Adam, or, as the marginal chronology of the Bible makes it, 590 years B.C. The Captivity lasts until the accession of Cyrus, King of Persia (Ezra i. 1), who, according to Ctésias, was born B.C. 599, being the son of Cambyses, and who conquered Babylon B.C. 536, or, according to the Bible chronology, exactly 3,622 years after the creation of Adam. We have now historic dates, and need no further texts; this makes about 4,158 years to the date fixed for the alleged birth of Jesus—viz., 1,875 years ago, or 6,033 from the creation of Adam to the present date. Doubtless these figures are incorrect; but up to the Captivity they are carefully taken from the English Bible, on which all blame of error must rest.

Thus it is clear that the Hebrew text and our English Bible teach in express terms that the first man (Adam) was created less than 6,000 years ago. Dr. John Lightfoote, in his "Harmony of the Old Testament," published 238 years since, had no doubt on this point, and three years earlier had expressly calculated "5,572 years since the creation." For almost 200 years more nine out of every ten clergymen of the Established Church taught the doctrine that man had only existed about 6,000 years. The last forty years have made a great change; but even to-day—while many, very many, clergymen of the Church of England know that the statement is not true—they are reticent; they keep the knowledge to themselves, and give no help to clear away the falsehood.

In truth, our orthodox version and the Hebrew Bible alike agree in making the whole universe older than the first man only by five clear days of twenty-four hours each. Many efforts have been made to evade this conclusion, but these efforts have been all miserably weak. Dr. Harold Browne, Bishop of Ely, in the Speaker's Commentary, that latest effort of pious weakness, tries the reconciliation of truth, as shown by science, and falsehood, as told by Genesis. The learned Bishop, aided by the counsel of other prelates and divines, says: "Countless ages *may have elapsed* between what is recorded in verse 1, and what is stated in verse 2," of the first chapter of Genesis. Yes, but they *may not have* elapsed. Supposition against supposition, and the Genesis story is not improved. In fact, there is no break in the Hebrew narrative for these "countless ages" between verses 1 and 2. The state of the earth, as given in verse 2, is evidently intended as its earliest state, immediately consequent on the creation; and no one dreamed of this non-natural reading of the text until the demands of science for a longer chronology became too imperative to be resisted. And even if, without any warranty, and only to evade the objection, you inserted the "countless ages" between those verses, it would not improve the story. You would equally need more "countless ages" between other verses to account for the time required for later changes in the earth's surface. Changes which have gone slowly on since the heat had so radiated off as to permit seas and lands to mark the earth. Long changes after these, vast in their lengths, and yet brief measured by the preceding enormous periods. Ages during which the flora of the world crept out, struggled into growth, and flourished in its richest luxuriance. Ages still, during which life-conditions gradually grow. Ages more, while the fauna of the earth were evolved from the merest sign of animal vitality to the huge monster, life-devouring, who roamed the forests or traversed the seas. And there are no verses in the Bible story between which you, by any pious hocus-pocus, or philosophic legerdemain, can insert these "countless ages."

An able writer in the orthodox *British Quarterly Review*, vol. xliii., pp. 120, 121, Egyptian Antiquities, says: "We are accustomed to suppose that we possess an undoubted canon of ancient chronology in the Holy Scriptures; but perhaps next to a clear acquaintance with what the sacred volume does undoubtedly contain, the most valuable knowledge is of what it does not. In the Universal History, above one hundred and twenty dates are given for the creation, most of them made out by persons who regard with most sincere reverence, and derive their arguments from, the sacred writings. The first of these places that event B.C. 6984; the last, 3616; differing by the moderate amount of more than three thousand years. The period of the Deluge is fixed with no greater uniformity. The Septuagint gives B.C. 3246; the Hebrew text (according to Usher) 2348. We shall add, as more connected with our subject, the extreme dates assigned to the Exodus, which is fixed by Josephus (according to Dr. Hales, nearly the same with Des Vignolles) B.C. 1648; by the English Bible (on the authority of Usher) 1491; by the vulgar Jewish chronology 1312. Our concern, however, is merely to show that the best Scripture chronology affords ample space for the highest antiquity which the great Egyptian kingdom can fairly claim. For the period between the Flood and the first connection of sacred history with Egypt we have four distinct authorities—the version of the LXX.; the Samaritan; Josephus, who professes to have adhered faithfully to the sacred volume; and the Hebrew chronology adopted in our Bibles. None of these, strictly speaking, agree, but the three first concur in assigning a much longer period between the Deluge and the birth of Abraham—the LXX. 1070 years the Hebrew only 292. If it should be urged that the translators of the Septuagint, environed on all sides by Egyptian antiquities, and standing in awe of Alexandrian learning, endeavoured to conform their national annals to the more extended chronological system; and that Josephus, either influenced by their authority, or actuated by the same motives, may have adopted the same views, yet the ancient Samaritan text still remains, an unexceptionable witness to the high antiquity of the more extended period. In fact, we are, perhaps, wasting our time in contesting this point, as we may fairly consider the Hebrew chronology of this period almost exploded."

Ordinarily, it is possible to check the chronological periods of nations by monuments, or later, by writings. Unfortunately for the student, neither the good nor bad qualities of the Jews provoked notice in any extant writer, outside their own nation, prior to 400 B.C. Much as has been done to discover evidences in Egypt, neither papyrus, pyramid, nor obelisk say aught about the 600,000 armed Jews who left the land of the Nile, laden with spoil, under Moses. Prior to David, all the Jewish chronology is the purest conjecture, and the conjecture is embarrassed by the mass of fabrication to be cleared away before real investigation becomes possible. The conquest of Judea, under Rehoboam (1 Kings xiv. 25), by Shiskak, or Sheshonk, King of Egypt, is the earliest ascertained and vouched period of contact between the Jews and other nations. Much stir has been made by the clergy, now and then, upon finding partial corroboration of names or dates occurring subsequently to Solomon, in the Old Testament. No necessity arises for the unbeliever to challenge the muster-roll of Jewish kings, from Solomon to the Captivity. There are blunders of names and dates, and facts, and unhistoric statements interwoven, but the list of kings is, probably, in the main part, correct; many of the reigns are probably fairly stated, and some of the wars referred to in Kings and Chronicles, doubtless, took place. What is needed to be remembered is, that verifying the names of some kings after Solomon does not prove the exactness of the chronology prior to David. Bunsen, so lauded as a Christian, says: "As regards the Jewish computation of time, the study of Scripture had long convinced me that there is, in the Old Testament, no connected chronology prior to Solomon." ("Egypt's Place in Universal History," vol. i., Preface.) And again (vol. iii., page 247) he affirms that the Hebrew tradition of earlier times "contains no chronology whatever."

G. R. Gliddon, in his archæological introduction to the tenth chapter of Genesis ("Types of Mankind," p. 627), gives five periods as specially marking changes in the Hebrew text, viz.:—

"First period, B.C.—'In most ancient times, the Hebrew text was corrupt;' and the Codex (says, 'Fragmentary Books') used by the Greek interpreters of the Old Testament, at Alexandria, was undoubtedly Hebrew, but a copy not sufficiently emended. Even Buxtorf is obliged to admit—'Judaos a tempore Esdra negligentiores fuisse circa textum Hebraum, et non curiosos circa lectionem veram'—the Jews in the time of Esdra neglected the Hebrew text, and were indifferent as to the true reading. The numerals were expressed by *letters;* the five *final* letters (ך ם ן ף ץ) had not then been invented; the words were still *undivided.*

"Second period, A.D. down to 500.—The texts were more corrupt in the time of Philo and Josephus. Neither in their day, nor in that of Origen, third century, were the *Commandments* (Exod. xx., 3—17) divided into ten, in the manner they are now. In Philo the division is *quinary*, after the fashion of Pythagoreans. About the latter epoch commences the Talmudic *Mishna;* and, in the fifth century, the *Gemara;* each of which books proves the increase of textual errors. So do the writings of the Fathers during all this age—notably St. Jerome; while the apostolic books demonstrate that the *Greek* differed, more or less, from the Hebrew original.

"Third period, A.D. 500 to 1000.—Aside from the later and less reliable Fathers, two Hebraical works establish that no expurgations of error had been made in the text, viz., the *Robboth*, after A.D. 700, and the *Pirke Eliezar*, after 800. About the sixth century, the Rabbis of Tiberias commenced the 'Masora;' a labour that would not have been undertaken but for the reasons above given, and the wretched condition of the text in their time; as proved by the multitudes of *Keri velo Kethib* (the read, but not the written) or *Kethib velo Keri* (the written, but not the read).

"Fourth period, A.D. 1000 to 1450.—The Jewish schools of Babylonia seek refuge in Spain about 1040; between which era and 1240 flourished the four great Rabbis. Their works prove not merely different readings, but absolute mistakes in copies of the text. Things then existing in manuscripts of the Old Testament now exist no longer, and *vice versâ;* while the 'Masora' itself, already in confusion inextricable, only rendered matters worse. It is of this age alone that we possess those Hebrew manuscripts by us called *ancient*—not one 900 years old!

"Fifth period, A.D. 1450 to 1750.—Printing invented; the art was first applied to *Psalms* in the year 1477; and to the whole Hebrew text in 1488; that entire edition, save one-third of a copy, being immediately by Neapolitan Jews. But here, upon editions now following each other with rapid succession, the Rabbis begin their restorations and their lamentations. Continental scholars now set to work upon *Hebrew* in earnest, without professorships; whilst, in England, King James's version is a splendid record of Professors without Hebraism, during the years 1603—1611. Fifty years later, Walton redeems the shame of Oxford; and yet, one hundred years later still, Kennicott himself chronicles: 'the reader will be *pleased* to observe, that as the study of the Hebrew language has only been *reviving* during the last one hundred years:' to end which sentence logically, we ourselves consider that there could be no 'revival' where, in 1600, there was scarcely a *beginning;* and, *ergo*, that the Doctor's attestation must refer to incipient efforts, in his century commencing, to resuscitate the *Hebrew tongue* after twenty centuries of burial."

The Rev. Dr. Porter, Professor of Biblical Criticism at Belfast, says: "Scientific teaching does not come within the province of revelation......Revelation does not give a scientific cosmology. That lies outside its province...... Revelation does not touch on geology; but it leaves room for the fullest development of the successive strata of the earth's crust, even though it could be proven that millions of years had been occupied in their formation. 'In the beginning God created the heavens and the earth.' No date is given." ("Science and Revelation: a Review of Tyndall, Huxley, Darwin, and Herbert Spencer," p. 35.) Professor Porter says no date is given. What meaning then does he attach to Exodus xx. 11, "In six days the Lord made heaven and earth, and all that in them is?" Genesis i. says that man was made on the sixth day. Where is there the fullest, or any room, for the "millions of years?" That Genesis does not give us a scientific cosmology is clear. But as it does give a cosmology full of details, as what kind of a cosmology would the learned Professor describe it? No date given. What, then, but dates are the added ages of Adam and his successors? Professor Porter says that "the historical record of creation seems to have a scientific basis, as if the writer, by a divine prescience, had anticipated the results of modern research." But if Genesis is God's revealed word, the writer would record actual facts not *fore-known*, but then known to God. But which part of Genesis i. has a scientific basis? Is it the creation of the firmament to divide the upper and lower waters? The firmament in which windows existed at the time of the deluge. Windows which God opened to let the waters down (vii. 11). A firmament in which God set the sun, moon, and stars. Has this firmament a scientific basis? Is there any scientific basis for the existence of seas on the earth's surface before the creation of the sun and moon? Where is the scientific basis for the earth bringing forth grass, herb, with seed, and fruit tree yielding fruit before there was yet sun to encourage and ripen vegetation?

But says Mr. Goodwin, in the famous "Essays and Reviews:" "It can scarcely be said that this chapter is not intended in part to teach and convey at least some physical truth, and taking its words in their plain sense it manifestly gives a view of the universe adverse to that of modern science. It represents the sky as a watery vault, in which the sun, moon, and stars are set. But the discordance of this description with facts does not appear to have been so palpable to the minds of the seventeenth century as it is to us. The mobility of the earth was a proposition startling not only to faith but to the senses. The difficulty involved in this belief having been successfully got over, other discrepancies dwindled in importance. The brilliant progress of astronomical science subdued the minds of men; the controversy between faith and knowledge gradually fell to slumber: the story of Galileo and the Inquisition became a school commonplace, the doctrine of the earth's mobility found its way into children's catechisms, and the limited views of the nature of the universe indicated in the Old Testament ceased to be felt as religious difficulties.

"The school books of the present day, while they teach the child that the earth moves, yet assure him that it is a little less than six thousand years old, and that it was made in six days. On the other hand, geologists of all religious creeds are agreed that the earth has existed for an immense series of years—to be counted by millions rather than by thousands; and that indubitably more than six days elapsed from its first creation to the appearance of man upon its surface."

Luke Burke, *Ethnological Journal* (p. 14), annihilates alike the chronologies of the Hebrew and other versions: "All careful investigation of the facts of natural history, will, he argues, "prove that there are determinate relations between the period of puberty and the total duration of life. In birds, the multiple is sometimes very high; in fishes, still more so; but in the mammalia generally, and especially in man, it will be found that the highest possible duration of life is seven times the age of finished puberty. Few human beings, especially in civilised life, ever reach this period; none, we believe, have ever exceeded it. The age of puberty greatly varies in different races of men, and the natural duration of their lives is longer or shorter accordingly. As, at the present day, all civilised and partially civilised nations are composed of an amalgamation of various primitive races, we find the period of puberty varying even in individuals in the same family; but still the law will be found equally applicable, in these individual cases, as when applied to the whole races of men. Now the chronology before us is at utter variance with this great law of nature. Mahalaleel begot Jared at the age of sixty-five, and lived 895 years afterwards, more than thirteen times the period of complete puberty. This is the same as saying that a person at the present day, whose natural life would extend to 80, 90, or 100 years, might be a man, and have children, at the age of six, seven, or eight years. In the postdiluvian period we have even a higher multiple than this. Sala begot Eber in his thirtieth year, and yet lived 433 years; more than fourteen times the age at which his son was born. Several other patriarchs have ages assigned to them ten, eleven, twelve, and thirteen times longer than the period of perfect puberty. Ought we not, then, to require that numbers which so directly contradict the known laws of nature, should come to us supported by evidence of a most unquestionable character? And what evidence is there in favour of these numbers, except that they, at present, form part of a treatise generally supposed to be of divine revelation? All genuine history is entirely opposed to the admission of such extreme longevity. Neither in ancient or modern times is there one authenticated instance of any human being having reached the age of 200 years, to say nothing of such enormous periods as 969 years." The believer is, by Luke Burke, placed in a worse strait than ever, for if the ages of the patriarchs are shortened to reasonable periods, another reduction will have to be made from the already too short chronology of 6000 years.

Dr. Kalisch, in his introduction to his "Commentary on Genesis" (p. 2) thus states the chronological difficulty:—"According to chronological computations based on the Old Testament, the earth, as a part of the universe, was created B.C. 4160, or about six thousand years hence. Even the larger chronologies of the Septuagint, Hales and others fix this date not further back than between seven and eight thousand years. But the researches of the natural sciences, especially geology, lead to widely different conclusions; they prove an antiquity of the earth of such vastness, that our imagination fails to conceive, and our numbers are almost unable to express it." And from the verified discoveries of Geologists he thus states the facts warranting the conclusions hostile to Genesis (p. 8): "The old red sandstone includes the fossils of zoophytes, conchifera, some tribes of fish, some traces of land plants; perhaps, also, the first perfect birds, some of small, others of gigantic size; and the foot-prints of those batrachians which have attracted the most zealous attention, and to which we shall later have occasion to allude in a very curious connection. But both in the new red sandstone, and still more in the subsequent oolitic strata, occur in great abundance the huge lizard-like animals, of extraordinary size, power, and armature; the voracious *ichthyosaurus*, of the length of a young whale, fitted both to live in the water and to breathe the atmosphere; of the general form of a fish, to which, however, were added the teeth and breast-bone of a lizard, the paddles of the whale tribes, the beak of a porpoise, and the teeth of a crocodile; the *plesiosaurus*, of similar bulk and equal rapacity, with a turtle-like body and paddles, a serpent neck, terminating in a formidable lizard head, and most extensively preying upon the finny tribes; further the *megalosaurus*, an enormous lizard, forty-five feet long, a carnivorous land creature; the *pterodactylus*, or *flying saurian*, a lizard with bat-like wings; *crocodiles*, some of which were herbivorous, as, for instance the iguanodon, reaching the amazing length of a hundred feet, or twenty times the size of the iguana of the Ganges, its present representative. Strongly, indeed, do these monstrous and terrible forms remind us of those strange creatures of fancy popular in ancient times and in the middle ages, the winged dragons and griffins, the gorgons, hydras, and chimeras; their huge jaws threatened with fearful teeth; their necks were almost equal in length to half that of the entire body of the boa-constrictor; they had enormous, mail-like impenetrable bodies, and terrific claws; and all darted upon their prey with irresistible vehemence. The oolitic beds contain, further, the remains of about twelve hundred other astonishing species and forms, the first specimens of insects, and about fifty plants.

"But only in deposits above the chalk formations do we meet with mammifers. About four thousand forms, all different from the present species, are found in the tertiary strata; some of them are most remarkable for their size and form, as the palæotherium, the ponderous dinotherium, with the bent tusks in its lower jaw, and many other thick-skinned animals *(pachydermata)*, like the hippopotamus and rhinoceros. Some of the species of elephants were of enormous magnitude; the mastodon, with his tusks projecting from both upper and under jaw, reached the height of twelve feet; the mammoth, the megatherium, with claw-armed toes more than two feet in length, and the megalonyx, were of gigantic proportions and iron-like organisation; we find, further, the bear, the horse, and the dog, seals, dolphins, and whales; massive oxen, camels, and other ruminants; the majestic Irish elk, with its broad plank-like horns; and even several felinæ or carnivora, and traces of monkeys (quadrumana): till at last the older creatures became extinct, and were succeeded by the existing occupants of the land and the water.

"Now, we ask, if the earth was created within six days, how, and for what conceivable purpose were these numberless, and often huge and appalling, forms of being, *exhibiting every stage of growth*, embedded in the different strata of the earth? We believe there is scarcely any man preposterous or blasphemous enough to impute to the Deity such planless and reckless destruction in the midst of his majestic acts of creation. Many species, and even many distinct genera, have thus entirely disappeared; they are no longer represented on the earth. Generally, even the organic beings of one formation exist no more in the next higher group of rocks.

Do not these circumstances compel us to suppose an indefinite antiquity of the earth's crust? Many have certainly ascribed all those destructions to the influence of the Noachian Deluge; they advance, that first submarine volcanoes, by ejecting their molten masses through different successive explosions, formed the massive layers below; and that then the land-floods, sweeping away the islands and continents, with their organic creations, produced the second or higher formations. But, besides failing entirely to account for the production of the tertiary strata, this theory introduces the agency of *fire* also in the Deluge, of which we read nothing in the Biblical record; it assumes a series of volcanic eruptions of such rapid succession as could only be caused by a miraculous intervention, of which nothing is mentioned; and it starts from the objectionable supposition, that strata, demonstrably separated from each other by immense periods, were formed within the space of a few months. For the facts, that very different fossils are found in the same formations, and that the same petrified species occur in different layers, cannot overthrow the general theory of slow successive stratification; the vast climatic changes which our planet has undergone, and the great variety in the internal structure of the various organic beings, are sufficient, together with other obvious circumstances, to account for these facts."

The argument from the fauna of the world is thus admirably summarised (p. 10): "Hitherto about 3,000 genera of fossil plants have been discovered in the beds of the earth; and this number is considered insignificant, compared with the probable real amount of vegetable life in the preceding conditions of our earth. Although some plants are less capable of resisting the action of water than others, and some are even totally decomposed if for some time immersed in that element, especially the simplest forms of flowerless (cryptogamic) vegetation; the proportion of the different families found in a fossil state leads, on the whole, to a safe conclusion with regard to the primitive flora of the earth; the plants which have been preserved are in themselves amply sufficient to serve as a basis for such conclusions. Now those vegetable remains—it is remarkable to observe—have more or less a *tropical* character, which is a sure proof of the higher temperature of our planet in former epochs; they show a surprising uniformity of plants over the whole earth, with but very little local difference, though they bear a different character in different periods, and consist, in each individual epoch, of but a very limited number of species, which are as many witnesses for the former more equal distribution of heat on the earth. It is most interesting to observe that every later period shows the *prevalence* of a more perfect genus of plants than the preceding one, so that the different epochs might be almost described by their predominant vegetation. The profoundest botanists have arrived at the conclusion that the earlier flora contained the same principal classes and families, though not all the minor species, of the present flora, but that the former possessed the simpler forms of vegetation in the highest possible perfection, whilst the latter only produced the higher and more complicated genera, *so that a successive and ascending development in the vegetable kingdom, which is still in endless progress, is manifest from the remotest periods; that the number of species has during the succeeding geological epochs steadily increased.*"

Dr. Kalisch, it is true, as a pious Theist, looks for some "supernatural cause" to account for all this; but, adopting the words of John Stuart Mill, the reader will be asked throughout this volume to understand by Nature "the aggregate of all powers and properties," "the sum of all phenomena, together with the causes which produce them, including not only all that happens, but all that is capable of happening." We here do no injustice to Dr. Kalisch in continuing to state his summary:—

"It appears that many of the plants are 'hereditary' through various geological epochs, and that certain species have traversed many thousands, perhaps hundreds of thousands, of years, in spite of the local and successive revolutions on the earth's surface. For submarine forests in several parts of the globe consist of trees which still cover the neighbouring continents, though the *animals* found in the same localities in a petrified state have ceased to exist, and many species of plants are not found in regions where they might thrive perfectly well, according to their structure, or to the present condition of the globe. They seem to be absent from such countries only because they did not exist there in former geological epochs. Ligneous plants existed formerly in many parts where the soil is at present not capable of producing them; the middle tertiary rocks present a mixture of exotic forms now peculiar to warm climates, together with others equally characteristic of temperate countries; the conditions of the earth and the atmosphere must, therefore, before the creation of man, have been more favourable, especially as regards the proportions of temperature. Sometimes islands and their neighbouring continents, at present insurmountably separated from them by the sea, contain the same species. It appears, therefore, that at a primitive epoch they joined together, and formed one continent. Summits of mountains very distant from each other offer the same species, and the same aquatic plants are found in very different countries; the transport which, in the present condition of the earth, is perfectly impossible, must have taken place at an anterior period. For, on the other hand, frequently countries very near each other offer very little resemblance, and often great difference, in their vegetable productions. All the plants did not proceed from one limited portion of the earth, for instance, the Paradise (as Linné main'ained); nor did they gradually spread from the Polar region southwards, in proportion as the globe cooled down (as Buffon asserted); nor did they first appear on the mountains, and thence extend to the lower parts of the earth as the waters receded; but the different species are aboriginal in numerous different regions, although these centres of creation cannot be indicated with certainty, in consequence of the vast changes which the surface of our planet has suffered. The production of the various species was probably progressive, ascending from the less to the more perfect plants; and every species has most likely commenced with a multiplicity of individuals. It is certain, both from ocular evidence and from inductive conclusions, that most of the animals discovered as fossils in the strata of the earth have died in a natural course on the spot where they enjoyed life. Now, as many of them are creatures of long life, and many reached an age far beyond the time now allotted to the creatures of the earth, it is impossible that they should have accomplished the full circle of their existence in a few days." And yet Exodus says: "In six days the Lord made heaven and earth, the sea, and all that in them is, and rested the seventh day."

The answer by defenders of the Bible is, that the word day used in the first chapter of Genesis, does not mean a period of twenty-four hours, but really represents an indefinite period of time, so that each day stands for a vast age. Dr. Kalisch says, p. 43: "In order to gain scope for the geological epochs, many critics have proposed to interpret the term 'day' יום

as a *period*, or an *indefinite epoch*. But this is equally inadmissible. In our plain, purely historical, and calm narrative, this metaphorical use of the word is rendered impossible by the repeated phrase, 'And evening was, and morning was,' both forming one natural day. Nor can the circumstance, that on the fourth day only the sun was created to divide the day from the night, prove that the word 'day' denotes, in the preceding verses at least, an unlimited time; if it means *day* in one verse, it has the same signification throughout the whole narrative, or we should be obliged to take the day of Sabbath likewise as 'a period of rest.'

"The word ביום 'in the day,' is sometimes used as a conjunction of time, in the general sense of *when;* but יום alone is in no prosaical part of the Scriptures applied in a similar signification.

"Hugh Miller once believed that the 'six days' were ordinary days of twenty-four hours each, and that the latest of the geologic ages was separated by a great chaotic gap from our own. But at that time his labours, as a practical geologist, had been restricted to the palaeozoic and Secondary Rocks; later, however, he directed his attention to the more recent formations also, and studied their peculiar organisms; and his unavoidable conclusions were, that 'for many ages ere man was ushered into being, not a few of his humble contemporaries of the fields and woods enjoyed life in their present haunts, and that for thousands of years anterior to even *their* appearance, many of the existing molluscs lived in our seas;' and, consequently, he *since then accepted the six days of creation as vastly extended periods*, perhaps 'millenniums of centuries.' We have introduced this opinion as a type of many similar views. It is perfectly unworthy of Biblical science, constantly to modify the interpretation according to the successive and varying results of other sciences, just as if the Biblical text were composed of indefinite and vague hieroglyphics, capable of every possible construction; it is a most objectionable practice to make the Hebrew narrative subservient to all the fluctuating movements of heterogeneous studies, which are based upon premises perfectly different from the Biblical notions, and which, as systematic sciences, neither derive support from them, nor require their authority and sanction. Scientific honesty and manly firmness prescribe a far different conduct, at once more simple and more decided. Let the true and authentis senses of the Biblical narrative be ascertained with all possible assistance of learning and philological knowledge: independently of this, let the other sciences bearing on the subject be zealously studied; and then let the results of both researches be compared, without bias and without anxious timidity. If careful geological studies press upon the mind the conviction, that even the present epoch commenced many ages before the appearance of man on earth; let it be admitted, without unavailing reluctance, that the Mosaic record speaks of a creation in six days, which is irreconcilable with those investigations, since it is philologically impossible to understand the word 'day' in this section in any other sense but a period of twenty-four hours.

"The device that the days denote epochs, is not only arbitrary, but ineffective; for the six 'epochs' of the Mosaic creation correspond in no manner with the gradual formation of the cosmos. More than one attempt has, however, been made to show this agreement; but they crumble into nothing at the slightest touch."

Before dealing with the authorised English and accepted Hebrew versions, I will present a few conflicting opinions on the value of the Samaritan and Septuagint texts, each of which I shall then take leave to dismiss as utterly valueless in the present inquiry.

The Reverend Dr. Irons, in dealing with the popular theory on the Bible, thus refers to the Septuagint version: "The striking fact, however, which confronts us is, that in the first century the Greek translation of the Old Testament was more in use among the *Jews* also than the Hebrew; and that this had possibly been the case for generations. It seemed even to be thought by some, that this Greek version fixed the sense of some passages of the Hebrew. Anyhow, this version lies in the pathway of the investigation, which evidently cannot be avoided, between the first century and the times of the old Prophets ending with Malachi. What is this Greek version, or 'Septuagint,' as it is called? Who made it? From what originals was it made? And when? And why? And what is its present state?

"It must be owned that we have here come to a somewhat difficult parenthesis—if it may be so termed—in our examination of the Old Testament of the Hebrew Prophets. The story used to be believed, however, that 270 years, or more, before Christ, some seventy Jews were employed by

Ptolemy Philadelphus to translate 'the Jewish Scripture' into Greek: Josephus says, that it was the Pentateuch. An account of the miraculous agreement of these seventy translators, working in seventy separate cells, is found in the letter of Aristæus to Philocrates. It has been respectfully referred to by Christian writers of such high name as Tertullian and St. Jerome (and our esteem for their sagacity cannot thereby be increased). Bellarmine, however, no more rejects it than did Josephus and Philo. It has been thought not unworthy of being 'done into English,' by Dr. Donne, Dean of St. Paul's. But this letter cannot be regarded in the nineteenth century (any more than the Talmud was) as 'historical.' We may pass it.

"Strictly speaking, no one knows who made the Septuagint. No one knows from what copies of the originals any parts of that version were made. It appears to be a growth of at least two generations; and, as might be expected, the style is not the same throughout. Has it, then, no authority at all, it may be asked? Was it not used by the Jews themselves, and bequeathed in fact by the Jewish Church to the Christian? Yes. That, such as it is, is the ground of its authority, for all purposes of practical edification. But this does not assist our investigation as to the literary condition of the Hebrew Scriptures at that time; unless we are to assume that the Septuagint corrects the sense of ancient Hebrew manuscripts now lost? Few would think, however, of thus setting aside the present Hebrew text in favour of the Septuagint, in those places where they now differ. The state of the text of the Septuagint itself is far, also, from satisfactory; and if it is to be set up as the principal authority for the Old Testament, the historical continuity of the originally Written Word is given up." ("The Bible and its Interpreters," p. 25).

He also says, "Versions in other tongues will not settle the Hebrew text," and that "the character which is used in the Hebrew Bible is thought by most learned men to be not the character used by Moses or the prophets."

It used to be pretended that the Septuagint version was made by seventy-two persons, shut up in the Island of Pharos, under Ptolemy Philadelphus; but as Hartwell Horne (vol. ii., pt. 1, cap. 5, sect. 1 § 2) admits that "the majority of the learned in our own time are fully agreed in considering the story as fictitious," there is no necessity for further comment. Justin Martyr, a pious Christian, improved the story by shutting up each translator in a separate cell, where each executed a distinct version, making the whole of their work agree word for word. Epiphanius, another pious Christian, in the fourth century, finding this story too much for his credulity, reduced the cells to thirty-six, and shut up the translators two and two.

The case in favour of the Septuagint is perhaps put most forcibly by a writer in the *Quarterly Review*, vol. xxiii., p. 321, which is here reproduced, that the reader may have both statements before him. The business of this work is not to occupy itself with the Septuagint, but rather to demolish the Hebrew record, which limits man's origin to one pair, and brings that pair into being less than 6,000 years from the present date:—

"According to all historical evidence, to the united testimony both of Jews and Christians, and the full belief of all competent judges, the Septuagint version, as it was carefully made for the use of Jews who spoke the Greek language, was, from its first formation, generally received by them, and publicly read in their synagogues, as a true, faithful, and accurate version of Scripture. Scaliger says that it was read in the synagogues through the whole of Asia, Greece, and Egypt. '*All persons*,' says Walton, '*agree in this*, that it was used, especially among the Hellenistic Jews, *ab ultima antiquitate*, both in public and in private, whence R. Azarias assures us that the interpretation of the Greeks was confirmed by the whole assembly of the Israelites.' The inspired Evangelists and Apostles often quoted from the Septuagint; this fact alone, if every other testimony were wanting, proves incontestably not only that they believed and knew it to represent Scripture faithfully, but also that it was familiarly used and received by the Jews as Scripture at that time.

"As to the assertion that our present Septuagint is not substantially the same with that originally designated by that name, it is borne down by such overwhelming proofs to the contrary, that it is perfectly astonishing how anyone could dare to make it. The general historical evidence of its identity may probably of itself be deemed sufficient; but this evidence applies with much greater force in the case of the Septuagint than in that of the works of any ancient author, from its having been publicly read as Scripture in many ancient churches, and therefore guarded with the most scrupulous care, the most sacred reverence. Nor is this all. The Apostles and the Evangelists undoubtedly quoted in many passages from different parts of the Septuagint; and the very passages which they quoted from the version as it existed in their day, remain in that version as it exists in ours. Again, many of the ancient Fathers, whose works have come down to us, have written commentaries on different books of Scripture, which they read according to the Septuagint; for instance, Augustin on the Psalms, Cyril on Isaiah, with many others; and any person comparing their commentaries with the text we now possess, must immediately perceive that it is substantially the same with that which they illustrated. Many of the early Fathers again have made direct quotations from the Septuagint, which appear in our present copies of that version; some have even incidentally remarked on passages in it, to which there are none corresponding in the Hebrew, and *vice versâ;* and the very same discrepancies which are noted by them are found to the present day."

Having thus given a very orthodox and one-sided plea for the Septuagint, it may be well to add one more reverend if not orthodox witness against it. The Rev. R. G. Browne, Vicar of Alnwick ("Mosaic Cosmogony," page 108), says:—"To think of the Septuagint version as an inspired or as a Divinely-preferred work is a perpetuation of the folly of Aristæus, and an erection of a superstructure of puerile conceits upon a fable and an imposition. It was, as in every translation, a merely human operation, bearing in its history and in its texture an endless tissue of human error and human inconsistency. We can never come to a true notion of God's ancient, and that his only genuine, word from the Septuagint version."

Luke Burke, in the *Ethnological Journal* (p. 23), says: "It must be evident, at the first glance, that the Samaritan chronology, taken as a whole, cannot be the original one. It is as inconsistent with itself as it is untrue to nature. At a time when it makes the duration of life from 230 to 438 years, it makes the generations twice as long as when men lived eight or nine hundred years. Nothing so absurd as this could ever have been drawn up by the writer of the book of Genesis, nor by any person, as an original draft. Such contradictions could only have arisen from the perversions and patchwork of subsequent times." Samuel Sharpe says, in his "Hebrew Nation and its Literature" (p. 265): "The Samaritan Pentateuch is not a version into a language different from the Hebrew. It is merely a transcript, which professes to make no change in the words, but to give the Hebrew words in the Samaritan letters. The Hebrew square characters declare their high antiquity by their pictorial form, and by their close resemblance to the Egyptian hieroglyphics, from which they seem to be copied. Moreover, it is very improbable that the Jews, reverencing their books so highly, should have ever ventured to change the characters in which they were first written. The Samaritans, on the other hand now (perhaps B.C. 480), for the first time building a temple, and proposing to have a priesthood of the line of Aaron, would naturally wish for a transcript of the sacred books, if the characters in which the Jews had written them were not so well understood on Mount Gerizim. The argument that the Samaritan letters are the oldest, because no Hebrew monuments can now be shown that are as old as the Samaritan letters on the Maccabee coins, is of little weight, because those coins are too modern to have much bearing in the controversy. Upon the whole it seems probable that the Hebrew Scriptures were in Jerusalem always written in square characters, much the same as those in which we now read them, and that the Samaritan transcript of the Pentateuch was made from the square characters soon after the time of Nehemiah. The Samaritan Bible does not reach beyond the Pentateuch, which circumstance alone should settle that it is a transcript, having no claim to be the original. The Samaritans seem never to have taken the trouble to complete the task."

The Rev. Dr. Wall, who was more favourable to the Samaritan codex, says ("Grounds for a Revision of the Authorised Version," p. 607): "The Samaritan Pentateuch was brought under notice and referred to by a series of Christian writers, extending from Eusebius, in the beginning of the fourth century, to Georgius Syncellus, about the end of the eighth; after which it was lost sight of in Christendom till the year 1631, when Father Morin, of the Oratory in Paris, published an account of two copies then recently brought from the East, which were purchased, one of them at Constantinople, by M. de Sancy, the French Ambassador there, and afterwards Archbishop of St. Maloes; and the other at Damascus, by Pietro della Valle, a Roman knight."

Noticing that Benjamin is written in "pure Hebrew" in the Samaritan Pentateuch, and in the orthodox Hebrew version only appears in "its Chaldaic corruption," Dr. Wall argues that: "It would appear, as far as a valid inference can be drawn from a single example, that, as the Samaritan characters approach nearer than the Jewish ones to the oldest known shapes of the Hebrew letters, so likewise, in the few instances in which the termination of corresponding words in the two editions differ, the Samaritan endings are those of greater antiquity."

The best that can be said for the Samaritan Pentateuch on the orthodox side is given in "Horne's Introduction" (part 1, chap. i., sect. 2); but as this admits a space "upwards of 1000 years," during which there is no trace of this Samaritan version, its evidence is not very valuable. There are two versions of this Samaritan Pentateuch, one being in Arabic, the other in Aramæn. It must not be supposed that the MSS. of these versions go anywhere near the date given by Mr. Sharpe, of 408 years B.C. The Darghestan roll of the Pentateuch is claimed by Mr. Forsyth, Q.C., to be the most ancient MS. of the Old Testament, and this dates only to A.D. 580, even if that date be conceded. This would leave a blank of centuries in which there is no record. Many critics would put the Darghestan roll as considerably more modern. Bishop Colenso commences part 4 of the Pentateuch with an essay on the Samaritan text, for which he fixes as a highly probable date, an epoch more modern by 200 to 250 years than that above stated by Mr. Sharpe.

But it is not simply a question of versions; the genuineness and authenticity of the whole text is challenged. Spinoza considered it "clear as the noonday light" that Moses was not the author of any part of the Pentateuch; and urges, that which to-day nearly all competent Biblicists admit, viz., that nothing is known as to when, where, or by whom the Book of Genesis was penned, or by whom it was preserved ("Tractatus Theologico-Politicus," caps. vii., viii., and ix.). He declares that many blemishes have crept into the Hebrew text itself, and that even the most ancient Jewish writers have animadverted on various doubtful readings and on several imperfect and truncated passages. He also urges that our Hebrew canon rests upon the decision of the Pharisees of the second Temple, who, on grounds to us unknown, selected the Books we have from amongst a great number, and that their decision was far from unanimous; one book (Ezekiel) becoming the Word of God, through the support given to it by Neghunja, the son of Hiskias; and another (Ecclesiastes) narrowly escaping suppression, because objected to by certain learned persons referred to in the Talmud, by Rabbi Jehuda, surnamed Rabi ("Tractatus Sabbathi," cap. ii., fol. 30, p. 2). These persons, he says, also desired to suppress the Book of Proverbs. Rabbi Jacob ben Chajim admits in his "Introduction to the Rabbinical Bible" (sec. 5) that "Some of the later great sages of blessed memory" taught that "during the Babylonish captivity, when the sacred books were lost and scattered about, and those wise men who were skilled in the Scriptures were dead, the men of the great synagogue found different readings in the sacred books ; and in every place where they met with a doubtful or perplexing case, they wrote down a word in the text, but did not put the vowels to it, or wrote in the margin and left it out in the text, not being sure what they found." And yet this is pretended to be God's infallible message to human kind. The same writer (sec. 10) quotes Ephodi as authority for a statement that Ezra, and the scribes who followed him, made the Keri and Kethiv (*i.e.*, various readings of words read but not written, and written but not read), "in every passage in which they met with some obliterations and confusion, not being sure what the precise meaning was." The word Ephodi is made of the initials of a phrase-signature used by Isaac Ha-Levi, a writer against Christianity about 470 years ago. Jacob ben Chajim (sec. 11) declares himself surprised that so holy a man as Rabbi Kimchi (who wrote at the end of the twelfth and the beginning of the thirteenth centuries) should say that "It appears that these marginal and textual readings originated because the sacred books were lost and scattered about during the Babylonian captivity, and the sages who were skilled in the Scriptures were dead."

In 1820, Mr. Whittaker, of St. John's College, Cambridge, writing then to defend the authorised version against Mr. Bellamy, says : "There are many passages, particularly in the Old Testament, of such acknowledged difficulty, that learned men never did, and perhaps never will, agree about them." And yet reverend men without hesitation circulate these as God's message to his creatures.

It is surprising, in the face of the researches of the most erudite Biblicists, that any educated men should maintain that the original Hebrew text of God's revelation to mankind has been preserved by the Jewish Rabbis uncorrupted, and without loss or variation of a single letter or word. And why do they speak of the original Hebrew in which

Moses wrote? It can hardly be pretended that the Deity selected the Hebrew for its flexibility and capacity for expressing his meaning. On the contrary, the Greek far excels the Hebrew as a written tongue. Nor is the Hebrew the most ancient written language. The construction of the various Hebrew roots affords reason to the contrary, and it is absolutely certain that the whole of the vowel-points (which in many cases entirely change the meaning of the text) are of comparatively modern date, say, from the second to the fifth century of the present era—probably not earlier than A.D. 450. The present square-letter form of Hebrew, and the twenty-two letter alphabet, are also of limited antiquity. The Hebrew Scriptures are neither the most ancient nor the most perfect of Scriptures. That the Hebrew text of Genesis has been corrupted there can be no doubt whatever; and that the authorised translation, circulated broadcast by the Bible Society as God's Word, is imperfect is admitted by the Church sanction to the revision now going on. Luke Burke, referring to the comparative merits of the Samaritan, Hebrew, and Septuagint versions, says: "The Jew naturally prefers the reading which exists in his own version, the Samaritan contends for the superiority of his copy, and the generality of Christians prefer of course the Septuagint [this refers to the first few centuries of our era]. Each party accuses the other of wilful corruption of the text, and some at least of these accusations must be true" (*Ethnological Journal*, p. 19). Dr. Wall speaks of the "blemishes in the existing condition of the Hebrew text," some of which he attributes to fraud, and others to gross ignorance ("Grounds for Revision of the Hebrew Bible," pp. 102 and 545); and it is declared by competent critics that the Hebrew text, even after the Masoretic correction and purification, was "deficient, imperfect, interpolated, and full of errors." Before the Christian era there were no divisions between words of the Hebrew text, and the five final letters were not invented. From then till A.D. 1000 the texts of the various codices were not only in a most corrupt and unreliable state, but nearly all the early fathers were unable to read the Hebrew character. The English translation (authorised version) is wretchedly imperfect. Errors abound in it, and some of them are of a most laughable description. On this account great calls have been made for the new translation, which is now in the course of manufacture, and also for a new edition of the Hebrew, which no one is competent to undertake; but neither a new translation nor a new Hebrew text will remove the difficulties developed during the last fifty years. Science has rendered the objections to the narrative insurmountable. The pretended revelation must in the end succumb before the scientific advocates it so long impeded.

Spinoza, treating of the true method of interpreting Scripture, says: "The first great 'difficulty' connected with our method arises from the consummate knowledge of the Hebrew tongue which its due application implies. But whence is this now to be obtained? The ancient masters of the Hebrew tongue have left nothing to posterity on the elements and principles of the language; we, at all events, have little or nothing of theirs—no dictionary, no grammar, no syntax. The Hebrew nation has lost all that it ever had of the elegances and ornaments of life (nor is this wonderful after such long ages of depression, disaster, and persecution), and has preserved nothing but a few fragments of its language and its literature. Then the meaning of many nouns and verbs which are met with in the Bible is either entirely unknown or is a subject of dispute. With all this, when we apply ourselves to study the syntax of this language, a matter of much moment, and seek to discover the idioms and modes of expression peculiar to the Hebrew people, we find that time, the consumer, has blotted them almost all from the memory of man. We shall, therefore, not be able, as we would wish, to determine the precise meaning of every passage which the common uses of the language would permit, and we shall come upon many sentences which, although expressed in words extremely well-known, are nevertheless of meaning most obscure, and are sometimes incomprehensible. To these difficulties must be added those which arise from the constitution and nature of the language itself, which occasion so many ambiguities that it is impossible to find such a method as shall assuredly teach us how to investigate the true sense of all the expressions of Scripture." After pointing out that doubt and obscurity result from the use of one letter in lieu of another, from the various meanings attaching to conjunctions and adverbs, and from the imperfections of the verb, Spinoza adds: "Besides the three causes of obscurity now noted in the Hebrew language, there yet remain to be mentioned two others, each of much more moment than all the rest. The first of these is that the Hebrew has no vowels; the second that it is without spaces between the words and sentences, and has no accents to indicate the proper pronunciation; and although these two deficiencies—viz., the vowels and sigr of accentuation, are wont to be supplied by points, it is impossible that we should acquiesce in the sufficiency of these, inasmuch as they are the invention and resource of men of these later times, whose authority can have no weight with us. The ancient Hebrews wrote without points (*i.e.*, without vowels and accents), as appears from the most ample testimony. The moderns supplied vowel-points and accents, as it seemed good to them that the Bible should be interpreted; wherefore they are to be regarded as mere interpretations of yesterday, and deserve no greater faith, as they have no higher authority, than the lucubrations of ordinary commentators" ("Tractatus Theologico-Politicus," cap. vii., p. 156). Gesenius admits that the ancient translators of the Hebrew, "evidently often translated by conjecture only" ("Hebrew Lexicon," by Leo, p. 17).

The learned Irenæus gives us a statement on the Hebrew, which shows either that he was utterly ignorant on the subject, or that since his time (A.D. 160) the language has entirely changed. He says ("Against Heresies," book 2, cap. xxiv., sec. 2): "For these ancient, original, and generally called sacred letters of the Hebrews, are ten in number (but they are written by means of fifteen), the last letter being joined to the first. And thus they write some of these letters according to their natural sequence, just as we do, but others in a reverse direction, from the right hand towards the left, thus tracing the letters backwards."

Bishop Colenso believes that he succeeds in identifying the work of at least four several authors in the Book of Genesis, and these he describes as 1st Elohist, 2nd Elohist (that is, two writers who respectively use the word Elohim אלהים ALEIM for God); 1st Jehovist, 2nd Jehovist (two writers who respectively use the word Jehovah יהוה IEUE for God); and Deuteronomist. Elohist No. 2 is supposed by the Bishop not to be a different writer from the 1st Jehovist, but to represent an earlier stage of the Jehovist's literary activity. In a synoptical table in Part V. of the Pentateuch the Bishop presents the results of the critical analysis of the Book of Genesis, and apportions the 1,533 verses of the Book of Genesis as follows: To the 1st Elohist, 336 verses; to the 2nd, 106 verses; to the 1st Jehovist, 1,028 verses; to the 2nd, 24 verses; and to the

Deuteronomist, 39 verses. The word Deuteronomist is used by Dr. Colenso for the later editor of the Pentateuch, and is fixed at about the time of King Josiah. These points are none of them material to the case to be made out in this volume, and are only given to show that modern Biblical criticism utterly rejects the notion of the Hebrew Pentateuch as the work of one pen.

The question of disputed authorship is not confined to the problem as to who wrote the first Book, or the first five Books, but extends to the whole Bible. Spinoza says ("Tractatus Theologico-Politicus," p. 158; Latin edition, cap. vii., sec. 58): "Of the authors—or, if you please, writers—of many of the Books, we either know almost nothing, or we entertain grave doubts as to the correctness with which the several Books are ascribed to the parties whose names they bear. Then we neither know upon what occasion, nor at what time, those Books were indited, the writers of which are unknown to us. Further, we know nothing of the hands into which the Books fell; nor of the codices which have furnished such a variety of readings, nor whether perchance there were not many other variations in other copies."

Peyrere followed Spinoza, and said: "God suffered the autographs to perish, and only very imperfect copies to come down to us" (De Wette, vol. i., dio. 1, sec. 84). In the Apocryphal Book of Esdras, it is distinctly stated that in consequence of the "law being burnt" (Esdras, cap. xiv., v. 31), Esdras took five rapid writers, and shut himself up forty days, so that they might "write all that had been done in the world since the beginning;" and it is alleged that these, having "understanding given them by the highest," wrote in forty days 204 books of things, "which they knew not." Eusebius, after speaking of the wonderful unanimity of the translators of the Septuagint, who, as before noticed, were alleged to have been shut up in seventy-two separate cells, and without intercourse with each other, to have made the whole translation in just the same words and letters, quoted from Irenæus. "Neither was it anything extraordinary that God should have done this, who, indeed, in the captivity under Nebuchadnezzar, *when their Scripture had been destroyed*, and the Jews returned to their country after seventy years, in the time of Artaxerxes, King of the Persians, *inspired Esdras, the priest of the tribe of Levi, to compose anew all the discourses of the ancient prophets, and to restore to the people the laws given them by Moses.*" ("Ecclesiastical History," book 5, cap. viii., Cruse's translation, p. 171.)

Bishop Colenso says: "It is quite possible—and, indeed, so far as our present inquiries have gone, highly probable—that Moses may be a historical character, that is to say, it is probable that legendary stories, connected with his name, of some remarkable movement in former days, may have existed among the Hebrew tribes, and these legends may have formed the foundation of the narrative. But this is merely conjectural. The result of our inquiries, as far as we have proceeded, is that such a narrative as that contained in the Pentateuch could not have been written in the age of Moses, or for some time afterwards."

Sharp says of Genesis ("Historic Notes on the Old and New Testaments," Moxon, 1854, p. 6): "We have no account of when this first of the Hebrew Books was written, or by whom. It has been called one of the Books of Moses, and some small part of it may have been written by that great law-giver, and leader of the Israelites. But it is the work of various authors and of various ages."

Michel Nicolas says ("Etudes Critiques sur la Bible, Ancien Testament," p. 2), quoting as his authorities Esdras, Irenæus, Jerome, and Augustine, "that there was a tradition generally received amongst the Israelites, that Esdras has been the restorer of the Mosaic writings, which had suffered great damage at the destruction of the Jewish kingdom, and which writings, according to some, had even been totally destroyed......St. Jerome held it indifferent to regard the Pentateuch as the work of Moses, or as retouched and put in order by Ezra." Nicolas adds that, although the Protestants have more firmly insisted on Moses as the author of the five Books than have their Catholic brethren, yet it is amongst the Protestants that the first doubts were raised amongst the Christian public as to the authorship.

Kurtz ("Colenso," part iv., p. 15), writing to prove that the whole Pentateuch as at present existing is from the hand of Moses, at last admits that the results of his examination have convinced him that several authors have taken part in the composition of the Pentateuch. Ewald, who commenced by asserting one author for Genesis, now admits that more than one hand may be traced in the Book. Delitzch, while contending for Moses, admits other authors, and the employment of pre-existing documents. Spinoza distinctly declares that the original writings of Moses [if they ever existed] are no longer extant, and that the present Books of the Old Testament are a selection from a greater number finally put together, and approved by a Council of Pharisees, so that it depended on the votes of certain Rabbis whether or no a particular Hebrew Book was or was not God's revelation to his people. It is quite certain that, if Moses wrote the Pentateuch, he did not write it in the square-letter Hebrew, which is comparatively a modern language, and which did not exist in his time. It is not contended that any other language was used by Moses, and there is no pretence for carrying modern Hebrew, or any proof in favour of carrying ancient Hebrew, as a language with written characters to such a period as that assigned to Moses. It is hardly possible that any work so voluminous as the Pentateuch could have been graven on stone in hieroglyph, and carried about on the Levites' shoulders in the ark, yet this is the only depository assigned to the Mosaic Books.

De Wette says: "Without doubt, it [the ancient Hebrew] originated in the land [of Canaan], or was still further developed therein after the Hebrew and other Canaanitish people had migrated thither from the mother country." (De Wette on the "Old Testament," part ii., secs. 30 and 35.) And he regards Hebrew, Arabic, and Aramean as branches from a common stem. In what language, then, is Moses to be supposed to have written? Some of the Talmudists taught that the ancient Hebrew language became entirely extinct during the captivity. Genesis itself does not speak of writing amongst the patriarchs; on the contrary, remarkable events were chronicled by the help of heaps of stones, trees, altars, &c., which were named after the events. The first allegation of writing is on the tables of stone; but surely this, if written, was not in Hebrew characters. The Hebrews had been slaves to the Egyptians, and might have gathered from them some of the hieroglyph lore of that age; but surely nothing more can be claimed for the ignorant slaves than was in use amongst their educated masters. De Wette says ("Book of Moses," sec. 163): "The opinion that Moses composed these Books is not only opposed by all the signs of a later date, which occur in the Book itself, but also by the entire analogy of the history of Hebrew literature and language."

The conclusions founded on the foregoing statements are very clear and simple.

1. The Bible alleges that man has existed on this earth not more than 6,000 years, and that all humankind are descended from one pair.

2. There is no corroboration to the Bible story, either in the character of its chronology or the coherence of its narrative.

3. The Bible itself is an unvouched and untrustworthy witness, its real authorship unknown, and with the additional disadvantage that authors have been claimed for parts of the Hebrew Bible who cannot by possibility have penned a word of it.

As some aid to modern divines in estimating the value of the Bible history, I quote the words of an early Father of the Church—Origen, who flourished in the third century; the "pious" Origen, the "illustrious" Origen, the "devout" Origen, for these and a score of like prefixes are given to him by good Christians. The extract is from "De Principiis," book 4, cap. i, sec. 16:—

"For who that has understanding will suppose that the first, and second, and third day, and the evening and the morning, existed without a sun, and moon, and stars? and that the first day was, as it were, also without a sky? And who is so foolish as to suppose that God, after the manner of a husbandman, planted a paradise in Eden, towards the east, and placed in it a tree of life, visible and palpable, so that one tasting of the fruit by the bodily teeth obtained life? and, again, that one was a partaker of good and evil by masticating what was taken from the tree? And if God is said to walk in the paradise in the evening, and Adam to hide himself under a tree, I do not suppose that any one doubts that these things figuratively indicate certain mysteries, the history having taken place in appearance, and not literally. Cain also, when going forth from the presence of God, certainly appears to thoughtful men as likely to lead the reader to inquire what is the presence of God, and what is the meaning of going out from him. And what need is there to say more, since those who are not altogether blind can collect countless instances of a similar kind recorded as having occurred, but which did not literally take place? Nay, the Gospels themselves are filled with the same kind of narratives—*e.g.*, the Devil leading Jesus up into a high mountain, in order to show him from thence the kingdoms of the whole world, and the glory of them. For who is there among those who do not read such accounts carelessly that would not condemn those who think that with the eye of the body—which requires a lofty height, in order that the parts lying [immediately] under and adjacent may be seen—the kingdoms of the Persians, and Scythians, and Indians, and Parthians, were beheld, and the manner in which their princes are glorified among men? And the attentive reader may notice in the Gospels innumerable other passages like these, so that he will be convinced that in the histories that are literally recorded, circumstances that did not occur are inserted."

That which the pious, illustrious, and devout Origen wrote more than 1,600 years ago is repeated by a living Bishop of the Church of England, who says (Colenso on "Pentateuch," part 4, cap. xi.) :—

"The statements in Genesis i., if regarded as statements of historical matter-of-fact, are directly at variance with some of the plainest facts of natural science, as they are now brought home, by the extension of education, to every village—almost, we might say, to every cottage—in the land. It is idle for any minister of religion to attempt to disguise this palpable discordance. To do so is only to put a stumbling-block in the way of the young—at all events, of those of the next generation—who, well-instructed themselves in these things, and having their eyes open to the real facts of the case, may be expected either to despise such a teacher as ignorant, or to suspect him as dishonest, and, in either case, would be very little likely to attach much weight to his instructions in things of highest moment."

In part 2, cap. iii, page 186, the same writer says :—

"It should be noticed that the Books of the Pentateuch are never ascribed to Moses in the inscriptions of Hebrew manuscripts, or in printed copies of the Hebrew Bible. Nor are they styled the 'Books of Moses' in the Septuagint or Vulgate, but only in our modern translations, after the example of many eminent Fathers of the Church, who, with the exception of Jerome, and, perhaps, Origen, were, one and all of them, very little acquainted with the Hebrew language, and still less with its criticism.

"The Jews do not speak of the first, second, &c., Book of Moses, but designate each Book by the first word which occurs in it in Hebrew, except that for Numbers they employ במדבר 'In the wilderness,' which word occurs in the first verse, and is probably chosen as more expressive than the first word ויהבר 'And he said,' which was used in the days of Jerome."

The Rev. Dr. Rowland Williams, in his "Rational Godliness," page 294, says: "The Scriptural writers, after all, were men, and the condition of mankind is imperfection. They spake of old; but all old times represent, as it were, the childhood of the human race, and therefore had childish things, which we must put away." And yet it is this collection of childish things, bound in one volume, and labelled "The Holy Bible," which is to be taught to-day to little children in our schools. If, by the admission of so high an authority, grown men are to put away the Bible as unfit for the knowledge of the present age, why should the clergy of the same Church persist in forcing the very Book on our schools as part of the every-day instruction of our boys and girls?

Having dealt with the case presented by the Bible, we now turn to the sciences of ethnology, anthropology, and geology, to see what aid they can give us in our inquiry.

"Ethnology," says Luke Burke (*Ethnological Journal*, page 1), "is a science which investigates the mental and physical differences of mankind, and the organic laws upon which they depend; and which seeks to deduce from these investigations principles for human guidance in all the important relations of social existence. Ethnology divides itself into two principal departments, the scientific and the historic. Under the former is comprised everything connected with the natural history of man, and the fundamental laws of living organisms; under the latter, every fact in civil history which has any important bearing, directly or indirectly, upon the question of races."

Anthropology was defined by my friend, the late Dr. James Hunt, as "the science of the whole nature of man." Mr. C. S. Wake says ("Aim and Scope of Anthropology," *Anthropological Journal*, July, 1870, pages 3 and 4):—"Mr. Bendyshe defines anthropology as that which 'deals with all phenomena exhibited by collective man, and by him alone, which are capable of being reduced to law;' while Dr. Broca declares it to be 'that science which has for its object the study of the human group, considered in its *ensemble*, in its details, and in its relations to the rest of nature.' Anthropology has relation chiefly to mankind *as a whole*, and is concerned with individual man only so far as he forms part of that whole. Of course, as Dr. Broca observes, 'a collection of individuals cannot be studied in its *ensemble*, if we do not commence with the study of the individual type which forms the unit of the number.' The latter study, however, has more especial reference to the *differences* which characterise man when compared with other natural objects; the identification of these differences resulting in the determinate idea of 'man' in his individual aspect. Anthropology, on the other hand, has rather to do with *resemblances*—its general aim being the generalisation of the phenomena which are displayed by mankind as a whole, so as to discover the laws of human being, in relation to its continued activity—past, present, and future—as well as, if possible, to define the nature of that being itself. When 'man,' as distinguished from other organic existences, has been clearly defined, the idea thus obtained requires to be extended, so as to embrace all those who answer to the definition. We have here the starting point of anthropology."

Here it is now proposed to show—by the aid of the sciences of Ethnology and Anthropology—the diversity existing of human type; and—by the aid of History and Anthropology—it is proposed to demonstrate:—first, that these diverse types of mankind can be traced back to a date prior to the Noachian deluge; and, next, by the additional aid of geology, it is intended to prove man's existence on earth long prior to the alleged creation of Adam.

"One feature," says Agassiz ("Types of Mankind," page 58), "in the physical history of mankind is the natural relations between the different types of man and the animals and plants inhabiting the same regions. The sketch here presented is intended to show, as far as it is possible in a mere outline delineation, that *the boundaries, within which the different natural combinations of animals are known to be circumscribed upon the surface of our earth, coincide with the natural range of distinct types of man.* Such natural combinations of animals circumscribed within definite boundaries are called *faunæ*, whatever be their home—land, sea, or river. Among the animals which compose the fauna of a country we find types belonging exclusively there, and not occurring elsewhere; such are, for example, the ornithorhynchus of New Holland, the sloths of America, the hippopotamus of Africa, and the walruses of the Arctics: others, which have only a small number of representatives beyond the fauna which they specially characterise, as, for instance, the marsupials of New Holland, of which America has a few species, such as the opossum; and, again, others which have a wider range, such as the bears—of which there are distinct species in Europe, Asia, or America—or the mice and bats, which are to be found all over the world, except in the Arctics. That fauna will, therefore, be most easily characterised which possesses the largest number of distinct types, proper to itself, and of which the other animals have little analogy with those of neighbouring regions, as, for example, the fauna of New Holland.

"The inhabitants of fresh water furnish also excellent characters for the circumscription of faunæ. The fishes, and other fluviatile animals from the larger hydrographic basins, differ no less from each other than the mammalia, the birds, the reptiles, and the insects of the countries which these rivers water. Nevertheless, some authors have attempted to separate the fresh-water animals from those of the land and sea, and to establish distinct divisions for them, under the name of fluviatile faunæ. But the inhabitants of the rivers and lakes are too intimately connected with those of their shores to allow of a rigorous distinction of this kind. Rivers never establish a separation between terrestrial faunæ. For the same reason, the faunæ of the inland seas cannot be completely isolated from the terrestrial ones, and we shall see hereafter that the animals of southern Europe are not bound by the Mediterranean, but are found on the southern shore of that sea, as far as the Atlas. We shall, therefore, distinguish our zoological regions according to the combination of species which they enclose, rather than according to the element in which we find them.

"If the grand divisions of the animal kingdom are primordial and independent of climate, this is not the case with regard to the ultimate local circumscription of species: these are, on the contrary, intimately connected with the conditions of temperature, soil, and vegetation. A remarkable instance of this distribution of animals with reference to climate may be observed in the Arctic fauna, which contains a great number of species common to the three continents converging towards the North Pole, and which presents a striking uniformity, when compared with the diversity of the temperate and tropical faunæ of those same continents.

"The Arctic fauna extends to the utmost limits of the cold and barren regions of the North. But from the moment that forests appear, and a more propitious soil permits a larger development of animal life and of vegetation, we see the fauna and flora, not only diversified according to the continents on which they exist, but we observe also striking distinctions between different parts of the same continent; thus, in the Old World, the animals vary, not only from the Polar circle to the equator, but also in the opposite direction—those of the western coast of Europe are not the same as those of the basin of the Caspian Sea, or of the eastern coast of Asia, nor are those of the eastern coast of America the same as those of the western.

"The first fauna, the limits of which we would determine with precision, is the Arctic. It offers, as we have just seen, the same aspects in three parts of the world, which converge towards the North Pole. The uniform distribution of the animals by which it is inhabited forms its most striking character, and gives rise to a sameness of general features which is not found in any other region. Though the air-breathing species are not numerous here, the large number of individuals compensates for this deficiency, and among the marine animals we find an astonishing profusion and variety of forms.

"In this respect the vegetable and animal kingdoms differ entirely from each other, and the measure by which we estimate the former is quite false as applied to the latter. Plants become stunted in their growth or disappear before the rigours of the climate, while, on the contrary, all classes of the animal kingdom have representatives, more or less numerous, in the Arctic fauna.

"Neither can they be said to diminish in size under these influences; for, if the Arctic representatives of certain classes, particularly the insects, are smaller than the analogous types in the tropics, we must not forget, on the other hand, that the whales and larger cetacea have here their most genial home, and make amends, by their more powerful structure, for the inferiority of other classes. Also, if the animals of the North are less striking in external ornament—if their colours are less brilliant—yet we cannot say that they are more uniform, for though their tints are not so bright, they are none the less varied in their distribution and arrangement.

"The limits of the Arctic fauna are very easily traced. We must include therein all animals living beyond the line where forests cease, and inhabiting countries entirely barren. Those which feed upon flesh seek fishes, hares, or lemmings, a rodent of the size of our rat. Those which live on vegetable substances are not numerous. Some gramineous plants, mosses, and lichens, serve as pasture to the ruminants and rodents, while the seeds of a few flowering plants, and of the dwarf birches, afford nourishment to the little granivorous birds, such as linnets and buntings. The species belonging to the sea-shore feed upon marine animals, which live, themselves, upon each other, or upon marine plants.

"The larger mammalia which inhabit this zone are—the white bear, the walrus, numerous species of seal, the reindeer, the musk ox, the narwal, the cachalot, and whales in abundance. Among the smaller species we may mention the white fox, the polar hare, and the lemming. The birds are not less characteristic. Some marine eagles, and wading birds in smaller number, are found; but the aquatic birds of the family of palmipedes are those which especially prevail. The coasts of the continents and of the numerous islands in the Arctic seas are peopled by clouds of gannets, of cormorants, of penguins, of petrels, of ducks, of geese, of mergansers, and of gulls, some of which are as large as eagles, and, like them, live on prey. No reptile is known in this zone. Fishes are, however, very numerous, and the rivers especially swarm with a variety of species of the salmon family. A number of representatives of the inferior classes of worms, of crustacea, of mollusks, of echinoderms, and of medusæ, are also found here.

"Within the limits of this fauna we meet a peculiar race of men, known in America under the name of Esquimaux, and under the names of Laplanders, Samojedes, and Tchuktshes in the north of Asia. This race, so well known since the voyage of Captain Cook and the Arctic expeditions of England and Russia, differs alike from the Indians of North America, from the whites of Europe, and the Mongols of Asia, to whom they are adjacent. The uniformity of their characters along the whole range of the Arctic seas forms one of the most striking resemblances which these people exhibit to the fauna with which they are so closely connected.

"The semi-annual alternation of day and night in the Arctic regions has a great influence upon their modes of living. They are entirely dependent upon animal food for their sustenance, no farinaceous grains, no nutritious tubercles, no juicy fruits, growing under those inhospitable latitudes. Their domesticated animals are the reindeer in Asia, and a peculiar variety of dog, the Esquimaux dog, in North America, where even the reindeer is not domesticated.

"Though the Arctic fauna is essentially comprised in the Arctic circle, its organic limit does not correspond rigorously to this line, but rather to the isotherme of thirty-two decrees Fahr., the outline of which presents numerous undulations. This limit is still more natural when it is made to correspond with that of the disappearance of forests. It then circumscribes those immense plains of the North, which the Samoyedes call *tundras*, and the Anglo-Americans, *barren lands*.

"The naturalists, who have overlooked this fauna, and connected it with those of the temperate zone, have introduced much confusion in the geographical distribution of animals, and have failed to recognise the remarkable coincidence existing between the extensive range of the Arctic race of men, and the uniformity of the animal world around the Northern Pole.

"The types which characterise best this fauna, are the white or Polar bear, the walrus, the seal of Greenland, the reindeer, the right whale, and the eider duck. The vegetation is represented by the so-called reindeer moss, a lichen which constitutes the chief food of the herbivorous animals of the Arctics and the high Alps during winter.

"To the glacial zone, which encloses a single fauna, succeeds the temperate zone, included between the isothermes of thirty-two degrees and seventy-four degrees Fahr., characterised by its pine forests, its amentacea, its maples, its walnuts, and its fruit trees, and from the midst of which arise, like islands, lofty mountain chains, or high table-lands, clothed with a vegetation which, in many respects, recalls that of the glacial regions. The geographical distribution of animals in this zone forms several closely-connected, but distinct, combinations. It is the country of the terrestrial bear, of the wolf, the fox, the weasel, the marten, the otter, the lynx, the horse and the ass, the boar, and a great number of stags, deer, elk, goats, sheep, bulls, hares, squirrels, rats, &c.; to which are added southward, a few representatives of the tropical zone.

"Wherever this zone is not modified by extensive and high table-lands and mountain chains, we may distinguish in it four *secondary* zones, approximating gradually to the character of the tropics, and presenting, therefore, a greater diversity in the types of its southern representation than we find among those of its northern boundaries. We have first, adjoining the Arctics, a *Sub-Arctic* zone, with an almost uniform appearance in the Old, as well as the New World, in which pine forests prevail, the home of the moose; next a *cold temperate zone*, in which amentaceous trees are combined with pines, the home of the fur animals; next, a *warm temperate zone*, in which the pines recede, whilst to the prevailing amentaceous trees a variety of evergreens are added, the chief seat of the culture of our fruit trees, and of the wheat; and a *sub-tropical zone*, in which a number of tropical forms are combined with those characteristics of the warm temperate zone. Yet there is, throughout the whole of the temperate zone, one feature prevailing; the repetition, under corresponding latitudes, but under different longitudes, of the same genera and families, represented in each botanical or zoological province by distinct so-called *analogous, or representative species*, with a very few subordinate types, peculiar to each province; for it is not until we reach the tropical zone that we find distinct types prevailing in each fauna and flora.

"Again, owing to the inequalities of the surface, the secondary zones are more or less blended into one another, as for instance, in the table-lands of Central Asia, and Western North America, where the whole temperate zone preserves the features of a cold temperate region; or the colder zones may appear like islands rising in the midst of the warmer ones, as the Pyrenees, the Alps, &c., the summits of which partake of the peculiarities of the Arctic and sub-Arctic zones, whilst the valleys at their base are characterised by the flora and fauna of the cold or warm temperate zones. It may be proper to remark, in this connection, that the study of the laws regulating the geographical distribution of natural families of animals and plants upon the whole surface of our globe, differs entirely from that of the associations and combinations of a variety of animals and plants within definite regions, forming peculiar faunæ and flora.

"Considering the whole range of the temperate zone from east to west, we may divide it in accordance with the prevailing physical features into—1st, an *Asiatic* realm, embracing Mantchuria, Japan, China, Mongolia, and passing through Turkestan into—2nd, the *European* realm, which includes Iran as well as Asia Minor, Mesopotamia, Northern Arabia, and Barbary, as well as Europe, properly so-called; the western parts of Asia, and the northern parts of Africa being intimately connected by the geological structure with the southern parts of Europe; and—3rd, the *North American* realm, which extends as far south as the table-land of Mexico.

"With these qualifications, we may proceed to consider the faunæ which characterise these three realms. But, before studying the organic characters of this zone, let us glance at its physical constitution. The most marked character of the temperate zone is found in the inequality of the four seasons, which give to the earth a peculiar aspect in different epochs of the year, and in the gradual, though more or less rapid, passage of these seasons into each other. The vegetation particularly undergoes marked modification; completely arrested, or merely suspended, for a longer or shorter time, according to the proximity of the Arctic or the tropical zone, we find it by turns in a prolonged lethargy, or in a state of energetic and sustained development. But in this respect there is a decided contrast between the cold and warm portions of the temperate zone. Though they are both characterised by the predominance of the same families of plants, and in particular by the presence of numerous species of the coniferous and amentaceous plants, yet the periodical sleep which deprives the middle latitudes of their verdure, is more complete in the colder region than in the warmer, which is already enriched by some southern forms of vegetation, and where a part of the trees remain green all the year. The succession of the seasons produces, moreover, such considerable changes in the climatic conditions in this zone, that all the animals belonging to it cannot sustain them equally well. Hence a large number of them migrate at different seasons from one extremity of the zone to the other, especially certain families of birds. It is known to all the world that the birds of Northern Europe and America leave their ungenial climate in the winter, seeking warmer regions as far as the Gulf of Mexico and the Mediterranean, the shores of which, even those of the African coasts, make a part of the temperate zone. Analogous migrations take place also in the north of Asia. Such migrations are not, however, limited to the temperate zone; a number of species from the Arctic regions go for the winter into the temperate zone, and the limits of these migrations may aid us in tracing the natural limits of the faunæ, which thus link themselves to each other, as the human rases are connected by civilisation.

"The temperate zone is not characterised, like the Arctic, by one and the same fauna; it does not form, as the Arctic does, one continuous zoological zone around the globe. Not only do the animals change from one hemisphere to another, but those differences exist even between various regions of the same hemisphere. The species belonging to the western countries of the Old World are not identical with those of the eastern countries. It is true that they often resemble each other so closely that until very recently they have been confounded. It has been reserved, however, for modern zoology and botany to detect these nice distinctions. For instance, the conifera of the Old World, even within the sub-Arctic zone, are not identical with those of America. Instead of the Norway and black pine, we have here the balsam and white spruce; instead of the common fir, the *Pinus rigida;* instead of the European larch, the hacmatac, &c.; and farther south the differences are still more striking. In the temperate zone proper, the oaks, the beeches, the birches, the hornbeams, the hophornbeams, the chestnuts, the buttonwoods, the elms, the linden, the maples, and the walnuts, are represented in each continent by peculiar species differing more or less. Peculiar forms make, here and there, their appearance, such as the gum-trees, the tulip-trees, the magnolias. The evergreens are still more diversified; we need only mention the camellias of Japan, and the kalmias of America, as examples. Among the tropical forms extending into the warm temperate zone, we notice particularly the palmetto in the southern United States, and the dwarf chamærops of southern Europe. The animal kingdom presents the same features. In Europe we have, for instance, the brown bear, in North America the black bear, in Asia the bear of Tubet: the European stag and the European deer are represented in North America by the Canadian stag, or wapiti, and the American deer; and in eastern Asia by the musk deer. Instead of the monflon, North America has the big-horn or mountain sheep, and Asia the argali. The North American buffalo is represented in Europe by the wild anerochs of Lithuania, and in Mongolia by the yak; the wild cats, the martens and weasels, the wolves and foxes, the squirrels and mice (excepting the imported house-mouse), the birds, the reptiles, the fishes, the insects, the mollusks, &c., though more or less closely allied, are equally distinct specifically. The types peculiar to the Old or New World are few; among them may be mentioned the horse, the ass, and the dromedary of Asia, and the opossum of North America; but upon this subject more details may be found in every text-book of zoology and botany. We would only add that in the present state of our knowledge we recognise the following combinations of animals within the limits of the temperate zone, which may be considered as so many distinct zoological provinces or faunæ :—

"In the *Asiatic realm*—1st, a north-eastern fauna, the *Japanese fauna*—2nd, a south-eastern fauna, the *Chinese fauna*, and a central fauna, the *Mongolian fauna*, following westwards by the *Caspian fauna*, which partakes partly of the European zoological character; its most remarkable animal, antelope saiga, ranging west as far as Southern Russia. The Japanese and Chinese fauna stand to each other in the same relation as Southern Europe and North Africa, and it remains to be ascertained by farther investigations whether the Japanese fauna ought not to be sub-divided into a more eastern insular fauna, the *Japanese fauna proper*, and a more western continental fauna, which might be called the *Mandshurian*, or *Tongonsian* fauna. But since it is not my object to describe separately all faunæ, but chiefly to call attention to the coincidence existing between the natural limitation of the races of man, and the geographical range of the zoological provinces, I shall limit myself here to some general remarks respecting the Mongolian fauna, in order to show that the Asiatic zoological realm differs essentially from the European and the American. The most remarkable animals of this fauna are the bear of Tubet (ursus thibetanus), the musk-deer (moschus moschiferus), the Tzeiran (antilope gutturosa), the Mongolian goat (capra sibirica), the argali (ovis argali), and the yak (bos grunniens). This is also the home of the Bactrian, or double-hunched camel, and of the wild horse (equus caballus), the wild ass (equus onager), and another equine species, the Dtschigetai (equus hemionus). The wide distribution of the musk-deer in the Altai, and the Himalayan and Chinese Alps, shows the whole Asiatic range of the temperate zone to be a most natural zoological realm, sub-divided into distinct provinces by the greater localisation of the largest number of its representatives.

"If we now ask, what are the nations of the men inhabiting those regions, we find that they all belong to the so-called Mongolian race, the natural limits of which correspond exactly to the range of the Japanese, Chinese, Mongolian, and Caspian faunæ, taken together, and that peculiar types, distinct nations of this race, cover respectively the different faunæ of this realm. The Japanese inhabiting the Japanese zoological province; the Chinese, the Chinese province; the Mongols, the Mongolian province; and the Turks, the Caspian province; eliminating, of course, the modern establishment of Turks in Asia Minor and Europe.

"The unity of Europe (exclusive of its Arctic regions), in connection with south-western Asia and northern Africa, as a distinct zoological realm, is established by the range of its mammalia and by the limits of the migration of its birds, as well as by the physical features of its whole extent. Thus we find its deer and stag, its bear, its hare, its squirrel, its wolf and wild-cat, its fox and jackal, its otter, its weasel and marten, its badger, its bear, its mole, its hedgehogs, and a number of bats, either extending over the whole realm in Europe, western Asia, and north Africa, or so linked together as to show that in their combination with the birds, reptiles, fishes, etc., of the same countries, they constitute a natural zoological association analogous to that of Asia, but essentially different in reference to species.

"Like the eastern realm, this European world may be subdivided into a number of distinct faunæ, characterised each by a variety of peculiar animals. In western Asia we find, for instance, the common camel, instead of the Bactrian, whilst Mount Sinai, Mounts Taurus and Caucasus have goats and wild sheep, which differ as much from those of Asia as they differ from those of Greece, of Italy, of the Alps, of the Pyrenees, of the Atlas, and of Egypt. Wild horses are known to have inhabited Spain and Germany; and a wild bull extended over the whole range of central Europe, which no longer exists there. The Asiatic origin of our domesticated animals may, therefore, well be questioned, even if we were still to refer western Asia to the Asiatic realm; since the ass, and some of the breeds of our horse, only belong to the table-lands of Iran and Mongolia, whilst the other species, including the cat, may all be traced to species of the European realm. The domesticated cat is referred by Rüppell to *felis maniculata* of Egypt; by others, to *felis catus ferus* of Central Europe; thus, in both cases, to an animal of the European realm. Whether the dog be a species by itself, or its varieties derived from several species which have completely amalgamated, or be it descended from the wolf, the fox, or the jackal, every theory must limit its natural range to the European world. The merino sheep is still represented in the wild state by the mouflon of Sardinia, and was formerly wild in all the mountains of Spain; whether the sheep of the patriarchs were derived from those of Mount Taurus, or from Armenia, still they differed from those of Western Europe; since, a thousand years before our era, the Phœnicians preferred the wool from the Iberian peninsula to that of their Syrian neighbours. The goats differ so much in different parts of the world, that it is still less possible to refer them to one common stock; and while Nepaul and Cashmere have their own breeds, we may well consider those of Egypt and Sinai as distinct, especially as they differ equally from those of Caucasus and of Europe. The common bull is derived from the wild species which has become extinct in Europe, and is not identical with any of the wild species of Asia, notwithstanding some assertions to the contrary. The hog descends from the common boar, now found wild over the whole temperate zone in the Old World. Both ducks and geese have their wild representatives in Europe; so also the pigeon. As for the common fowls, they are decidedly of East Asiatic origin; but the period of their importation is not well known, now even the wild species from which they are derived. The wild turkey is well known as an inhabitant of the American continent.

"Now, taking further into account the special distribution of *all* the animals, wild as well as domesticated, of the European temperate zone, we may sub-divide it into the following eight faunæ:—1st, Scandinavian fauna; 2nd, Russian fauna; 3rd, the fauna of Central Europe; 4th, the fauna of Southern Europe; 5th, the fauna of Iran; 6th, the Syrian fauna; 7th, the Egyptian fauna; and 8th, the fauna of the Atlas.

"Here, again, it cannot escape the attention of the careful observer, that the European zoological realm is circumscribed within exactly the same limits as the so-called white race of man, including, as it does, the inhabitants of South-Western Asia, and of North Africa, with the lower parts of the valley of the Nile. We exclude, of course, modern migrations and historical changes of habitation from this assertion. Our statements are to be understood as referring only to the aboriginal, or ante-historical distribution of man, or rather to the distribution as history finds it. And in this respect there is a singular fact, which historians seem not to have sufficiently appreciated, that the earliest migrations recorded, in any form, show us man meeting man, wherever he moves upon the inhabitable surface of the globe, small islands excepted.

"It is, farther, very striking, that the different subdivisions of this race, even to the limits of distinct nationalities, cover precisely the same ground as the special faunæ or zoological provinces of this most important part of the world, which in all ages has been the seat of the most advanced civilisation. In the south-west of Asia we find (along the table-land of Iran) Persia and Asia Minor; in the plains southward, Mesopotamia and Syria; along the sea shores, Palestine and Phœnicia; in the Valley of the Nile, Egypt; and along the southern shores of Africa, Barbary. Thus we have Semitic nations covering the North African and South-West Asiatic fauna, while the South European peninsulas, including Asia Minor, are inhabited by Græco-Roman nations, and the cold temperate zone, by Celto-Germanic nations; the eastern range of Europe being peopled by Sclaves. This coincidence may justify the inference of an independent origin for these different tribes, as soon as it can be admitted that the races of men were primitively created in nations; the more so, since all of them claim to have been *autochthones* of the countries they inhabit. This claim is so universal that it well deserves more attention. It may be more deeply founded than historians generally seem inclined to grant. Though temperate America resembles closely in its animal creation the countries of Europe and Asia belonging to the same zone, we meet with physical and organic features in this continent which differ entirely from those of the Old World. The tropical realms, connected there with those of the temperate zone, though bound together by some analogies, differ essentially from one another. Tropical Africa has hardly any species in common with Europe, though we may remember that the lion once extended to Greece, and that the jackal is to this day found upon some islands in the Adriatic, and in Morea. Tropical Asia differs equally from its temperate regions, and Australia forms a world by itself. Not so in Southern America. The range of mountains which extends, in almost unbroken continuity, from the Arctic to Cape Horn, establishes a similarity between North and South America, which may be traced also, to a great degree, in its plants and animals. Entire families which are peculiar to this continent have their representatives in North as well as South America, the cactus and didelphis, for instance; some species, as the puma, or American lion, may even be traced from Canada to Patagonia. In connection with these facts, we find that tropical America, though it has its peculiar types, as characteristic as those of tropical Africa, Asia, and Australia, does not furnish analogues of the giants of Africa and Asia; its largest pachyderms being tapirs and pecaris, not elephants, rhinoceroses, and hippopotami; and its largest ruminants, the llamas and alpacas, and not camels and giraffes; whilst it reminds us, in many respects, of Australia, with which it has the type of marsupials in common, though ruminants and pachyderms, and even monkeys, are entirely wanting there. Thus, with due qualification, it may be said, that the whole continent of America, when compared with the corresponding twin-continents of Europe, Africa, or Asia—Australia is characterised by a much greater uniformity of its natural productions, combined with a special localisation of many of its subordinate types, which will justify the establishment of many special faunæ within its boundaries.

"With these facts before us, we may expect that there should be no great diversity among the tribes of man inhabiting the continent of America; and, indeed, the most extensive investigation of their peculiarities has led Dr. Morton to consider them as constituting but a single race, from the confines of the Esquimaux down to the southernmost extremity of the continent. But, at the same time, it should be remembered that, in accordance with the zoological character of the whole realm, this race is divided into an infinite number of small tribes, presenting more or less difference one from another.

"As to the special faunæ of the American continent, we may distinguish, within the temperate zone, a Canadian fauna, extending from Newfoundland across the great lakes to the base of the Rocky Mountains, a fauna of the North American table-land, a fauna of the North-west coast, a fauna of the middle United States, a fauna of the Southern United States, and a Californian fauna, the characteristic features of which I shall describe on another occasion.

"When we consider, however, the isolation of the American continent from those of the Old World, nothing is more striking in the geographical distribution of animals than the exact correspondence of all the animals of the northern temperate zone of America with those of Europe.

"In tropical America we may distinguish a central American fauna, a Brazilian fauna, a fauna of the Pampas, a fauna of the Cordilleras, a Peruvian fauna, and a Patagonian fauna.

"The slight differences existing between the faunæ of the temperate zone have required a fuller illustration than may be necessary to characterise the zoological realms of the tropical regions, and the southern hemisphere generally. It is sufficient for our purpose to say here, that these realms are at once distinguished by the prevalence of peculiar types, circumscribed within the natural limits of the three continents, extending in complete isolation towards the southern pole. In this respect there is already a striking contrast between the northern and the southern hemisphere. But the more closely we compare them with one another, the greater appear their differences. We have already seen how South America differs from Africa, the East Indies, and Australia, by its closer connection with North America. Notwithstanding, however, the absence in South America of those sightly animals so prominent in Africa and tropical Asia, its general character is, like that of all the tropical continents, to nourish a variety of types which have no close relations to those of other continents. Its monkeys and edentata belong to genera which have no representatives in the Old World; among pachyderms it has pecaris, which are entirely wanting elsewhere; and though the tapirs occur also in the Sunda Islands, that type is wanting in Africa, where in compensation we find the hippopotamus, not found in either Asia or America. We have already seen that the marsupials of South America differ entirely from those of Australia. Its ostriches differ also generically from those of Africa, tropical Asia, New Holland, &c.

"If we compare, further, the southern continents of the Old World with one another, we find a certain uniformity between the animals of Africa and tropical Asia. They have both elephants and rhinoceroses, though each has its peculiar species of these genera, which occur neither in America nor in Australia; whilst cercopitheci and antelopes prevail in Africa, and long-armed monkeys and stags in tropical Asia. Moreover, the black orangs are peculiar to Africa, and the red orangs to Asia. As to Australia, it has neither monkeys nor pachyderms, nor edentata, but only marsupials and monotremes. We need, therefore, not carry these comparisons further, to be satisfied that Africa, tropical Asia, and Australia constitute independent zoological realms.

"The continent of Africa south of the Atlas has a very uniform zoological character. This realm may, however, be sub-divided, according to its local peculiarities, into a number of distinct faunæ. In its more northern parts we distinguish the fauna of the Sahara, and those of Nubia and Abyssinia; the latter of which extends over the Red Sea into the tropical parts of Arabia. They are inhabited by two distinct races of men, the Nubians and Abyssinians, receding greatly in their features from the woolly-haired Negroes with flat, broad noses, which cover the most central parts of the continent. But even here we may distinguish the fauna of Senegal from that of Guinea and that of the African Table-land. In the first, we notice particularly the chimpanzee; in the second, the gorilla. There is no anthropoid monkey in the third. A fuller illustration of this subject might show how peculiar tribes of Negroes cover the limits of the different faunæ of tropical Africa, and establish in this respect a parallelism between the nations of this continent and those of Europe.

"The East Indian realm is now very well known zoologically, thanks to the efforts of English and Dutch naturalists, and may be sub-divided into three faunæ—that of Dukhun, that of the Indo-Chinese peninsula, and that of the Sunda Islands, Borneo, and the Philippines. There is, however, one feature in this realm, which requires particular attention, and has a high importance with reference to the study of the races of men. We find here upon Borneo (an island not so extensive as Spain) one of the best known of those anthropoid monkeys, the orang-outan, and with him, as well as upon the adjacent islands of Java and Sumatra, and along the coasts of the two East Indian peninsulæ, not less than ten other different species of Hylobates, the long-armed monkeys; a genus which, next to the orang and chimpanzee, ranks nearest to man. One of these species is circumscribed within the island of Java, two along the coast of Coromandel, three upon that of Malacca, and four upon Borneo. Also, eleven of the highest organised beings which have performed their part in the plan of the creation within tracts of land inferior in extent to the range of any of the historical nations of men.

"In accordance with this fact, we find three distinct races within the boundaries of the East Indian realm: the Telingan race in anterior India, the Malays in posterior India and upon the islands, upon which the Negrillos occur with them. Such combinations justify fully a comparison of the geographical range covered by distinct European nations with the narrow limits occupied upon earth by the orangs, the chimpanzees, and the gorillas; and though I still hesitate to assign to each an independent origin (perhaps rather from the difficulty of divesting myself of the opinions universally received, than from any intrinsic evidence), I must, in presence of these facts, insist at least upon the probability of such an independence of origin of all nations; or, at least, of the independent origin of a primitive stock for each, with which at some future period, migrating or conquering tribes have more or less completely amalgamated, as in the case of mixed nationalities. The evidence adduced from the affinities of the languages of different nations in favour of a community of origin is of no value when we know that among vociferous animals every species has its peculiar intonations, and that the different species of the same family produce sound as closely allied, and forming as natural combinations, as the so-called Indo-Germanic languages compared with one another. Nobody, for instance, would suppose that because the notes of the different species of thrushes, inhabiting different parts of the world, bear the closest affinity to one another, these birds must all have a common origin; and yet, with reference to man, philologists still look upon the affinities of languages as affording direct evidence of such a community of origin among the races, even though they have already discovered the most essential differences in the very structure of these languages.

"Ever since New Holland was discovered, it has been known as the land of zoological marvels. All its animals differ so completely from those of other parts of our globe, that it may be said to constitute a world in itself, as isolated in that respect from the other continents as it truly is in its physical relations. As a zoological realm, it extends to New Guinea and some adjacent islands. New Holland, however, constitutes a distinct fauna, which at some future time may be still further subdivided, differing from that of the islands north of it. The animals of this insular continent belong to two families only, considering the class of mammalia alone, the marsupials, and the monotremes.

Besides these there are found bats, and mice, and a wild dog; but there are neither true edentata, nor ruminants, nor pachyderms, nor monkeys, in this realm, which is inhabited by two races of men, the Australian in New Holland, and the Papuans upon the Islands."

We get thus eight realms with distinct types of man, and accompanying fauna and flora. 1. The Arctic with the Esquimaux. 2. The Mongol with the Chinaman. 3. The European with the Caucasian. 4. The American with the Indian. 5. The African with the Negro. 6. The Hottentot with the Bushman. 7. The East Indian with the Malay. 8. The Australian with the Papuan. And the question is —supposing an universal deluge A.M. 1656—have all these diverse human beings developed from the family of one man Noah, since B.C. 2348? or rejecting the story of the universality of the Deluge, have the differing races developed from one man Adam, and one woman Eve, in less than 6,000 years?

The late Professsor J. W. Jackson, in a remarkable paper published in the *Anthropological Review* for 1869, thus presents the Caucasian race: "The three great religions of existing Caucasian man are Judaism, Christianity, and the faith of Islam, all of Semitic origin; while, on the other hand, our science, literature, and art are mostly of Aryan lineage. So strongly pronounced, indeed, are these racial proclivities that the religion of the Aryan ever tends to assume the form of a philosophic Pantheism, eventuating in a deification and worship of nature, as among the ancient Hindoos and modern Europeans; while, conversely, the science of the Semite is ever prone to sink into a superstition, as in the astrology of the Chaldæans and the alchemy of the Saracens. This is only saying in other words that, influenced by his predominant moral principles, the Semite believes and worships, where the Aryan, guided by his preponderating intellectual faculties, investigates facts and deduces conclusions.......What is the Caucasian, whereof Aryan and Semite are but the two great sub-divisions? And we reply, that he is pre-eminently the man of civilisation. All pure savages incline either to the Negroid or the Turanian type; they do so from the absence of adequate nervous force for their effective development into the truly human form. This is not the utterance of prejudice, but the simple statement of a fact. The coarser types are differenced from the finer by their inferiority, that is, by the comparative weakness of the moral and intellectual elements, and the preponderating power of the passional and impulsive. This is clearly indicated, to a properly-qualified observer, in their physical organisation. In the Negroid type, the brain lacks volume; the nervous system is not adequately centralised; and this brain, thus deficient in quantity, is equally wanting in quality. The rude mould of the features, where all the indications of intelligence are weak, while those which imply sensuality are large; the rudimentary character of the hands, the semi-quadrumanous structure of the feet; and the generally unfinished build of the whole body, to say nothing of the porous skin and its woolly envelope, are ample and undeniable evidence of the exceedingly coarse quality of the Negroid family. And this brain, thus deficient both in quantity and quality, is also equally wanting in form. The cranium is compressed laterally and retreats anteriorly, indicating an utter incapacity either for breadth of view or depth of thought. But it is elevated coronally and developed posteriorly, showing that here, in this rootman of the South, we have the invaluable germs of moral sentiment and domestic affection.

"Diametrically opposed to this, as if formed under transverse influences, we have the broad-built Turanian, in whom, however, with somewhat more of the human, there is still much of the animal element. He has, in excess, that which is wanting in his Negroid brother—breadth. His volume of brain is enormous, though its quality is coarse and its form rude. He has attained to a higher grade of centralisation—and we have reason to believe, therefore, of specialisation—than the primitive man of the South. His deficiency is in altitude. He lacks the higher moral sentiments, and the creative portion of the intellectual faculties. But he has practical power and executant ability of a high order. In other words, he has force, but is wanting in susceptibility to the higher motives for its noblest exercise. As an instrument in the hands of a superior race, he may prove invaluable; but as a leader and pioneer of humanity, he is fatally deficient.

"What, then, is the savage? and we reply, that he is man on the plane of nature, adapted—by the limitation of his faculties and the bluntness of his susceptibilities—to the only social and physical life possible in the wilderness and the forest, at the dawn of human existence on earth......

"Such mental deficiencies, when characteristic of a race,

are of necessity reflected in their organisation; that is, in the volume and contour of the brain, in the form of the features, in the expression of the face, in the build of the body, and in the fashion of its extremities. And thus, then, it is that we have the savage, precisely as we have the lion and the eagle, the jackal and the vulture, we have him as an organic adaptation to a certain environment with which he is in harmony, because, as the advocates of development would say, he was its product. Now, that this primitive savage always inclines either to the Negroid or the Turanian type, is a fact of no slight significance in the science of man......

"The Caucasian is emphatically the man of civilisation, as contra-distinguished from the savage. What, then, is this Caucasian? And we reply, the highest type to which man has yet attained. He presents us with that form of humanity in which cerebration and respiration are most powerful in proportion to alimentation and reproduction. He is the most effectually developed type of man, the one in whom the functions, that are specially human, are the most powerful in proportion to those which are also bestial. This, of course, implies an organic structure, adapted as an instrument for the efficient discharge of these higher duties. And accordingly we find that his brain is equal in volume to that of the Turanian, while it is superior in form and finer in quality; thus conducing, through intensity and activity, not only to greater mental power, but also to power of a higher order. His thoughts are more logically concatenated, and his conceptions are more beautiful and artistic. His special superiority to the Turanian is, however, in the moral sentiments. He is better developed coronally; and hence, is more amenable to the influence of 'faith, hope, and charity,' and, we may add, justice. Thus, in a sense, it may be said that he unites the excellences of the two inferior races without the defects of either. He has the breadth of the Turanian without his coarseness, and the altitude of the negro without his narrowness, while in temperament he immeasurably transcends them both. Of course, with such a brain, so powerful in structure, so fine in quality, so complex in its convolutions, and so intense in its functions, there must be a face to correspond; that is, with features distinctly marked, and delicately chiselled, and susceptible, in duly cultured individualities, of all the varying shades of intellectual expression......

"But this high-caste Caucasian, this man of civilisation,

is organically, lingually, and theologically, divisible into two well-marked families, Aryans and Semites, or Indo-Europeans and Arabians; the former especially located in Europe, and the latter in Asia, although the first are the predominant population of Persia and India, and the last extend throughout all Northern Africa. It may thus be said that the Caucasian occupies the temperate zone of the world, from India to Britain, with the Negroid races to the south, and the Turanian to the north, the Semites, resting on and through Moors, Tuaricks, Nubians, and Abyssinians, gradually shading off into the former; while the Aryans rest on and through Slavons, Muscovites, and Cossacks, gradually shade off into the latter. Thus, whether we regard their geographical position, their mental constitution, or their organic specialities, we shall find that the Semites are allied, as flower and root, to the Negroid type of the south, and the Aryans to the Turanian type of the north."

On this statement there are only two alternatives. Either, as stated in the Bible, all mankind originated from one pair, and the different races, with their peculiarities now found existing, are to be attributed to subsequent changes, an assumption for which, as Louis Agassiz says, "there is no evidence whatever;" or, we must acknowledge that the diversity amongst animals, including man, is a primordial fact.

Mr. Lawrence dealt with this question very distinctly, more than fifty years since, in his "Lectures on Man" (sec. 2, cap. i.), on the varieties of the human species; but the researches of the last half century have opened out so many new stores of evidence that it seems quite unnecessary here to do more than pay tribute to the exertions of the intrepid physiologist.

"If," say Dr. J. C. Notts ("Types of Mankind," p. 57), "the *unity* of the races or species of men be assumed, there are but three suppositions on which the *diversity* now seen in the white, black, and intermediate colours, can be accounted for, viz.:—

"1st. A *miracle*, or direct act of the Almighty, in changing one type into another.

"2nd. The gradual action of physical causes, such as climate, food, mode of life, etc.

"3rd. Congenital, or accidental varieties.

"There being no evidence whatever in favour of the first hypothesis, we pass it by. The second and third have been sustained with signal ability by Dr. Prichard, in his 'Physical History of Mankind.'

"Is it not strange that all the remarkable changes of type spoken of by Prichard and others should have occurred in remote ante-historic times, and amongst ignorant, erratic tribes? Why is it that no instance of these remarkable changes can be pointed out which admits of conclusive evidence? The civilised nations of Europe have been for many centuries sending colonies to Asia, Africa, and America; amongst Mongols, Malays, Africans, and Indians; and why has no example occurred in any of these colonies to substantiate the argument? The doubtful examples of Prichard are refuted by others, which he cites on the adverse side, of a positive nature. He gives examples of Jews, Persians, Hindoos, Arabs, &c., who have emigrated to foreign climates, and, at the end of one thousand or fifteen hundred years, have preserved their original types in the midst of widely different races. Does nature anywhere operate by such opposite and contradictory laws?

"A few generations in animals are sufficient to produce all the changes they usually undergo from climate, and yet the races of men retain their leading characteristics for ages, without approximating to aboriginal types.

"In fact, so unsatisfactory is the argument based on the influence of climate to Prichard himself, that he virtually abandons it in the following paragraph: 'It must be observed,' says he, 'that the changes alluded to do not so often take place by alteration in the physical character of a whole tribe simultaneously, as by the *springing up* of some new *congenital* peculiarity, which is afterwards propagated, and becomes a character more or less constant in the progeny of the individual in whom it first appeared, and is *perhaps* gradually communicated by intermarriages to a whole stock or tribe. This, it is obvious, can only happen in a long course of time.

"We beg leave to fix your attention on this vital point. It is a commonly-received error that the influence of a hot climate is gradually exerted on successive generations, until one species of mankind is completely changed into another, a dark shade is impressed on the first, and transmitted to the second; another shade is added to the third, which is handed down to the fourth; and so on, through successive generations, until the fair German is transformed, by climate, into the black African!

"This idea is *proven to be false*, and is abandoned by the

well-informed writers of all parties. A sun-burnt cheek is never handed down to succeeding generations. The exposed parts of the body alone are tanned by the sun, and the children of the white-skinned Europeans in New Orleans, Mobile, and the West Indies, are *born* as fair as their ancestors, and would remain so, if carried back to a colder climate. The same may be said of other acquired characters (except those from want and disease). They die with the individual, and are no more capable of transmission than a flattened head, mutilated limb, or tattooed skin. We repeat, that this fact is settled, and challenge a denial.

"The only argument left, then, for the advocates of the *unity* of the human species to fall back upon, is that of '*congenital*' varieties or peculiarities, which are said to spring up, and be transmitted from parent to child, so as to form new races.

"Let us pause for a moment to illustrate this fanciful idea. The Negroes of Africa, for example, are admitted not to be offsets from some other race, which have been gradually blackened and changed in moral and physical type by the action of climate; but it is asserted that, 'once in the flight of ages past,' some genuine little Negro, or rather many such, were born of Caucasian, Mongol, or other light-skinned parents, and then have turned about and changed the type of the inhabitants of a whole continent. So in America, the countless aborigines found on this continent, which we have reason to believe (see Squier's work), were building mounds before the time of Abraham, are the offspring of a race changed by accidental or congenital varieties. Thus, too, old China, India, Australia, Oceanica, etc., all owe their types, physical and mental, to *congenital* or *accidental varieties*, and all are descended from Adam and Eve! Can human credulity go farther, or human ingenuity invent any argument more absurd? Yet the whole groundwork of a common origin for some nine or ten hundred millions of beings, embracing numerous distinct types, which are lost in an antiquity far beyond all records or chronology, sacred or profane, is narrowed down to this 'baseless fabric.'

"In support of this argument, we are told of the porcupine Samily of England, which inherited for some generations a peculiar condition of the skin, characterised by thickened warty excrescences. We are told also of the transmission from parent to child of club feet, cross eyes, six fingers, deafness, blindness, and many other familiar examples of congenital peculiarities. But these examples merely serve to disprove the argument they are intended to sustain. Did any one ever hear of a club-foot, cross-eyed, or six-fingered *race*, although such individuals are exceedingly common? Are they not, on the contrary, always swallowed up and lost? Is it not strange, if there be any truth in this argument, that no race has ever been formed from those congenital varieties which we *know* to occur frequently, and yet races should originate from congenital varieties which cannot be proved, and are not believed, by our best writers, ever to have existed? No one ever saw a Negro, Mongol, or Indian, born from any but his own species. Has any one heard of an Indian child born from white or black parents in America, during more than two centuries that these races have been living there? Is not this brief and simple statement of the case sufficient to satisfy any one that the diversity of species now seen on the earth cannot be accounted for on the assumption of congenital or accidental origin? If a doubt remains, would it not be expelled by the recollection of the fact that the Negro, Tartar, and white man existed, with their present types, at least one thousand years before Abraham journeyed to Egypt as a supplicant to the mighty Pharaoh?"

As no miraculously-originated diversity of race is even alleged in the Bible, it is needless to waste time in discussing the first of the three suppositions put forward by Dr. Nott. On the second and third hypotheses the question arises, Will the period which elapsed from Adam to that date at which we distinctly trace diversity of type, be sufficient to cover the possibility of the gradual creation of the diverse races? Not only will the answer be that diversities as distinct as those we find to-day may be traced back at least 4,000 years, but that the antiquity of man reaches back to an age long anterior to that of Adam.

Sir John Lubbock writes, in his "Pre-Historic Times," p. 328: "Our belief in the antiquity of man rests not on any isolated calculations, but on the changes which have taken place since his appearance; changes in the geography, in the fauna, and in the climate of Europe. Valleys have been deepened, widened, and partially filled up again; caves through which subterranean rivers once ran are now left dry; even the configuration of land has been materially altered, and Africa finally separated from Europe.

"Our climate has greatly changed for the better, and with it the fauna has materially altered. In some cases, for instance, in that of the hippopotamus and of the African elephant, we may probably look to the diminution of food and the presence of man as the main causes of their disappearance; the extinction of the mammoth, the *Elephas antiquus*, and the *Rhinoceros tichorhinus*, may possibly be due to the same influences; but the retreat of the reindeer and the musk ox are probably in great measure owing to the change of climate. These and similar facts, though they afford us no means of measurement, impress us with a vague and overpowering sense of antiquity. All geologists, indeed, are now prepared to admit that man has existed on our earth for a much longer period than was until recently supposed to have been the case.

"But it may be doubted whether even geologists yet realise the great antiquity of our race."

And in his "Origin of Civilisation," page 352, the same author says: "From the careful study of the remains which have come down to us, it would appear that the pre-historic archæology may be divided into four great epochs.

"Firstly, that of Drift, when man shared the possession of Europe with the mammoth, the cave-bear, the woolly-haired rhinoceros, and other extinct animals. This we may call the Palæolithic period.

"Secondly, the later or polished Stone Age; a period characterised by beautiful weapons and instruments made of flint and other kinds of stone, in which, however, we find no trace of the knowledge of any metal, excepting gold, which seems to have been sometimes used for ornaments. This we may call the Neolithic period.

"Thirdly, the Bronze Age, in which bronze was used for arms and cutting instruments of all kinds.

"Fourthly, the Iron Age, in which that metal had superseded bronze for arms, axes, knives, &c.; bronze, however, still being in common use for ornaments, and frequently also for the handles of swords and other arms, but never for the blades.

"Stone weapons, however, of many kinds were still in use during the Age of Bronze, and even during that of Iron. So that the mere presence of a few stone implements is not in itself sufficient evidence that any given 'find' belongs to the Stone Age.

"In order to prevent misapprehension, it may be as well

to state at once, that I only apply this classification to Europe, though in all probability it might also be extended to the neighbouring parts of Asia and Africa. As regards other civilised countries, China and Japan for instance, we, as yet, know nothing of their pre-historic archæology. It is evident, also, that some nations, such as the Fuegians, Andamaners, &c., are even now only in an Age of Stone."

Mdlle. Clemence Royer points out (Ages Primitifs de l'Industrie, Encyclopédie Generale, vol. i., p. 270) that while the recent discoveries of flint implements have thrown back to a distant period in the geologic past the existence of man, yet that these discoveries are only the evidences of the accuracy of the ancient traditions which pointed to remote periods anterior to the use of iron, when bronze was used, and again to a prior age when no metal was known, and the weapons of mankind were rudely-fashioned stones. Agreeing very much with Sir John Lubbock in the above division of pre-historic antiquity, she shows how, prior to the Neolithic period, there come long ages, of incalculable duration, during which the stone weapons become more rude, fit only to divide the flesh of animals, and not even fit to cut wood, as though man's intelligence was as yet only slightly awakened. Mdlle. Royer contends that, as early as the Miocene period of the tertiary strata, there is evidence that man existed—or, at any rate, that an animal existed—using with his hands sharp stones to separate the flesh of animals from their bones. The testimony she adduces is that of the bones scratched, or cut, or marked, as if struck or rubbed with some hard cutting surface, not marked as if by the natural teeth of carnivorous animals. She contends that in the same strata with the striated bones have been found stones—evidently artificially though rudely sharpened—capable of making the marks which the fossil bones actually show. That it seems as if the man of that period ate the raw flesh which he got but clumsily off the bones by means of his roughly-fashioned stone knives. The man of the Pliocene period, judged by the stone record, gives no testimony of improved condition; and it is not until the glacial changes, which almost entirely destroy the pliocene fauna, that Mdlle. Royer thinks you begin to trace human progress.

But, if a tithe of this argument be true, then, perhaps millions of years before the Bible Adam, men dwelt on the earth, lacking nearly all the intellectual ability of modern men; men who knew not how to build them any dwellings, but crouched in the caves with the other fauna of the earth; men who knew not the use of fire, but who, like the beasts of prey of to-day, ate the flesh of the animals they killed, only supplementing their teeth and fingers with the rudely-sharpened flint. These men have all gone back into Nature's mighty womb; she has devoured her human offspring, and the rough-cut stone, and the bone it scraped, are the only signs left to-day of that far-off human presence. Now, in a later period—still far remote from all possible history—we find not man, but the evidences of his work, proving the exercise of higher intelligence. His stone weapons have distinct forms, are cut to pattern, and the use of fire is certainly traceable. If the researches of the early cavern period in Belgium are reliable, the man of that age was cannibal. Nearer still to us, and yet ages away, comes the reindeer period, when tools accompany weapons, and both are better finished, and traces of art begin to slowly manifest themselves. Now, in more modern times, not satisfied with destroying, man domesticates some of the animals, makes himself rude dwellings, and wears some clothes, polishes highly his weapons and his tools; and even yet we are not out of the Neolithic period, the length of which no man knows, except that your Hebrew fathom-line only hangs at its surface, being too short by innumerable chiliads of years to sound its mighty depths.

A form of the inquiry has been presented by the Duke of Argyll, in his "Primeval Man," as involving the following questions:—

"1st. The origin of man, considered simply as a species, that is to say, the method of his creation, or introduction into the world.

"2nd. The antiquity of man; or the time in the geological history and preparation of the globe at which this creation or introduction took place.

"3rd. His mental, moral, and intellectual condition when first created."

The Bible teaches that man was originated by special fiat of Deity, one man and one woman being first created, and all other human beings being descended by birth from this one pair. It is here maintained that outside the Bible, or equivalent mythic records, there is no more reason for attributing all human kind to one pair than there is for suggesting that all bees are descended from one male and one female bee, or all elephants from one male and female elephant. That while it may or may not be true that change of food, climate, and soil, may gradually modify race, yet there is no reason to suppose that the diverse types of mankind now existing on the earth could have possibly been developed from one stock in the limited period accorded by the Bible chronology. That, on the contrary, not only does science show traces of man on the earth, long prior to the 4004 B.C. of the authorised Bible, but that it is actually possible to trace the distinct types of mankind existing to-day, and existing also at a period when, if the Bible testimony is to be relied on, all the families of the world, save that of Noah, had been entirely swept away by the Deluge. On the question of the absolute origin of the human family, man's experience can teach him nothing. Even on the alleged origin of any form of vegetable or animal life, it is doubtful whether the experiments advanced to vouch "spontaneous generation," have been sufficiently exact to avoid the possibility of error. But whether or not life can be artificially originated, it can clearly be moulded, augmented, and diminished in its presentations. By artificial processes and modes of culture, varieties of vegetable and animal life may most certainly be produced, departing more or less from the parent stock. How far such varieties, so artificially created, can become permanent, or whether their permanency is possible, is an open question. Some contend that such varieties "are not permanent, and either die out or revert to their original types." To the query: Whence came man? no answer is serious which pretends that the totality of existence is insufficient to possibly account for human life. To the query: How came man? it is only possible to open out the page of development of life as revealed to us by geology and ethnology, tracing here first, the gradations of existing life, like steps on some mighty ladder, and then looking back to where the evidences of the higher forms of life become more rare, and the lower are more plentiful. Wherever and whenever in the mighty laboratory of the universe life conditions are, there the life, the outcome of those conditions, must be.

The theory of the origin of the human race from Adam and Eve would have long since been abandoned but for the fact that Adam and his fall have been made the cornerstones of the whole Christian system. If Adam be myth, then the Fall and Atonement cease to be acceptable as truths. The redemption scheme is based on the story of the Fall, and the abandonment of Adam's original sin involves the rejection of the Gospel of Jesus' sacrifice to restore mankind to their original state of perfection.

Nor is the theory of man's gradual development more difficult than the dogma of Adam's sudden creation. No man has ever witnessed the introduction of a new species of living animal, and yet geology affirms the introduction and cessation of many types and species. Vast periods have been necessary for these evolutions, periods transcending the limits of any possible Bible chronology. According to the Bible, the first man's intellectual condition must have been of the highest order; according to science, early man groped in a state of utter barbarism, out of which he has slowly and only partially emerged.

The evidences of man's antiquity on the earth have much increased during the last generation. While in historic investigation doubt has been thrown on the vast ages claimed, fifty years since, in Hindostan and Assyria, it has become clear that to pre-historic man an age must be accorded, beside which the long chronologies of India and Egypt dwindle into the pettiest arrays of insignificant figures. At present an endeavour will be made to marshal some few of the facts demonstrating man's existence on the earth prior to the date given in Genesis.

The difficulty of obtaining evidence of the antiquity of man has, until very lately, been of no ordinary character. Every discovery which seemed to show man to be older than Adam was ignored, explained away, or suppressed. Sir John Lubbock shows us, in the ninth chapter of his "Pre-Historic Times," how, when stone implements of undoubted human manufacture were found near Abbeville, the finder was derided as a madman, because, if real, they demonstrated a vast antiquity for the human family. To-day the flint implements found in France, England, and other countries are too numerous and too well vouched to be prayed down or frowned down as mere Infidel inventions. Three questions arising on these records of the stone age are thus stated by Sir J. Lubbock:—

"1st. Are the so-called flint implements of human workmanship?

"2ndly. Are the flint implements of the same age as the beds in which they are found, and the bones of the extinct animals with which they occur?

"3rdly. What are the conditions under which these beds were deposited? and how far are we justified in imputing to them a great antiquity?"

Answering the two first questions in the affirmative (pp. 276 and 283), Sir John Lubbock speaks of "the enormous time which must have elapsed since the first appearance of man in Western Europe." Referring to a human skull found by Dr. Schmerling in the Cave of Engis, Sir John Lubbock says: "There seems no reason to doubt that it really belonged to a man who was contemporaneous with the mammoth, the cave-bear, and other extinct mammalia."

If one account given by Dr. A. Koch to the Academy of Science at St. Louis be true—and there is no reason for disbelieving it, so far as I am aware, except that it proves the Genesis story to be false—then, at some remote pre-historic period, man had hunted the mastodon in the Mississippi Valley, for the bones of the mastodon, and the arrow heads used by the primitive hunters were found mingled together at Gasconade County, in Missouri ("Pre-Historic Times," p. 234).

It was at one time the fashion to entirely deny the possibility of human fossil remains, but such human fossils have been discovered sufficiently often to preclude the further repetition of such a denial. Sir Charles Lyell, "Antiquity of Man," p. 44, and Agassiz, "Types of Mankind," p. 352, give the case of the jaws with perfect teeth and bones of the foot, found by Count F. de Pourtalès in a bluff on the shores of Lake Monroe, in Florida, having, according to Agassiz, a minimum age of ten thousand years. Those who turn to Nott and Gliddon's work will find there a full statement of the human fossils discovered down to the time of the publication of the "Types of Mankind." Fossil remains of man and the mastodon, similar in appearance, have been discovered together at Natchez, near Vicksburg, Mississippi. To avoid the force of this discovery it was suggested that, although found together and alike in appearance, they belonged to different eras.

Sir Charles Lyell, in his "Antiquity of Man," p. 204, says: "My reluctance in 1846 to regard the fossil human bone as of postpliocene date arose, in part, from the reflection that the ancient loess of Natchez is anterior in time to the whole modern delta of the Mississippi. The table-land, was, I believe, once a part of the original alluvial plain or delta of the great river before it was upraised. It has now risen more than two hundred feet above its pristine level. After the upheaval, or during it, the Mississippi cut through the old fluviatile formation of which its bluffs are now formed, just as the Rhine has in many parts of its valley excavated a passage through its ancient loess. If I was right in calculating that the present delta of the Mississippi has required, as a minimun of time, more than one hundred thousand years for its growth, it would follow, if the claims of the Natchez man to have co-existed with the mastodon are admitted, that North America was peopled more than a thousand centuries ago by the human race. But even were that true, we could not presume, reasoning from ascertained geological data, the Natchez bone was anterior in date to the antique flint hatchets of St. Acheul." In plain words, that the men who wielded these last-named hatchets trod the earth at some period even yet more ancient than 100,000 years ago.

"At the forty-third meeting of the German Scientific and Medical Society at Innspruck, in September, 1869, Mr. Karl Vogt (of Geneva) summed up the main results of the recent Congress of Palæontologists at Copenhagen. After vindicating the place of Primeval History as one of the exact physical sciences, he divided the subject under three headings. 1. *The Age of the Human Race.* There is no longer any doubt that man existed in Europe—probably the latest-peopled part of the world—at a time when the great Southern animals—the elephant, mammoth, rhinoceros, hippopotamus—were found there, which are now extinct. Even where no human remains or tools have been found, the acute researches of Steenstrup have found traces of man by distinguishing the bones which have been gnawed by animals from those which show signs of having been split by man for the sake of the marrow, or otherwise handled by him. It is equally certain that posterior to the advent of man the Straits of Gibraltar, of Dover, and the Dardanelles, as well as Sicily and Africa, were still united by isthmuses; the whole Mediterranean area was separated from Africa by a sea in the basin of Sahara; the Baltic was a sea of ice covering the whole of the low levels of North Germany and Russia, and cutting off Finland, Sweden, and Norway into what would have been an island but for its junction with Denmark. The astonishing researches of Lartel in France, of Fraas in Germany, and of Dupont in Belgium, have proved that this period was succeeded by another, in which men hunted in the countries of Central Europe the reindeer and other Arctic animals, in an Arctic climate, and surrounded by an Arctic flora. We may also speak with confidence of the migrations of these primeval races; the human contemporaries of the most ancient animals —the mammoth, the cave-bear, and the cave-lion—can only be traced in the western and southern parts of Europe. In Central Europe and Switzerland, their remains are unknown. In the 'reindeer period,' again we find man in Switzerland and Suabia; but no trace of him in North Germany and Denmark. 2. *The Growth of Primeval Civilisation* is shown by the striking similarity of the tools dug up in caves of the 'reindeer period' in the South of France with those of the Esquimaux and Greenlanders collected in the Museum at Copenhagen. Our primeval Europeans were, no doubt, savages in the fullest sense, even those with a white skin being distinctly inferior, so far as we can make out, to the lowest type of modern savage, the Australian. They were cannibals, as has been lately shown by researches in Copenhagen. The lake villages in Switzerland, on the other hand, show that agriculture and the pastoral life flourished whilst the metals were still unknown, and that the introduction of them was connected with barter and trade. We are acquainted at present with a number of primeval manufacturing localities, and of the commercial routes which were used in the rudest times. It can be shown, moreover, that our civilisation came, not from Asia, but from Africa; and Heer has proved that cultivated plants in the Swiss lake villages are of African, and, to a great extent, Egyptian origin. 3. *The Corporeal Development of Man*, and the different families, kinds, and races of men, have been far less investigated than the corresponding divisions of the ape type. In many places, the skulls discovered have been few, but less than a year ago a whole cemetery of more than forty human skulls and skeletons, belonging to the 'reindeer period,' was discovered near Solutri, in France. We, therefore, now have considerable material for arriving at conclusions respecting primeval man of this period. There can be no doubt that man approaches more nearly in bodily conformation to the animal, and especially his nearest relative, the ape, the lower his stage of culture. As time goes on, these characteristics gradually vanish, the foreheads becomes more upright, the skull higher and more dome-shaped, and the projecting countenance gradually recedes under the skull. These changes are the result of man's conflict with his circumstances, and to the mental labour which that conflict entails." (*Anthropological Review*, 1870, p. 219.)

Sir John Lubbock ("Pre-Historic Times," p. 320) says that the calculations made by M. Morlot and Professor Gilliéron as to the age of the lake-habitation at Pont de Thièle, near the Lake of Neufchâtel, indicate that "6,000 or 7,000 years ago Switzerland was already inhabited by men who used polished stone implements; but how long they had been there, or how many centuries had elapsed before the discovery of metal, we have as yet no evidence to show."

The *Quarterly Review*, vol. cxxv., p. 438, treating this subject, says: "A very few years ago—in fact, since the discovery of the Swiss lake dwellings—evidence was prominently brought forward in England to prove that the antiquity of man on the earth far transcended the common estimate of six or seven thousand years, seeing that tribes of men making and using very rude stone implements were already living in the time of the extinct quaternary animals. Since then the inquiry has been taken up with great vigour, and the search in gravel beds and limestone caverns has at any rate placed it beyond doubt that savage tribes of men inhabited Europe while the mammoth, the tichorine, the rhinoceros, the cave-bear, and the cave-hyena were still surviving in the land. Various attempts have been made to calculate the age of this period of early human history, and, loose as these estimates have been, it seems at any rate to have been very remote. These investigations, however, beside their inherent interest to all intelligent persons, gained a special attention from being looked upon as hostile to Christianity by a large public, who accordingly either feared them, or sometimes triumphed in them. But those theologians who most thoroughly understand the bearings of the case see at once the uncharitableness and injustice of bringing against such inquiries the imputation of heresy. Dates arrived at by the process of adding up generations and years and days, in such computations as that printed in the margin of our Bibles, can scarcely be regarded as limiting the age of the savages of Brixham and St. Acheul, when they would not be put in evidence against the high antiquity of the mammoths among whom these men lived. And however great may be the merit and use of calculations based on the Bible, they carry upon their face the confession of their indefiniteness, and obviously cannot be taken as binding upon men's faith."

One most interesting piece of evidence as to man's comparative antiquity is that afforded by the remains discovered in the delta of the Mississippi, and on this we quote from Messrs. Nott and Gliddon's "Types of Mankind," p. 337, adding only Sir Charles Lyell's remark, "that nowhere in the world could the geologist enjoy a more favourable opportunity for estimating in years the duration of certain portions of the recent epoch" ("Antiquity of Man," p. 44) : "The average depth of the Gulf of Mexico, between Cape Florida and the mouth of the Mississippi, is about 500 feet. Borings have been made near New Orleans to a depth of 600 feet, without reaching the bottom of the alluvial matter; so that the depth of the delta of the Mississippi may be safely taken at 500 feet. The entire alluvial plain is 30,000 square miles in extent, and the smallest complement of time required for its formation has been estimated at 100,000 years. This calculation merely embraces the deposits made by the river since it ran in its present channel ; but such an antiquity dwindles into utter insignificance when we consider the geological features of the country. The bluffs which bound the valley of the Mississippi rise in many places to a height of 250 feet, and consist of loam containing shells of various species still inhabiting the country. These shells are accompanied with the remains of the mastodon, elephant, and tapir, the megalonyx, and other megatheroid animals, together with the horse, ox, and other mammalia, mostly of extinct species. These bluffs must have belonged to an ancient plain of ages long anterior to that through which the Mississippi now flows, and which was inhabited by occupants of land and fresh-water shells agreeing with those now existing, and by quadrupeds now mostly extinct.

"The plain on which the City of New Orleans is buil rises only nine feet above the sea, and excavations are often made far below the level of the Gulf of Mexico. In these sections, several successive growths of cypress timber have been brought to light. In digging the foundations for the gas works, the Irish spadesman, finding they had to cut through timber instead of soil, gave up the work, and were replaced by a corps of Kentucky axe-men, who hewed their way downwards through four successive growths of timber —the lowest so old that it cut like cheese. Abrasions of the river banks show similar growths of sunken timber, while stately live-oaks flourishing along the bank directly above them, are living witnesses that the soil has not changed its level for ages. Messrs. Dickeson and Brown have traced no less than ten distinct cypress forests at different levels below the present surface, in parts of Louisiana, where the range between high and low-water is much greater than it is at New Orleans. These groups of trees (the live oaks on the banks, and the successive cypress beds beneath), are arranged vertically above each other, and are seen to great advantage in many places in the vicinity of New Orleans.

"Dr. Bennett Dowler ('Tableaux of New Orleans,' 1852) has made an ingenious calculation of the last emergence of the site of that city, in which these cypress forests play an important part. He divides the history of this event into three eras: 1. The era of colossal grasses, trembling prairies, &c., as seen in the lagoons, lakes, and sea coast. 2. The era of the cypress basins. 3. The era of the present live oak platform. Existing types, from the Balize to the highlands, show that these belts were successively developed from the water in the order we have named; the grass preceding the cypress, and the cypress being succeeded by the live oak. Supposing an elevation of five inches in a century (which is about the rate recorded for the accumulation of detrital deposits in the valley of the Nile, during seventeen centuries, by the nilometer mentioned by Strabo), we shall have 1,500 years for the era of aquatic plants until the appearance of the first cypress forest; or, in other words, for the elevation of the grass zone to the condition of a cypress basin.

"Cypress trees of ten feet in diameter are not uncommon in the swamps of Louisiana; and one of that size was found in the lowest bed of the excavation at the gas-works in New Orleans. Taking ten feet to represent the size of one generation of trees, we shall have a period of 5,700 years as the age of the oldest trees now growing in the basin. Messrs. Dickeson and Brown, in examining the cypress timber of Louisiana and Mississippi, found that they measured from 95 to 120 rings of annual growth to an inch, and, according to the lower ratio, a tree of ten feet in diameter will yield 5,700 rings of annual growth. Though many generations of such trees may have grown and perished in the present cypress region, Dr. Dowler, to avoid all ground of cavil, has assumed only two consecutive growths, including the one now standing; this gives us, as the age of two generations of cypress trees, 11,400 years.

"The maximum age of the oldest tree growing on the live oak platform is estimated at 1,500 years, and only one generation is counted. These data yield the following table:—

GEOLOGICAL CHRONOLOGY OF THE LAST EMERGENCE OF THE PRESENT SITE OF NEW ORLEANS.

	Years.
Era of aquatic plants	1,500
Era of cypress basin	11,400
Era of live oak platform	1,500
Total period of elevation	14,400

Each of these sunken forests must have had a period of rest and gradual depression, estimated as equal to 1,500 years for the duration of the live-oak era, which, of course, occurred but once in the series. We shall then certainly be within bounds, if we assume the period of such elevation to have been equivalent to the one above arrived at; and, inasmuch as there were at least ten such changes, we reach the following result:—

	Years.
Last emergence as above	14,400
Ten elevations and depressions, each equal to the last emergence	144,000
Total age of the delta	158,400

In the excavation at the gas-works, above referred to, burnt wood was found at the depth of sixteen feet; and, at the same depth, the workmen discovered the skeleton of a man. The cranium lay beneath the roots of a cypress tree belonging to the fourth forest level below the surface, and was in good preservation. The other bones crumbled to pieces on being handled. The *type* of the cranium was, as might have been xpected, that of the aboriginal American race.

	Years.
we take, then, the present era at	14,400
nd add three subterranean groups, each equal to the living, (leaving out the fourth, in which the skeleton was found)	43,200
We have a total of	57,600

From these data it appears that the human race existed in the delta of the Mississippi more than 57,600 years ago; and the ten subterranean forests, with the one now growing, establish that an exuberant flora existed in Louisiana more than 100,000 years earlier; so that 150,000 years ago the Mississippi laved the magnificent cypress forests with its turbid waters."

Coming to Europe for testimony, we take the Etruscans, utilising here the researches of Nicolucci :—"The primitive Etruscans occupied Tuscany, part of the Perugian province, and part of what became patrimony of St. Peter. They extended their possessions into three directions; and as centres of their new acquisition they founded Felsina (now Bologna), the port of Luni, and Volturno (now Capua). After a period of long duration, however, the Sanmites put an end to the Etruscan dominations in Lower Italy, destroying most of the inhabitants of Volturno; pouring like a torrent over the Alps, invading New Etruria, and ended the power of the Etruscans in Upper Italy, so that Etruria found herself reduced to her former limits; and it was there that the strength of the whole nation, endured with its liberty, its laws, and its name, until it merged into Rome.

"Proofs abound to show that during the stone-age the Etruscan territory was inhabited, for stone utensils and weapons are being found almost everywhere. Stone weapons abound in the Upper Valley of the Tiber (which was Etruscan ground) at Ponte Molle, Tor di Quinto, and Acqua Traversa, on the right bank of the river; and, as they are always found embedded in gravel, and never in sand or clay, it is clear that the primitive seat of the most ancient populations was the slopes of the Appennines, whence these *débris* were carried into the valley. Numerous bones of Elephas meridionalis, antiquies et primigenius, Rhinoceros tichorinus, Hippopotamus major, Bos primigenius, Cervus elaphus, Dama romana, are found in the same strata. And it was during the cutting of the Arezzo and Perugia Railway that Signor Cocchi found, at a depth of forty-eight feet in the valley of Chiana, the human skull known by the name of the Olmo skull. A brown flint lance-point was found at the same place.

"That man inhabited the same regions during the period of the polished stone weapons is abundantly proved by these implements of all kinds being found in the same regions. But still more conclusive are the proofs of the presence of man in that country during the bronze period; and Signor Mellini, in 1854, found in a sepulchral grotto upon Monte Calamita (Elba) three skulls, with a cup and a kind of tumbler in terra-cotta, and other ornaments. Professor Vogt having described these skulls, and Signor Bechi having made an analysis of the bronze, it was recognised that the ancient inhabitants, during the bronze period at least, could in no way belong to the Phœnician or Etruscan types afterwards peopling the same country. Professor Nicolucci thinks that the Umbrians were the masters of Middle Etruria during the bronze period. The cranial indices are nearly the same in the bronze-age man as in the Umbrian skulls found atMisanello, near Bologna" (*Anthropological Journal*, 1870, p. 80).

Probably the strongest English testimony to man's existence at a remote date is that afforded by the discoveries at Kent's Hole, near Brixham (*Westminster Review*, January, 1876, and "Report of Transactions of Plymouth Institution," 1875, on Flint Implements found in Kent's Cavern, by W. Pengelly, F.G.S.) Under two stalagmite floors—one of granular stalagmite five feet thick, and a second floor twelve feet thick, deposited, it is calculated, at the rate of the twentieth part of an inch in 250 years—have been found implements used by man. The following is Mr. Pengelly's own story: "That the deposits, with the constructive and destructive processes described, were not only distinct and successive, but also very protracted terms in the cavern chronology, is strikingly seen in considering the changes they indicate. 1st. During the period of the breccia (*i.e.*, the lowest deposit yet known) there was machinery capable of transporting from Lincombe or Warberry Hill, or both, or from some greater distance, fragments of dark-red grit, varying in size from pieces four inches in diameter to mere sand, and lodging them in the cavern. This so completely passed away, that nothing whatever was carried in, but the deposit already there was covered with a thick sheet of stalagmite, obtained through the solution, by acidulated water, of portions of the limestone in the heart of which the cavern lay. This stage having also ended, the stalagmite was broken up by some natural agency, the exact character of which it is difficult to ascertain, but which achieved its work, not by one effort, but by many in succession, and much of at least the breccia it covered was dislodged and carried out of the cavern. This re-excavating period having in like manner come to a close, a second deposit was introduced; but instead of consisting of dark-red sand and stone, as in the former instance, it was made up of a light-red clay, and in it were embedded small fragments of limestone, which, from their angularity, could not have been rolled, but were in all probability supplied by the waste of the walls and roof of the cavern itself. 2nd. The paleontology of the two deposits is perhaps even more significant of physical changes, and the consequent absorption of time. When the cavern-hunting habits of the hyena are remembered, it will be seen that his entire absence from the fauna of the breccia, and his remarkable preponderance in that of the cave-earth, renders it eminently probable that he was not an occupant of Britain during the earlier period. To accept this, however—and there seems to be no escape from it—is to accept the opinion that, between the eras of the breccia and of the cave-earth, it had become possible for the hyena to reach this country, since he was actually here, and in great force; in other words, the men of the breccia, the ursine period of the cavern, saw this country an island as we see it—unless, indeed, their era was prior to this insularity—when it was also occupied by bears and lions, but not by hyenas; whilst in the time of their descendants or successors the whole of western Europe had been so elevated that the channel which previously and subsequently separated it from the continent was dry, and Britain was in a continental condition."

This evidence goes to show that, even allowing for a much more rapid deposit of the stalagmite than any evidence justifies, a quarter of a million years, and perhaps ten-fold that time, before death came into the world by the first man Adam's sin, barbaric men had lived and died in Devonshire and Cornwall—men whose race we do not know, but whose weapons—more durable than themselves—remain to give testimony to their presence. Two readable lectures by Mr. Pengelly on the Cave-men of Devonshire, detailing, in popular language, the evidence on the subject, are recommended to the reader. When Mr. Vivian first brought the Kent Hole remains to the knowledge of the Geological Society, his paper was suppressed. To-day the same Geological Society has become much more liberal.

We read in the *Times* that on Wednesday evening, April 4th, 1876, at the Geological Society, a joint paper, by the Rev. J. M. Mello and Professor Boyd Dawkins, F.R.S., was read on the mammalia and traces of man found in the Robin Hood Cave. Mr. Mello referred to the explorations, the plan of the cave, and the successive beds met with; and Professor Dawkins described the fossil remains found. Between the present floor of the cave and the rock below four distinct beds can be traced. Beginning at the bottom, the lowest is a bed of sand with limestone fragments, about two feet thick, and containing no bones. Above this is a red sand of three feet thick, containing a large assemblage of bones all marked with hyena teeth. There seems no doubt that the bones were carried into the cave by hyenas. Among the remains is sufficient indication to identify the following—woolly rhinoceros, mammoth lion, grisly bear, brown bear, bison, and reindeer. There is, however, not the slightest trace of man yet met with. Above this sand is a bed of "cave earth," varying from one foot to three feet in thickness. It contains the same assemblage of animal remains as the last bed, but with them are found traces of man—rude, rough implements of quartzite, of the pattern of the valley gravels and the lowest beds of Kent's Hole. Among them one flint scraper has been found. Quartzite pebbles abound close at hand in abundance, and hence the raw material. Above this "cave earth" is a thickness of stalamitic breccia. Here flint implements are the rule and quartzite the exception. Flints for the manufacture of implements are to be met with further off than the quartzite. These implements are of a higher type—that of the spear head. The animal remains in this bed are lion, cave hyena, fox, wolf, grisly and brown bear, Irish elk, reindeer, bison, horse, wild boar, hare. The evidence which this cave affords, with the sequence of superposition of beds so clear, Professor Dawkins spoke of as of the highest importance with reference to the grouping of paleolithic implements. It fits in, too, in a remarkable way with the theories founded on the examination of Continental caves.

No allegation need be, or ought to be, made by Freethinkers as to the antiquity of the human race other than this:—That at a period farther back than any record save that which geology affords, and sufficiently remote to leave no means of fixing it with anything like certainty, undeniable traces of man's presence are found in different portions of the world, and that historic man is certainly carried back to an earlier date than the Mosaic era.

"It is natural," says Paul de Remusat (*Revue des Deux Mondes*, 1870, p. 886), "to inquire whether there does not rest in man some *souvenir* of the years, of the ages, which have preceded what is known as the historic period? Is there nothing, either in the habits or traditions of man, which in any degree recalls the tertiary world and its inhabitants?" Pointing out that many domesticated animals preserve habits inexplicable until illustrated by their condition in a savage state, M. Remusat thus summarises the views of M. Edgar Quinet and Dr. Louis Büchner: "The first ages of man were passed in the midst of gigantic and terrible animals, which it was necessary should be destroyed before there could be any dream of progress or civilisation, for civilisation is impossible without security. It is even possible that the disappearance of some of these monstrous beings, hitherto attributed by geologists to geologic causes, is due to man himself, for a long period incapable of all the arts, but, from the very earliest date, ready to kill. The remembrance of these combats would transmit itself from age to age, and the heroes of these ancient times would be the men who had destroyed the greatest number of animals. Now, the traditions of all peoples represent those of their ancestors whom they admire, and of whom they respect the memory, as sustaining frightful combats against dragons, monsters, and animals strangely formed and of huge size. Was not this because man had really battled with the grand and singular animals of the diluvium and of the tertiary era? The lion of Némée appears very different from the modern lion, and very much like the lion of the cave period. All those monsters destroyed by Hercules and Theseus were perhaps the gigantic animals which no longer exist. And not only the sentiment of their hugeness is perpetuated in the tradition, but their forms even, differing from modern shapes, have not been forgotten. The dragon has not been invented. The poets have described from tradition the pterodactylus." But adds M. de Remusat, "all this is not certain. Pure imagination would have been sufficient to enlarge the beings fought with by our fathers, just as our fathers themselves owe to imagination an exaggerated fame for their strength and courage. The reality of a gigantic animal is not necessary, and in human tradition imagination may figure higher than memory. The mixture of diverse faculties given to the same animal can be explained without invoking pre-historic existence. Men do not know how to entirely invent; they are constrained to increase what they see, or to unite upon some one animal the various gifts naturally distributed over many species. Without having recourse to paleontology, it is easy to understand the fables of the ancients; even the same fables are found amongst different races having no relation with each other."

Not only have human remains of vast antiquity been found, but at Brux, in Bohemia; at Neanderthal, between Düsseldorf and Elberfeld; at Caunsladt, at Lozère, at Engis, in the valley of the Meuse, in Belgium, and at Eguisheim, human skulls have been discovered, some of which are remarkable also for their extreme variance from the skulls of modern races, located in the same countries. The Brux cranium is alleged to belong to the most ancient alluvium, the löss; and this, and the Neanderthal skull, present an illustration of arrested development worthy careful examination by those who mock Mr. Darwin's theory (*Anthropologia*, October, 1874, p. 331). M. Gustave Lagneau, in No. 4 of the *Revue d'Anthropologie*, for 1873, contends that two distinct races are traceable in the North of France back to the age of the mammoth and the reindeer. In Professor Huxley's "Man's Place in Nature," p. 120, he says: "There can be no doubt that the physical geography of Europe has changed wonderfully since the bones of men and mammoths, hyenas and rhinoceroses, were washed pell-mell into the Cave of Engis;" and he explains, in terms easy to the English reader, the distinction used by M. Lagneau, and generally by ethnologists and anthropologists, of "brachycephalic" and "dolichocephalic" skulls. "In some skulls [p. 146] the brain case may be said to be 'round,' the extreme length not exceeding the extreme breadth by a greater proportion than 100 to 80, while the difference may be much less. Men possessing such skulls were termed by Retzius *brachycephalic.* Other skulls have a very different, greatly elongated, form, and may be termed 'oblong.' In this skull the extreme length is to the extreme breadth as 100 to not more than 67, and the transverse diameter of the human skull may fall even below this proportion. People having such skulls were called by Retzius *dolichocephalic.*" Of the Neanderthal skull, Professor Huxley wrote, p. 156: "Under whatever aspect we view this cranium, whether we regard its vertical depression, the enormous thickness of its supraciliary ridges, its sloping occiput, or its long and straight squamosal suture, we meet with ape-like characters, stamping it as the most pithecoid of human crania yet discovered." But, after examination of other bones of the skeleton, he adds, that "in no sense can the Neanderthal bones be regarded as the remains of a human being intermediate between men and apes. At most they demonstrate the existence of a man whose skull may be said to revert somewhat towards the pithecoid type—just as a carrier, or a pouter, or a tumbler, may sometimes put on the plumage of its primitive stock. And, indeed, though truly the most pithecoid of known human skulls, the Neanderthal cranium is by no means so isolated as it would appear to be at first, but forms, in reality, the extreme term of a series leading gradually from it to the highest and best-developed of human crania."

Freethinkers are under no obligation to trace the development of man from some other genus; it is enough to show in antiquity such variations of human type as render impossible the hypothesis of a common origin in one pair less than 6,000 years ago.

Paul Broca, in an essay on L'Anthropologie, in the "Almanach de l'Encyclopédie," ridiculing the petty attempts of theologians to lengthen the Hebrew chronology by the aid of the Septuagint, says: "Il faudra prendre des mesures plus radicales, car ce n'est pas par années ni par siècles, mais par centaines, par milliers de siècles que se supputent les periodes geologiques." That is, that it is not enough to add years or centuries, but that hundreds and thousands of centuries are required. Without regarding the facts as conclusively demonstrated, M. Broca holds that the researches of MM. Desnoyers, Bourgeois, De Launay, and Issel, tend to verify the existence of man in the tertiary period, co-existing with the meridional elephant and the mastodon, and he quotes the discovery by M. Withney, Director of the Geological Survey in California, of the remains of a human skull in a bed of volcanic cinders, and at a depth of 153 feet, and which had above it five layers of volcanic lava and five strata resulting from watery deposit. This discovery was made while sinking a well on the eastern slope of the Sierra Nevada. M. Paul de Remusat, in a critique on M. Edgar Quinet's "La Création," affirms that M. l'Abbé Bourgeois has demonstrated the existence of man in the tertiary period (*Revue des Deux Mondes*, 1870, p. 866). It is scarcely needed that the reader should be reminded that a strong denial is yet maintained against the reality of tertiary man.

The Rev. Bouchier Wrey Savile, intending to damage the

advocates of man's antiquity, says (Journal of the Victoria Institute, 1875, No. 33, p. 39): "Probably at no period has there been such a variety of conjectures concerning the age of man on earth as those put forward in the present day." This is perfectly true; but it is so because, in the present day, specialists have made discoveries in history, anthropology, and geology, each of which discoveries has warranted a fresh conjecture. "The late Baron Bunsen contended," says Mr. Savile, "that man existed on earth about 20,000 B.C., and that there is no valid reason for assuming a more remote beginning of the human race ('Egypt's Place in Universal History,' iii. xxviii.). Mr. Jukes, a distinguished English geologist, places the age of man at 100,000 years." And so the Rev. Mr. Savile would pair off the two scientists as self-contradictory, and therefore availing nothing against the Bible. But Mr. Savile omits two things: 1. That both Baron Bunsen, the historian, and Mr. Jukes, the geologist, concur in carrying man back thousands of years before Adam. 2. That it is precisely in the quarter of a century which has elapsed since Bunsen commenced the publication of his great work on Egypt, that geology, ethnology, and anthropology have united in accumulating for us evidences of man's antiquity. To finish the Rev. Mr. Savile's enumeration: "Professor Fülroth affirms, in his work 'Der Fossile Mensch aus dem Neanderthal,' that it reaches back to a period of from 200,000 or 300,000 years. Dr. Hunt, the late President of the Anthropological Society, not content with the comparatively modest chronology of the Brahmins, which allows the human race an antiquity of 4,300,000 years, according to Sir William Jones, affirms that man has really existed on earth for the prolonged period of 9,000,000 years. While Professor Huxley, though cautiously declining to commit himself by naming a definite number of years, having affirmed in his lecture on the Fossil Remains of Man that the human race was existing when a tropical fauna and flora flourished in our northern clime, *i.e.*, during the Carboniferous era, we might fairly credit his theory concerning the antiquity of man with nine or even ninety millions of years." The Rev. Mr. Savile intends this as a sneer; but, in drawing the reader's attention to this sentence, and the one which follows, I make little doubt that all will see that, in truth, the vast measure of man's sojourn on the earth is not compressible within any limit at present ascertained. "Indeed," adds Mr.

Savile, of Professor Huxley, "in his speech at the Norwich meeting of the British Association, he asked his audience if the distribution of the different types of skulls did not point to a vastly remote time, when the distant localities between which there now rolls a vast ocean were parts of one tropical continent? And if so, does it not throw back the appearance of man on the globe to an era immeasurably more remote than has ever yet been assigned to it by the boldest speculators?" In a note the Rev. Mr. Savile adds: "A French Speculator boldly declares that the horse was killed and eaten in Europe before the commencement of the quarternary (*i.e.*, the post tertiary) up to the period termed the Age of Bronze—that is to say, during a period which cannot be estimated at less than 300,000 years" ("Les Origines du Cheval Domestique," par C. A. Piétrement, quoted by M. Chabas in his "Etudes sur l'Antiquité Historique, d'apres les Sources Egyptiennes"). The Rev. B. W. Savile affirms—and in this we quite agree with him—that "the chronology of Scripture points distinctly to a period of about 6,000 years since the creation of man."

J. E. Howard, pleading on behalf of the Bible view, in a paper on "The Early Dawn of Civilisation Considered in the Light of Scripture," having commenced the human family with the Bible Adam (*Journal of Victoria Institute*, vol. ix., No. 39), is actually obliged to quote with approval the declaration of M. Lenormant, that "we possess no chronometer to determine, even approximately, the duration of the ages and the thousands of years which have elapsed since the first men of whom we find traces."

It may be fairly taken that, whatever the period of man's antiquity, it enormously exceeds the Bible chronology, and the next point treated will be that of the antiquity of type. Man has been here traced back long prior to Adam, and the question that remains for us is, can diversity of race be traced back prior to the alleged date of the Deluge?

At the meeting of the Society of Biblical Archæology on Tuesday, April 4th, 1876, a paper on "The Tertiary Race" was read by the Rev. H. S. Warleigh, M.A., which illustrates the difficulties actually recognised by the clergy, and the strange explanations to which divines are driven. The following were the author's conclusions: "According to the geologists, certain works of art are in existence, which prove that man must have been living as far back as the tertiary period of the earth's crust; and Egyptologists affirm that the advanced state of early civilisation and art prove that man was made more than 6,000 years ago. On the other hand, some theologians say that man was not in existence till the present era, and that therefore mankind could not have produced these works, nor could they be the subjects of this alleged civilisation. These works of art, however, do exist, and they were made during the tertiary period ; but other manufacturers, besides those of the human race, may have produced them. The Bible mentions a race of intelligent and bodily-erect beings as existing before the tertiary period, who were capable of making these works of art, and who were in circumstances which would call for their production. The historical fragments which speak of this race are Genesis vi. 4 and Numbers xiii. 33. The passages which allude to it are Genesis i. 28, iv. 14—25. Thus it is evident that a powerful race, not of human origin, existed in the time of Adam, that it was of immense antiquity, and that it was not extinct in the days of Moses. This race might be called Genus Tertiarum ; or it might receive its Biblical appellation, Ha Nephilim—The Nephilim. This race may have lived in a highly civilised state in the valley of the Nile, and have left the stamp of their power there ; and some of them may have emigrated northward, and built the giant cities of Bashan. Perhaps some parts of ancient mythology relate to them ; and indeed the discovery of such a race throws much light on many obscure subjects of study, and at any rate, if proven on one point, supports the harmony of science and the Bible." The texts relied on by the Rev. Mr. Warleigh do not at all sustain his position, except so far as that Cain's marriage at a time when he had no other relatives than his father and mother is a flat contradiction to the theory of the development of the whole human race from one pair. The Rev. Mr. Warleigh argued that Cain's wife was of the race of the Nephilim, and maintained that—" 1. Though works of art have been found belonging to the tertiary period, this fact does not prove that they were manufactured by any of the human race, or that Adam was created earlier than about 6,000 years ago. They may have been made by the tertiarian race. 2. If the civilisation of Egypt can be proved to be as early as the last modified opinion of Bunsen makes it, this does not prove that it was the civilisation of the human race. It may have been that of the Nephilim, or other races. 3. If the Cyclopean works which are found in various parts of the earth are proved to be earlier than 6,000 years ago, and are of too ponderous a nature to have been executed by the mechanical contrivances in early human times, here is a race with sufficient bodily strength to execute them all with tolerable ease. 4. Many of the heathen mythologies and heroes may have been originated by persons and incidents which took place in times long prior to the days of Adam. 5. Comparative philologists tell us that the two oldest known languages, Hebrew and Sanskrit, bear tokens that they were derived from a common original language. This very language may have been spoken, not only by Adam, but also by these Nephilim; or, at any rate, by the kindred of Cain's wife. 6. If theologians should conclude that the utterances of scientists are inconsistent with the Bible, it may be well for them to reconsider whether these utterances contradict the Bible itself or only our traditions of the Bible. 7. Scientists should not hasten to conclude that the Bible is not defensible when it does not happen to fall in with the present amount of their knowledge. They should distinguish between what they now know and what there is for them yet to learn. 8. The Bible need not decline the test of true and mature science; but partial acquirements are not competent to judge it. 9. The Bible speaks of other powerful races, and it is not improbable that some of their descendants are existing now. 10. All of the *genus homo* have descended from Adam and Eve; but this fact does not prove that other similar, though inferior, *genera* do not exist." These propositions seem to grow out of one of the more than ordinarily weak efforts to reconcile the irreconcileable. If all the *genus homo* are descended from Adam, and if the Nephilim were not descended from Adam, then they were not human beings. If Cain married one of the females of the Nephilim, then he took his wife from amongst inferior animals. The whole hypothesis is pregnant with absurdity, and yet we find the Rev. Dr. Robinson Thornton, Vice-President of the Victoria Institute, saying ("Journal of the Transactions," vol. ix., No. 33, p. 31): "Many, both believers and unbelievers, imagine that, if the supposed discovery of traces of pre-Adamite man were confirmed, it would go very far to invalidate the authority of the Scriptures, and would at all events be inconsistent with the Biblical cosmogony. Is this so certain? I am far from saying that it has yet been satisfactorily made out, or even that reasonable grounds have been shown, for thinking it probable that any rational beings—in human, or even in gorilla, form—did exist before Adam; but is it so clear from the words of the Bible that there could not have been a prior type of humanity, which appeared and disappeared in one of those periods of mundane existence, anterior to the present state of things, at which Scripture hints, though it makes no definite revelation?" That which the Rev. Mr. Warleigh states boldly the Rev. Dr. Thornton, more astutely, puts hypothetically. The facts as to man's existence the Rev. Mr. Warleigh frankly admits, while the Rev. Dr. Thornton uncandidly uses language which may be read both ways. Dr. Hall had, in the introductory synopsis of the Natural History of Man prefixed to Pickering's "Races of Man," stated the point as raised by the Rev. H. S. Warleigh (see Pickering's "Races of Man," Bohn's edition, p. 33). Unless the Rev. Mr. Warleigh means that Egyptian civilisation endured through and despite the alleged Deluge of Noah, his argument is good for nothing; and if Mr. Warleigh means this, then he flatly contradicts Genesis ix. 18, 19, which limits the repeopling of the earth to the descendants of the three sons of Noah. The view, that "from two human beings the universal race of men drew their origin," is strongly maintained by Dr. Hall in the work to which we have just referred, and to which the reader can turn for the orthodox, but unsound, arguments, which may be used against him on this head. Dr. Hall pleads "that the truth and credibility of the Mosaic records are proved by the most striking testimonies of natural and civil history." After dealing with the antiquity of the various types of man, some observations will be offered on this point.

A fine instance of the permanence of type is given in the case of the Egyptian fellah; another in that of the Jew. The first—it is true, always living under one climate, and upon one soil—may be traced back for at least 3,500 years. The second, like the Gipsy, preserves his identity "in all the climates of the earth, and under all forms of government, through extremes of prosperity and adversity." Mr. Layard has found us the Jew, about 2,600 to 2,800 years ago, prominent in the monumental evidence Assyria presents, and this type is traced in Egypt to as far back as 1671 B.C., where in the 17th Theban Dynasty you will find a Greek-faced man and Hebrew-faced woman rulers in Egypt; and these, with other Greek, Jewish, Negro, Nubian, Egyptian, and Asiatic faces, are repeated on the monuments of Egypt.

Four distinct types are shown on one monument, dating about 3,300 years ago. The monuments of the 12th Dynasty—commencing about B.C. 2,337, or 11 years after the Deluge, according to Archbishop Usher's chronology—show Egypto-Caucasian, Asiatic, and Negro faces. It surely is not necessary to argue gravely against the Bible on this point; no sane person could pretend to find all these races only a few years after the Noachic flood had swept the world of life. Dr. Bertillon, in his elaborate article on "Anthropologie" ("Encyclopédie Général," v. ii., p. 348), says: "The permanence of human types, studied in historic times, appears extreme. Upon the monuments of Egypt 4,000 years old we have represented to us of the following types: African Negro, Fellah, Jew, Mongol, Greek, and Hindoo, with the respective characteristics which we know are theirs to-day. And the celebrated New Orleans skull—found underneath the superposed *débris* of four successive gigantic cypress forests buried under the deposits of the Mississippi, and which, according to the very lowest calculation, is more than 15,000 years old—represents the exact type of the North American red skin. Take then the Lydians, or blond Kabyles, with blue eyes—of whose struggles against Egypt 1,600 B.C. the Egyptian hieroglyphs tell the story; whom Scylax notes 1,200 years later, established in the neighbourhood of Mount Auress, precisely where our officers find them to-day; and whom General Faidherbe has studied between our Algerian frontiers and Morocco—clearly proving how tenacious are the human type characteristics, and notably the persistence during from 3,000 to 4,000 years of this blond population on African soil. All these show what enormous resistance race-character opposes to the influence of surroundings (as climate, food, soil, and mode of life) when these are not combined with the otherwise powerful effects of admixtures of race. They prove how destitute of value are efforts indulged in to give an air of reasonableness to Bible History, which—examined by the unimpeachable monuments of Egypt—does not allow as much as 2,000 years to humanity to change from white to black, from the Jewish type to the Ethiopian; when 4,000 years of African sun have not been enough to brown the skin, the hair, or the eyes of the fair Kabyles of Mount Auress. Thus all the evidence, historic and paleontologic, combines to prove the long resistance of type, and how little the imprint of race, that is to say, of heredity, can be effaced by surrounding conditions. From this it results that, if we do not go beyond the historic period, all the probabilities (it is necessary even to say the certainty) are in favour of polygenesis. But to-day, now that it is demonstrated that man has survived several geologic periods, that already he was active in the tertiary period, and that it is necessary to allow millions of years for his history, one ought to avow that in such immensities of time the problem of monogenesis or polygenesis would find itself suppressed. On the one hand, there is no longer any reason to deny that a type, even very inferior, might have been able, under fortunate circumstances, and by a selection of immense duration, to modify itself and to elevate itself by example from an Australian type to an European type. But, on the other hand, there is no more reason to refuse to the creative or evolvive cause of the human type, a simultaneous or successive action in diverse centres of appearance, for creative or evolvive causes almost identical exhibiting themselves as the land emerged would probably produce very similar creations and evolutions. Thus botanists and zoologists explain the similitudes, the relations, and the differences of the diverse flora and fauna, and it is not less rational to suppose different centres of evolution for the human type." But, as Dr. Bertillon adds, these are hypotheses for which we are at present almost without hope of verification. There is no burden on the Freethinker, who finds evidence to reject the Bible story of man, that he should adopt therefore without reservation the views of Mr. Charles Darwin or of Mr. Herbert Spencer. There is only the duty of careful examination of every important hypothesis.

The orthodox editor of the Transactions of the Victoria Institute appears to believe in the rapid transmutability of type. He writes (p. 75, vol. ix.), "Dr. Kitchen Parker has called my attention to the distinct race the Americans are becoming, and how short a time has produced a considerable change." He adds, "The Yankee is a good sub-species already." Principal Dawson, in his address as President of the Montreal Natural History Society (May, 1874), says, in regard to changes culminating rapidly, and then becoming stationary, each "specific type has capacities for the production of varietal and race forms, which are usually exercised to the utmost in the early stages of its existence; and then remain fixed or disappear and reappear as circumstances may arise. Finally, the races fall off one by one as it approaches extinction." If this argument be fully accepted, it may carry us much farther than would be approved by the pious editor of the journal of the Victoria Institute. Admitting that all vegetables and animals transported to countries differing essentially in soil and climate must be affected by the new surroundings, and this in a degree proportioned to the quality of the plant or animal and difference of surroundings, it is here denied that the amalgam in the United States of differing races, under conditions new and abnormal for nearly all the races, furnishes any evidence in favour of the orthodox theory.

At the close of the essay in the "Types of Mankind," on the Comparative Anatomy of Races, p. 465, Dr. Nott stated a number of positions which, so far as they seem to me to be borne out by the evidence, I shall here repeat, with some verbal variation, for which Dr. Nott must not be held responsible :—

1. That the surface of our globe is naturally divided into several zoological provinces, each of which is a distinct centre of evolution, possessing a peculiar fauna and flora; and that every species of animal and plant originated in its appropriate province.

2. That the human family offers no exception to this general law, but fully conforms to it : mankind being divided into several groups of races, each of which constitutes an element in the fauna of its particular province.

3. That history affords no evidence of the transformation of one type into another, nor of the origination of a new and permanent type ; but that pre-historic records do tend to show types of man then existing, which we cannot trace to-day.

4. That certain types have been permanent for at least 15,000 years.

5. That permanence of type is a sure test of specific character.

6. That certain types have existed, the same as now, in and round the valley of the Nile, for a period prior to any alphabetic chronicles.

7. That the ancient Egyptians had already portrayed mankind as known to them, in diverse types, prior to any date assignable to Moses.

8. That high antiquity for distinct races is amply sustainable by scientific testimony.

9. That the existence of man, myriads of years since, in widely-separate portions of the globe, is proven by the dis-

covery of his osseous and industrial remains in alluvial deposits and diluvial drifts; and more especially of his fossil bones imbedded along with the vestiges of extinct species of animals.

Dr. John Charles Hall says: "For that period of the world's history, from the Creation to the Deluge, we are solely indebted to the Mosaic records, the truth and credibility of which are proved by the most striking testimonies of natural and civil history" (Pickering's "Races of Man," p. 35). If by Mosaic records he meant the Pentateuch, it is enough to say that, so far as civil history is concerned, there is not even a fragment of corroborative testimony for the Pentateuch to be found in civil history; and wherever natural history is capable of being called on for evidence, there is the most distinct contradiction between its version and that of the Bible.

It is hardly necessary to remind the careful reader of Genesis of the narrow and purely local creation conception of the Genesaic writer or writers. There is no broad or grand view of the universe given in the Bible story. You have an all-important earth, with a fixed firmament or sky above, in which are also fixed the sun, moon, and stars, to give light to the earth. Above this firmament are stores of water to be let down when God shall open the windows of heaven. This the limited view of cosmos stated by a very poor narrator. That the earth was only one, and not the chief, member of the solar system—that myriads of worlds, and countless thousands of mighty suns, revolved in the vast expanse—all this was a conception, utterly beyond the untrained brain which bequeathed us the story of the creation of Adam and Eve. Kalisch says (Genesis, p. 51): "The Bible is not silent on creation; it attempts, indeed, to furnish its history; but in this account it expresses facts which the researches of science cannot sanction, and which were the common errors of the ancient world."

The creation account is in the highest degree self-contradictory, as will be shown by the following epitome, which has been used by many writers before our time, and was published by us in the earliest edition of "The Bible: What it is," in 1856 (see last edition, Genesis, p. 20).

FIRST ACCOUNT (Genesis i. 1, to Genesis ii. 3).	SECOND ACCOUNT (commencing Genesis ii. 4).
Water abundant (i. 2, 5, 6, 9, 10).	Water deficient (ii. 5, 6).

Vegetation proceeds at God's fiat (i. 11, 12).	Vegetation does not take place for want of moisture and tillage (ii. 5).
Plants and herbs grow in the earth prior to the existence of man (i. 12).	Plants are not in the earth, and herbs do not grow because there is not a man to till the ground (ii. 5).
Animals are created before man (i. 20, 21, 24, 25).	Animals are created after man (ii. 19).
Man and woman created same day (i. 26, 27).	Man created first (ii. 7) and alone (18), then an interval for the creation and naming of animals (19, 20), then the subsequent creation of woman (21, 22), there having been no helpmeet found for him amongst the cattle, beasts, and fowl (20).
Man made to have dominion over all the earth (i. 28).	Man made to dress and keep the Garden of Eden (ii. 15).
Every fruit given to man for food (i. 29).	One kind forbidden (ii. 17), and another withheld (iii. 22).
Concludes with blessing (ii. 3).	Concludes with cursing (iii. 14 to 19).

(See also Kalisch on Genesis, p. 83).

The question with which this section opened has now its distinct answer, so far as it is possible here to give it. The Genesis story of man's origin is not true; the "whence and how" of man is not traceable in the Pentateuchal narrative. On page 65 we have alluded to the hypothesis which, accepting the universe as sufficient for all its phenomena, affirms the evolution of life instead of inventing a life-creator other than the universe, in order to account for life. It does not, however, come within our scope to trace out and examine the evolution theory in detail. Mr. Herbert Spencer, in his "First Principles," his "Principles of Biology and Psychology," and his "Descriptive Sociology," stands as teacher at the head of one school of English Evolutionists, and to him the reader is referred. Nor can we attempt here to follow, step by step, the gradual ascent from the earliest-recorded simple life-form of primeval time to the complex organisations now spread over the globe. This has been done by such men as Mr. Alfred Wallace, and, with untiring patience, by Dr. Charles Darwin. The latter, in his "Origin of Species" and "Descent of Man," suggests how, "under the laws of growth, with reproduction; inheritance almost implied by reproduction; variability from the indirect and direct action of the external conditions of life, and from use and disuse; a ratio of increase so high as to lead to a struggle for life, and as a consequence to natural selection, entailing divergence of character and extinction of less improved forms;" life-forms adapt themselves to the conditions around them. These life-forms, by the survival of those best suited to their environment, have, he maintains, ascended in a long gradation, becoming more and more complex as they ascend, evolving through countless generations the organs most fitted to maintain and to preserve life, modified by the conditions surrounding them, and, in their turn, modifying those conditions, and thus, by a continual inter-action, evolving the races of animal life now existent.

Amongst the objections to Mr. Darwin's "Theory of Natural Selection" are :—

1. The absence of transitional forms, it being an admitted fact that species are now, if not fixed in their boundaries, yet remarkably well-defined. To this Mr. Darwin rejoins that the records are fragmentary, and the researches incomplete.

2. The inconceivability of the proposition that the highest organisms have arisen through successive modifications by natural selection from the lowest forms. This is, however, an objection of a nature often hazarded in the infancy of mighty theories.

3. The special difficulty of conceiving the "instincts" of the bee and ant as having so arisen.

4. The fact that sterility results from hybridism. This objection, it is maintained, is not fairly against Mr. Darwin, but against a misconception of his teachings.

The general evolution theory, as distinguished from that of Mr. Darwin, is that "the multitudinous kinds of organisms that now exist, or have existed during past geologic eras, have arisen by insensible steps through actions such as we see habitually going on."

Professor Huxley says ("Lectures on Organic Nature," p. 26): "We have gradually traced down all organic forms, or, in other words, we have analysed the present condition of animated nature, until we found that each species took its origin in a form similar to that under which all the others commenced their existence. We have found the whole of the vast array of living forms, with which we are surrounded, constantly growing, increasing, decaying, and disappearing; the animal constantly attracting, modifying, and applying to its sustenance the matter of the vegetable kingdom which derived its support from the absorption and conversion of inorganic matter."

The evolution of man from lower forms of life scarcely, as yet, takes rank as a scientific truth; it is rather a grand hypothesis, which, if verified, may throw light on many problems of existence, and is, at least, in analogy with the workings of nature, so far as we know them. When we first catch a glimpse of man, he is, as has been already shown, but a half-human animal dwelling in caves, disputing with his co-brutes for existence; we can trace him thence upwards to the civilised European; it seems reasonable, then, to trace him downwards also to the unintelligent life in its lowest forms, halting only when organic and inorganic blend together in the far-off yesterday.

INDEX TO SECTION I. OF PART I.

WORKS QUOTED.

SUBJECTS.

RELIGION: WHAT & WHY?

OR, GOD = X.

It has been broadly contended that man is a religious animal, and it is no unfrequent thing to hear it asserted that all men, however barbarous, have some religion. The Rev. Mr. Pearson, in his prize essay on "Infidelity," p. 7, says: "Faith in God is so inherent in the heart of humanity, and so essential to our reason, that many wise and good men have doubted if ever there lived an intelligent mortal so absolutely destitute of religious belief as is implied in Atheism." Sir John Lubbock ("Origin of Civilisation," p. 121) says: "The opinion that religion is general and universal has been entertained by many high authorities. Yet it is opposed to the evidence of numerous trustworthy observers. Sailors, traders, and philosophers, Roman Catholic priests and Protestant missionaries, in ancient and modern times, in every part of the globe, have concurred in stating that there are races of men who are devoid of religion. The case is stronger, because in several instances the fact has greatly surprised him who records it, and has been entirely in opposition to all his pre-conceived views. On the other hand, it must be confessed that in some cases travellers denied the existence of a religion merely because the tenets were unlike ours. The question as to the general existence of religion among men is, indeed, to a great extent, a matter of definition. If the mere sensation of fear, and the recognition that there are other beings more powerful than man, are sufficient alone to constitute a religion, then we must, I think, admit that religion is general to the human race. But when a child dreads the darkness, and shrinks from a lightless room, we never regard that as an evidence of religion. Moreover, if this definition be adopted, we can no longer regard religion as peculiar to man. We must admit that the feeling of a dog or a horse towards its master is of the same character, and the baying of a dog to the moon is as much an act of worship as some ceremonies which hav been so much described by travellers."

The inhabitants of the world are roughly calculated at about 1,300,000,000, whose religions are, in the "Statesman's Year-Book," given as follows :—

Buddhists...	405,600,000
Christians...	399,200,000
Mahomedans	204,200,000
Brahminists	174,200,000
Nondescript Heathens	111,000,000
Jews	5,000,000

This calculation is loose and inaccurate, as it makes no allowance for Sceptics in Europe or America ; and, notwithstanding that every man, woman, and child, is put down as either Protestant, or Catholic, or Jew, there are certainly a very large number of men and women on both Continents who ought not to be classified as Christians. For example, in Great Britain and Ireland, where Earl Russell said, in a speech, that there were "millions of Atheists," we have the whole population, except the Jews, recorded as if they were, every one, either Catholic or Protestant. We think that Earl Russell erred considerably in his enumeration of English Atheists, but it is, nevertheless, certain that there are, in Great Britain, very large numbers of Freethinkers. We find the Bishop of Ripon, in his triennial charge, prominently mentioning the growth of Scepticism ; the Home Secretary, Mr. Cross, in the House of Commons, recently testified to the increase in numbers and influence of English Freethinkers ; and the Rev. Gervase Smith, the President of the Wesleyans, gave similar testimony. In France, where 98½ per cent. of the population are returned as Catholics, and the other 1½ per cent. as Protestants, we find a large number of Bishops, headed by l'Evêque d'Orleans, declaring that nearly all the members of the medical profession in that country are Materialists, and that the professional schoolmasters are anti-Christian (Les Alarmes de l'Episcopat justifiées par les Faits). It is, too, a noticeable fact that, in the large centres of industry, funerals without any religious ceremonies are extremely frequent, and are attended by very large gatherings of persons, who openly favour the abstaining from religious rites.

In Germany, and in the various States united as the Germa-

Empire, although here, too, every one is put down as either Protestant or Roman Catholic, the Freethinking element is very large indeed. Besides those who are really Freethinkers, there is, in France and Germany, a very large proportion of the male population who are utterly indifferent to Christianity. "Germany," says the Rev. Thos. Pearson, "of all the countries of modern Europe, is the most prolific soil of Pantheism" (p. 28). "And Pantheism reaches the point to which it is ever tending—the very verge of Atheism. Such has been, and is, in a great measure, still the faith of immense multitudes of people on the Continent in the middle of the nineteenth century" (p. 33).

In the United States the number of sects of Christians is very large, and many Unitarians are classified as Christians, although they are Theists only. Outside these there is a very large mass of Americans who are certainly not Christians, although so reckoned in the above figures. Mr. Pearson says: "The Emerson school, which numbers many disciples in our land, is unquestionably Pantheistic. Emerson himself, with all his gorgeous mysticism, is a Pantheist" (p. 34).

Besides these exceptions, there are also, throughout the world, many persons without any religion at all, and a larger number still whose views on religion are utterly at variance with either Christianity, Mahomedanism, Buddhism, Brahminism, or Judaism. These probably are estimated above amongst the "Nondescripts."

In answer to the frequently-repeated allegation, that even the most savage peoples have some religion, it is sufficient to cite the following cases:—

"The Mincopies, or inhabitants of the Andaman Islands, have been described by Dr. Mouatt and Professor Owen, who consider that they 'are, perhaps, the most primitive or lowest in the scale of civilisation of the human race.'...... They have no idea of a Supreme Being, no religion, nor any belief in a future state of existence" ("Pre-historic Times," by Sir Jno. Lubbock, pp. 345—6).

The natives of Australia "have no religion, nor any idea of prayer," says the same writer; but as he adds, "most of them believe in evil spirits," we presume that he meant that they had no belief in a Supreme Being (p. 353).

The Tasmanians are described by the Rev. T. Dove as distinguished "by the absence of all moral views and impressions. Every idea bearing on our origin and destiny as rational beings seems to have been erased from their breasts" (p. 465). When the Rev. T. Dove says that the idea has been erased, he merely means that he found no trace of any such idea.

The Samoans "had no religion" (p. 357).

"According to Crantz, the Greenland Esquimaux have neither a religion nor idolatrous worship, nor so much as any ceremonies to be perceived tending towards it" (p. 409).

The following tribes of Indians had not "any ideas of religion:" "Charruas, Minuanas, Aucas, Guaranys, Guayanas, Nalicuégas, Guasarapos, Guatos, Ninaquiguilas, Guanas, Lenguas, Aguilots, Mocobys, Abissons, and Paraguas" (p. 427).

"According to the Missionaries, neither the Patagonians nor the Auracanians had any ideas of prayer, or any vestige of religious worship" (p. 431).

Of the inhabitants of Tierra Del Fuego, Adolph Decker says: "There is not the least spark of religion or policy to be observed amongst them" (p. 432). "Like Decker, Admiral Fitzroy never witnessed, or heard, any act of a decidedly religious nature" (p. 437).

After making various statements showing the intellectual inferiority of savages, Sir John Lubbock says (p. 467): "It has been asserted over and over again that there is no race of men so degraded as to be entirely without a religion—without some idea of a Deity. So far from this being true, the very reverse is the case. Many, we might almost say all, of the most savage races are, according to the nearly universal testimony of travellers, in this condition." Burton states that some of the tribes in the Lake districts of Central Africa "admit neither God, nor angel, nor devil" (p. 468). "In the Pellew Islands Wilson found no religious buildings nor any sign of religion..........Some of the tribes (of Brazilian Indians), according to Bates and Wallace, were entirely without religion. The Yenadies and the Villees are, according to Dr. Short, without any belief in a future state. Captain Grant could find no distinct form of religion in some of the comparatively civilised tribes visited by him. And again Hooker tells us that the Lepchas of Northern India have no religion" (p. 468). "It is evident," says M. Bik, "that the Arafuras of Vockay (one of the Southern Arus) possess no religion whatever. Of the immortality of the soul they have not the least conception" ("Origin of Civilisation," Sir J. Lubbock, p. 122).

"Among the Koossa Kaffirs, Lichtenstein affirms that

there is no appearance of any religious worship whatever (p. 123).

"It might be the proper time now," says Father Baegert, "to speak of the form of government and the religion of the Californians previous to their conversion to Christianity, but neither the one nor the other existed among them.......Religious worship or ceremonies were unknown to them, and they neither believed in the true and only God, nor adored false deities.......I made diligent inquiries amongst those with whom I lived, to ascertain whether they had any conception of God, a future life, and their own souls, but I never could discover the slightest trace of such a knowledge. Their language has no words for 'God' and 'Soul'" (p. 124).

"Several tribes," says Robertson, "have been discovered in America which have no idea whatever of a Supreme Being, and no rites of religious worship" (p. 124).

It is denied ("Encyclopédie Générale," article, Athées Peuples) that the islanders of Molugues and New Guinea have any idea of God. Sir J. Emerson Tennant affirms that the Veddahs of Ceylon have no idols, no altars, no religion, no prayers, no knowledge of God, no conception of future life. This is confirmed by Bailey, who resided a long time amongst these people. After a residence of many years in Australia Dr. Aram affirms that the Aborigines near Cape York were utterly destitute of any religion until they had been taught by the Europeans ("Bulletin de la Société d'Anthropologie," 1868, quoted in "Encyclopédie Générale").

Sir Samuel Baker says that the indigenous races of Ounyoro have no idea of God or of a future state, and that they worship nothing. The Obbos are in the same state; and an interesting conversation between Sir Samuel Baker and Commoro, King of the Latoukas, shows that the Latouka had not even a superstitious sentiment or any conception by which Sir Samuel Baker could explain to him any religious idea (same authority).

Moffat, the missionary who passed twenty-three years in Southern Africa, affirms that the Caffres, the Bechuanas, the Hottentots, and the Bushmen were utterly without any kind of religious notions except after having had communication with the Europeans. M. Casalis confirms this as to the Bassoutos, a Bechuanan tribe.

Not only do we find so many peoples entirely without religion, but we also find "that religion, as understood by the lower savage races, differs essentially from ours; nay, it is not only different, but even opposite. Thus then the deities are evil, not good; they may be forced into compliance with the wishes of man; they require bloody, and rejoice in human, sacrifices; they are mortal not immortal; a part of, not the author of, nature; they are to be approached by dances rather than by prayers; and often approve what we call vice, rather than what we esteem as virtue" ("Origin of Civilisation," Sir J. Lubbock, p. 116). He urges that "Hitherto it has been usual to classify religions according to the nature of the object worshipped; Fetichism, for instance, being the worship of inanimate bodies, Sabæism that of the heavenly bodies. The true test, however, seems to me to be the estimate in which the Deity is held. The first great stages in religious thought may, I think, be regarded as—

"Atheism; understanding by this term, not a denial of the existence of a Deity, but an absence of any definite ideas on the subject.

"Fetichism; the stage in which man supposes that he can force the Deity to comply with his desires.

"Nature-worship, or Totemism; in which natural objects, trees, lakes, stones, animals, &c., are worshipped.

"Shamanism; in which the superior deities are more powerful than man, and of a different nature. Their place of abode is also far away, and accessible only to Shamans.

"Idolatry, or Anthropomorphism; in which the gods take still more completely the nature of men, being, however, more powerful. They are still amenable to persuasion; they are a part of nature, and not creators. They are represented by images or idols.

"In the next stage the Deity is regarded as the author, not merely a part, of nature. He becomes for the first time a really supernatural being."

All these stages, except the first, we should include in the first stage," "the theological state," of M. Auguste Comte, who says (chap. 1, Positive Philosophy, Harriet Martineau's translation): "In the theological state, the human mind, seeking the essential nature of beings, the first and final causes (the origin and purpose) of all effects—in short, absolute knowledge—supposes all phenomena to be produced by the immediate action of supernatural beings."

"In the metaphysical state, which is only a modification of the first, the mind supposes, instead of supernatural beings, abstract forces, veritable entities (that is, personified abstractions) inherent in all beings, and capable of producing all phenomena. What is called the explanation of phenomena is, in this stage, a mere reference of each to its proper entity."

"In the final, the positive state, the mind has given over the vain search after absolute notions the origin and destination of the universe, and the causes of phenomena, and applies itself to the study of these laws,—that is, their invariable relations of succession and resemblance. Reasoning and observation, duly combined, are the means of this knowledge. What is now understood when we speak of an explanation of facts is simply the establishment of a connection between single phenomena and some general facts, the number of which continually diminishes with the progress of science.

The great confusion of thought and looseness of language common to religious writers is admirably illustrated by the declaration of the Rev. Dr. J. Pye Smith ("First Lines of Christian Theology," p. 108) that "indeed, the difference between a Deist and an Atheist is practically very inconsiderable." It is in truth only the difference between recognising a God and not recognising any God, and this the great Christian controversialist thought a "very inconsiderable" difference. The variety of religions amongst different peoples arises as Mr. Henry Buckle puts it: "A very ignorant people will, by virtue of their ignorance, incline towards a religion full of marvels, a religion which boasts of innumerable gods, and which ascribes every occurrence to the immediate authority of those gods. On the other hand, a people whose knowledge makes them better judges of evidence, and who are accustomed to that most difficult task, the practice of doubting, will require a religion less marvellous, less obtrusive, one that taxes their credulity less heavily" ("History of Civilisation," vol. i., p. 254).

Speaking of David Hume's "Natural History of Religion" Mr. Buckle says (vol. iii., p. 345): "The object of Hume in writing it was to ascertain the origin and progress of religious ideas; and he arrives at the conclusion, that the worship of many gods must, everywhere, have preceded the worship of one god. This he regards as a law of the human mind, a thing not only that always has happened, but that always must happen. His proof is entirely speculative. He argues that the earliest state of man is necessarily a savage state; that savages can feel no interest in the ordinary operations of nature, and no desire to study the principles which govern those operations; that such men must be devoid of curiosity on all subjects which do not personally trouble them; and that, therefore, while they neglect the usual events of nature, they will turn their minds to the unusual ones. A violent tempest, a monstrous birth, excessive cold, excessive rain, sudden and fatal diseases, are the sort of things to which the attention of the savage is confined, and of which alone he desires to know the cause. Directly he finds that such causes are beyond his control, he reckons them superior to himself; and being incapable of abstracting them, he personifies them; he turns them into deities; polytheism is established; and the earliest creed of mankind assumes a form which can never be altered as long as men remain in this condition of pristine ignorance."

E. B. Tylor, treating on the use of idols, says: "The idol answers to the savage in one province of thought, the same purpose that its analogue the doll does to the child. It enables him to give a definite existence and a personality to the vague ideas of higher beings, which his mind can hardly grasp without some material aid..........It does not appear that idols accompany religious ideas down to the lowest levels of the human race, but rather that they belong to a period of transition and growth.........It does not seem, indeed, that the growth of the use of images may be taken as any direct measure of the growth of religious ideas, which is complicated with a multitude of other things. But it seems that when man has got some way in developing the religious element in him, he begins to catch at the device of setting a puppet or a stone as the symbol and representative of the notions of a higher being which are floating in his mind. He sees in it, as a child does in a doll, a material form which his imagination can clothe with all the attributes of a being which he has never seen, but of whose existence and nature he judges by what he supposes to be its works. He can lodge it in the place of honour, cover it up in the most precious garments, propitiate it with offerings such as would be acceptable to himself" ("Early History of Mankind," p. 110).

What is the religious sentiment for which so much is claimed, which is so often named, so little explained? In a savage it is the result of the prostration of the yet untrained intellect at the threshold of the unknown. In a St. Augustin it is still the prostration of the intellect on the same threshold. The "religious sentiment" is neither less nor greater than the area within which—either from inherited pre-disposition to habit-thought, or from intellectual incompetence—no inquiry is made, and where "God" is the symbol-word used, in lieu of all research, as the answer to all inquiry from without.

What is religion? Mr. John Stuart Mill says: "We venture to think that a religion may exist without belief in a God;" and in answer to the question, "What are the conditions necessary to constitute a religion?" he responds: "There must be a creed, or conviction, claiming authority over the whole of human life; a belief, or set of beliefs, deliberately adopted, respecting human destiny and duty, to which the believer inwardly acknowledges that all his actions ought to be subordinate. Moreover, there must be a sentiment connected with this creed, or capable of being invoked by it, sufficiently powerful to give it, in fact, the authority over human conduct, to which it lays claim in theory;" and "if a person has an ideal object, his attachment and sense of duty towards which are able to control and discipline all his other sentiments and propensities, and prescribe to him a rule of life, that person has a religion" ("Auguste Comte and Positivism," p. 133).

Disagreeing almost entirely with Mr. Mill on this head, we venture to affirm that the word religion must always be taken, and except in the case of the Positivists has always been taken, to involve some assertion of the supernatural. That the creed accepted on authority must, if it be entitled to be classed as religious, contain affirmations admittedly incapable of verification by experience, and that Saint Augustin, in his "Confessions," is here a truer exponent of religion than Mr. Mill in his presentation of what the Positivists call "the religion of humanity." In his essay on he "Utility of Religion," Mr. Mill does identify religion with belief in the supernatural.

Mr. H. G. Atkinson writes to Miss Martineau ("Man's Nature and Development," Letter XX., p. 229): "He who does not suppose a personal god, or look for a future, may, nevertheless, be most unselfish and deeply religious; so religious, that he shrinks from all the forms of worship, because he sees in them all but forms of worship—forms of fancy, and not the spirit of truth. There are thousands upon thousands who have no clear knowledge on any one question relating to their religion."

In Auguste Comte's "Catechism of Religion," Conversation 1, we find the woman saying to the Positivist priest: "Your doctrine rejects every form of belief in a supernatural power: why do you persist in calling it a religion?" And the Positivist priest answers that the term religion "has no necessary connection with any opinions whatever.........In itself it expresses the state of perfect unity which is the distinctive mark of man's existence, both as an individual and in society, when all the constituent parts of his nature, moral as well as physical, are made habitually to converge towards one common purpose.........Religion, then, consists in regulating each one's individual nature, and forms the rallying point for all the separate individuals."

This is a meaning given to the word religion by M. Comte, but it is not a meaning which many religious people would accept outside the ranks of his own disciples.

M. Auguste Comte repudiates "all philosophical or historical connection between Positivism and what is called Atheism," but scarcely does justice to Atheism. He says that the tendency of Atheism "is to prolong the metaphysical stage indefinitely by continuing to seek for new solutions of theological problems, instead of setting aside all inaccessible researches on the ground of their utter inutility" ("System of Positive Polity," vol. i., p. 36, Dr. Bridge's translation).

Dr. Congreve, the authorised English exponent of Positivism, says: "It is by sympathy, by the due training and encouragement of the sympathetic instincts, that man attains victory over his selfish personality, and constitutes his inward unity in the only way in which it is reconcileable with the service of others. And I believe that the older faith of our earlier years was right in thinking that this internal unity was unattainable, except in submission, in the recognition of some external power, some power outside and above the individual; that it was with reason that the love of God was made the first and great commandment. We change the language, but keep the truth it embodied. The power outside and above the individual is for us Humanity; and in the love and service of Humanity must we find that motor force which can secure the triumph of our altruistic over our self-regarding nature" ("Essays: Political, Social, and Religious," p. 363).

Louis de Blois ("Le Directeur des Ames Religeuses," chapter i.), in the sixteenth century, takes the extreme opposite, where he affirms that, to enter into a religious order, "C'est afin de mourir au monde et à vous-même; c'est afin de ne vivre que pour Dieu seul." That is, that in devoting oneself to religion, one becomes dead to the world and to oneself, and lives for God alone. This renunciation of the world in accepting religion is formally embodied, though in milder language, in the Church of England renunciation of the "pomps and vanities of this wicked world." Dr. John Pye Smith observes that "religion is a sense of the relation between ourselves and the absolutely perfect being, the Deity, and of the duties and expectations thence arising;" and defines religion as—1. "Theology in its most general acceptation—the declarations of fact upon which religion is built as the just consequence." 2. "Natural theology: those principles of knowledge concerning the attributes and government of the Deity which the human mind is naturally competent to discover, by observation, reflection, and inference." 3. "Revealed, and particularly Christian, theology—the principles of knowledge concerning the attributes and government of God, and their connections and consequences, which are either assumed or disclosed by the declarations of a positive revelation" ("First Lines of Christian Theology," book i., chap. i.). He also (chap. ii.) defines Natural Religion to be "such opinions on the method of honouring Deity and obtaining his favour as may be acquired by human research and reasoning, without any Divine revelation."

A writer in the *Westminster Review* (vol. xcvi., p. 457) says: "Every religion is an attempt to solve the mystery of things, to furnish an explanation, not only of the physical world about us, but also of that moral world which reveals itself to the introverted gaze. The religion of the savage has few or no moral elements in it, because his own moral nature has scarcely as yet glimmered upon his consciousness. But, as a race advances, it begins to crave for a solution of other questions than those connected with outward things, and its religion deepens in tone. Thenceforward we find religions serving the double purpose of a physical theory of the universe and an explanation of moral problems."

Thomas Pearson, in his prize essay on "Infidelity" (p. 5), includes the following as amongst "the commonly-understood doctrines of natural and revealed religion"—viz., "The independent existence of one absolutely perfect Being, the creator, preserver, and governor of all things; the doctrine of the Trinity, or of three persons in the Godhead—the Father, the Son, and the Holy Spirit."

A writer in the *Quarterly Review* (vol. cix., p. 289), attacking the "Essays and Reviews," says: "There can be no religious system which is not founded upon definite teaching as to God, and as to his relation to us. The very name of a theology testifies to man's universal sense of this truth, even where it is held unconsciously and instinctively, and not reasoned out into a proposition. Even a false faith, if it is to be effectual at all, must rest upon a theology."

Bishop Butler says "religion implies a future state" ("Analogy of Religion," chap. i.).

The Duke of Argyll says: "M. Guizot's affirmation, that belief in the supernatural is essential to all religion, is true only when it is understood in a special sense. Belief in the existence of a living will—of a personal god—is indeed a requisite condition" ("Reign of Law," p. 51).

On the whole, then, as all believers in God include in the word "religion" some belief in a Deity, and as they certainly have a prior claim to the term, it appears to me to be wiser, franker, more honest, to avoid using an old word in a new sense, and thus to prevent the certainty of misconception on the part of those around us.

It should be clearly and specially insisted by Freethinkers that the words used by theologians should have their meanings clearly and definitely stated, and that the definitions should be such as can be tested by the records of experience. In dealing with God and his attributes, it is intended here to argue from the commonly-received meaning of words; although orthodox speakers and writers often write of God's love, goodness, benevolence, mercy, or justice, and then object to having to defend acts in contradiction of the ordinary sense of those words.

It is contended by some that God, being infinite, cannot at all be judged by finite man, and that, therefore, when any matters are alluded to as being inconsistent with Divine power, wisdom, or goodness, we are to consider that these attributes, alleged to exist in God, are not liable to criticism by man. It is on this point that John Stuart Mill specially conflicted with Mr. Mansel (see "Examination of Sir W. Hamilton," p. 121).

"It is a fact," says Mr. Mansel ("Limits of Religious

Thought," preface to 4th edition, p. 13), "which experience forces upon us, and which it is useless were it possible to disguise, that the representation of God after the model of the highest human morality which we are capable of conceiving, is not sufficient to account for all the phenomena exhibited by the course of his natural providence. The infliction of physical suffering, the permission of moral evil, the adversity of the good, the prosperity of the wicked, the crimes of the guilty, involving the misery of the innocent, the tardy appearance and partial distribution of moral and religious knowledge in this world—these are facts which, no doubt, are reconcileable, we know not how, with the infinite goodness of God, but which certainly are not to be explained on the supposition that its sole and sufficient type is to be found in the finite goodness of man." "In other words," replies Mr. Mill, "it is necessary to suppose that the infinite goodness ascribed to God is not the goodness which we know and love in our fellow creatures, distinguished only as infinite in degree, but is different in kind, and another quality altogether. When we call the one finite goodness, and the other infinite goodness, we do not mean what the words assert, but something else; we intentionally apply the same name to things which we regard as different. Accordingly, Mr. Mansel combats, as a heresy of his opponents, the opinion that infinite goodness differs only in degree from finite goodness...... When we mean different things we have no right to call them by the same name, and to apply to them the same predicates, moral and intellectual. Language has no meaning for the words just, merciful, benevolent, save that in which we predicate them of our fellow creatures; and, unless that is what we intend to express by them, we have no business to employ the words. If, in affirming them of God, we do not mean to affirm these very qualities, differing only as greater in degree, we are neither philosophically nor morally entitled to affirm them at all......What belongs to it (infinite goodness), either as absolute or infinite, I do not pretend to know, but I know that infinite goodness must be goodness, and that what is not consistent with goodness, is not consistent with infinite goodness. If in ascribing goodness to God, I do not mean what I mean by goodness; if I do not mean the goodness of which I have some knowledge, but an incomprehensible attribute of an incomprehensible substance, which, for aught I know, may be a totally different quality from that which I love and venerate; what do I mean by calling it goodness? and what reason have I for venerating it? If I know nothing about what the attribute is, I cannot tell that it is a proper object of veneration. To say that God's goodness may be different in kind from man's goodness, what is it but saying, with a slight change of phraseology, that God may possibly not be good? To assert in words what we do not think in meaning is as suitable a definition as can be given of a moral falsehood. Besides, suppose that certain attributes are ascribed to the Deity in a religion, the external evidences of which are so conclusive to my mind as effectually to convince me that it comes from God; unless I believe God to possess the same moral attributes which I find in, however inferior a degree, in a good man, what ground of assurance have I of God's veracity? All trust in a revelation presupposes a conviction that God's attributes are the same, in all but degree, with the best human attributes.

"If, instead of the 'glad tidings,' that there exists a being in whom all the excellences which the highest human mind can conceive, exist in a degree inconceivable to us, I am informed that the world is ruled by a being whose attributes are infinite, but what they are we cannot learn, nor what are the principles of his government, except that the highest human morality which we are capable of conceiving does not sanction them; convince me of it and I will bear my fate as I may. But when I am told that I must believe this, and at the same time call this being by the names which I express and affirm the highest human morality, I say, in plain terms, that I will not. Whatever power such a being may have over me, there is one thing which he shall not do; he shall not compel me to worship him. I will call no being good who is not what I mean, when I apply that epithet to my fellow creatures; and if such a being can sentence me to hell for not so calling him, to hell I will go."

"Neither is this to set up my own limited intellect as a criterion of divine or any other wisdom. If a person is wiser and better than myself, not in some unknown and unknowable meaning of the terms, but in their known human acceptation, I am ready to believe that what this person thinks may be true, and what he does may be right, when, but for the opinion I have of him, I should think otherwise. But this is because I believe that he and I have at bottom the same standard of truth and rule of right, and that he probably understands better than I the facts of the particular case. If I thought it not improbable that his notion of right might be my notion of wrong, I should not defer to his judgment. In like manner, one who sincerely believes in an absolutely good ruler of the world, is not warranted in disbelieving any act ascribed to him, merely because the very small part of its circumstances, which we can possibly know, does not sufficiently justify it. But if what I am told respecting him is of a kind which no facts that can be supposed added to my knowledge could make me perceive to be right; if his alleged ways of dealing with the world are such as no imaginable hypothesis respecting things known to him and unknown to me, could make consistent with the goodness and wisdom which I mean when I use the terms, but are in direct contradiction to their signification, then, if the law of contradiction is a law of human thought, I cannot both believe these things, and believe that God is a good and wise being" ("Examination of Sir William Hamilton," p. 123).

Another word in very common use among theologians in dealing with the God question is the word "creation;" here, again, a strict definition is needed. Sir William Hamilton says ("Discussions on Philosophy," p. 609): "When aware of a new appearance, we are utterly unable to conceive that therein has originated any new existence, and are, therefore, constrained to think that what now appears to us under a new form, had previously an existence under others—others conceivable by us or not. These others (for they are always plural) are called its cause; and a cause, or more properly causes, we cannot but suppose: for a cause is simply everything, without which the effect would not result, and all such concurring the effect cannot but result. We are utterly unable to construe it in thought as possible that the complement of existence has been either increased or diminished. We cannot conceive, on the one hand, nothing becoming something, or, on the other, something becoming nothing."

The words "creation" and "destruction" have no value, except as applied to phenomena. You may destroy a sovereign by melting, but you do not destroy the metal. You may dissolve the metal gold, but you have only destroyed the condition, not the substance. Creation and destruction are the loosely-worded equivalents for change.

The Rev. Baden Powell, in his essay on the "Study of the Evidences of Christianity" ("Essays and Reviews," p. 166), speaking of organic life, says: "Creation is only another name for our ignorance of the mode of production."

The word "matter" is one to which many absurd meanings have been given by theologians. It is here only used in exactly the sense in which Mr. J. S. Mill uses "nature." He says ("Three Essays," p. 5): "As the nature of any given thing is the aggregate of its powers and properties, so Nature in the abstract is the aggregate of the powers and properties of all things. Nature means the sum of all phenomena, together with the causes which produce them; including not only all that happens, but all that is capable of happening; the unused capabilities of causes being as much a part of the idea of nature as those which take effect." George Henry Lewes, in his "Problems of Life and Mind" (vol. ii., p. 262), defines matter as "the felt," and force as "activity of the felt." Poisson says: "La matière est tout ce qui peut affecter nos sens d'une manière quelconque." Matter is all that we can in any manner sensate. Mr. Lewes adds (p. 264): "Matter is the symbol of all the known properties, statical and dynamical, passive and active—*i.e.*, subjectively, as feeling and change of feeling; or objectively, as agent and action." Dr. Priestley says: "It has generally been supposed that there are two distinct kinds of substance in human nature, and they have been distinguished by the terms matter, and spirit, or mind. The former of these has been said to be possessed of the property of extension—viz., of length, breadth, and thickness, and also of solidity or impenetrability, and consequently of a *vis inertiæ;* but it is said to be naturally destitute of all other powers whatever. The latter has of late been defined to be a substance entirely destitute of all extension, or relation to space, so as to have no property in common with matter; and therefore to be properly immaterial, but to be possessed of the powers of perception, intelligence, and self-motion. Matter is alleged to be that kind of substance of which our bodies are composed, whereas the principle of perception and thought belonging to us is said to reside in a spirit, or immaterial principle, intimately united to the body; while higher orders of intelligent beings, and especially the Divine Being, are said to be purely immaterial. It is maintained that neither matter nor spirit (meaning by the latter the subject of sense and thought) correspond to the definitions above mentioned. For that matter is not that inert substance that it has been supposed to be; that powers of attraction or repulsion are necessary to its very being, and that no part of it appears to be impenetrable to other parts; I therefore define it to be a substance possessed of the property of extension, and powers of attraction or repulsion; and since it has never yet been asserted that the powers of sensation and thought are incompatible with these (solidity or impenetrability, and, consequently, a *vis inertiæ*, only having been thought to be repugnant to them), I therefore maintain that we have no reason to suppose that there are in man two substances so distinct from each other as have been represented. It is likewise maintained that the notion of two substances that have no common property, and yet are capable of intimate connection and mutual action, is absurd."

M. Emanuel Briard says ("La Pensée Nouvelle," 1ère année, No. 36), "Un mode d'existence est inséparable de l'existence elle-même. Le monde existe, il existe d'une certaine manière, de la manière que nous voyons. Qu'est-ce que cela peut prouver en faveur d'une Providence?...... Pour pouvoir affirmer qu'il y a de l'ordre dans la nature, il faudrait pouvoir comparer la nature à quelque chose d'autre, ce qui est impossible, puisque tout est dans la nature....... Quand donc vous dites: il y a de l'ordre dans la nature, vous ne faites que reporter à la nature l'idée que vous en avez tirée; vous dites seulement ceci, la nature est comme elle est." "A mode of existence is inseparable from existence itself. The universe exists, it exists in a certain manner, the manner we see. What can this prove in favour of a Providence? To be able to affirm that there is order in nature, you should be able to compare nature with something else, which is impossible, because everything is in nature. When, therefore, you say there is order in nature, all you do is to attribute to nature the idea you have drawn from nature. You only say, that nature is as she is."

From the pretended "general consent of mankind" to the affirmation of Theism, it is alleged that there is in man an innate idea, an intuitive perception, an instinctive sense of Deity. We challenge the existence of the general consent except as an imperfect thought-growth varying amongst all peoples. We utterly deny any ideas which are not the results of perseption or reflection on perception; we deny intuition except in the sense in which it is used by Mr. George Henry Lewes ("Problems of Life and Mind," vol. I., p 373): "'We call judgment *intuitive* when the relations seem to embody experiences which are not specified or cannot now be specified, although originally they were capable of being so." "The conclusion which is seen so rapidly that its premisses are but faintly or nor at all recognised, is said to be seen intuitively; it is an organised judgment." In this sense alone we accept the word intuition, and we reject instinctive sense, except so far as by it is intended inherited predisposition.

Baron D'Holbach says: "If a faithful account was rendered of man's ideas upon the divinity, he would be obliged to acknowledge, that for the most part the word gods has been used to express the concealed, remote, unknown causes of the effects he witnessed; that he applies this term when the spring of natural, the source of known causes ceases to be visible; as soon as he loses the thread of these causes, or as soon as his mind can no longer follow the chain, he solves the difficulty, terminates his research, by ascribing it to his gods; thus giving a vague definition to an unknown cause, at which either his idleness, or his limited knowledge, obliges him to stop. When, therefore, he ascribes to his gods the production of some phenomenon, the novelty or the extent of which strikes him with wonder, but of which his ignorance precludes him from unravelling the true cause, or which he believes the natural powers, with which he is acquainted, are inadequate to bring forth, does he, in fact, do anything more than substitute for the darkness of his own mind a sound to which he has been accustomed to listen with reverential awe? Ignorance may be said to be the inheritance of the generality of men; these attribute to their gods, not only those uncommon effects that burst upon their senses with an astounding force, but also the most simple events; the causes of which are the most easy to be known to whoever shall be willing to meditate upon them. In short, man has always respected those unknown causes, those surprising effects, which his ignorance prevented him from fathoming"—(Mirabaud's "System of Nature," vol ii., cap. 1).

And again (cap. 4): "The unanimity of man, in acknowledging the Divinity, is commonly looked upon as the strongest proof of his existence. There is not, it is said, any people on the earth who have not some ideas, whether true or false, of an all-powerful agent who governs the world. The rudest savages, as well as the most polished nations, are equally obliged to recur by thought to the first cause of everything that exists; thus it is affirmed the cry of nature herself ought to convince us of the existence of the God-head: of which she has taken pains to engrave the notion in the minds of men: they therefore conclude that the idea of God is innate."

"If, disengaged from prejudice, we analyse this proof, we shall see that the universal consent of man, so diffused over the earth [and which later experiences enable us to say is not so universal as D'Holbach conceded] actually proves little more than that he has been in all countries exposed to frightful revolutions, experienced disasters, been sensible to sorrows, of which he has mistaken the physical causes; that those events to which he has been either the victim or the witness have called forth his admiration, or excited his fear; that for want of being acquainted with the powers of nature, for want of understanding her laws, for want of comprehending her infinite resources, for want of knowing the effects she must necessarily produce under given circumstances, he has believed these phenomena were due to some secret agent, of which he has had vague ideas; to beings whom he has supposed conducted themselves after his own manner, who were operated upon by similar motives with himself.

"The consent, then, of man in acknowledging a variety of gods proves nothing, except that in the bosom of ignorance he has either admired the phenomena of nature, or trembled under their influence; that his imagination was disturbed by what he beheld or suffered; that he has sought in vain to relieve his perplexity upon the unknown cause of the phenomena he witnessed, which frequently obliged him to quake with terror: the imagination of the human race has laboured variously upon these causes, which have almost always been incomprehensible to him: although everything confessed his ignorance, his inability to define these causes, yet he maintained that he was assured of their existence; when pressed he spoke of a spirit; a word to which it was impossible to attach any determinate idea; which taught nothing but the sloth, which evidenced nothing but the stupidity of those who pronounced it."

"For the most part, the notions on the Divinity, which obtain even at the present day, are nothing more than a general terror, diversely acquired, variously modified in the mind of nations: which do not tend to prove anything, save that they have received them from their trembling ignorant ancestors. These gods have been successively altered, decorated, subtilised, by those thinkers, those legislators, those priests, who have meditated deeply upon them; who have prescribed systems of worship to the uninformed; who have availed themselves of their existing prejudices, to submit them to their yoke; who have obtained a dominion over their mind, by seizing on their credulity; by making them participate in their errors; by working on their fears; these dispositions will always be a necessary consequence of man's ignorance, when steeped in the sorrows of his heart."

In treating the question of general consent, Mr. Mill points out ("Three Essays on Religion," p, 157) that "the religious belief of savages is not belief in the god of natural theology, but a mere modification of the crude generalisation, which ascribes life, consciousness, and will to all natural powers of which they cannot perceive the source or control the operation. And the divinities believed in are as numerous as those powers. Each river, fountain, or tree, has a divinity of its own. To see in this blunder of primitive ignorance the hand of the Supreme Being, implanting in his creatures an instinctive knowledge of his existence, is a poor compliment to the Deity. The religion of savages is Fetichism of the grossest kind, ascribing animation and will to individual objects, and seeking to propitiate them by prayer and sacrifice. That this should be the case is the less surprising, when we remember that there is not a definite boundary line, broadly separating the conscious human being from inanimate objects. Between these and man there is an intermediate class of objects, sometimes much more powerful than man, which do possess life and will, *i.e.*, the brute animals, which in an early stage of existence play a very great part in human life; making it the less surprising that the line should not at first be quite distinguishable between the animate and the inanimate part of nature. As observation advances, it is perceived that the majority of outward objects have all their important qualities in common with entire classes or groups of objects, which comport themselves exactly alike in the same circumstances; and in these cases the worship of visible objects is exchanged for that of an invisible being, supposed to preside over the whole class. This step in generalisation is slowly made, with hesitation, and even terror; as we still see in the case of ignorant populations with what difficulty experience disabuses them of belief in the supernatural powers and terrible resentment of a particular idol. Chiefly by these terrors the religious impressions of barbarians are kept alive, with only slight modifications, until the Theism of cultivated minds is ready to take their place. And the Theism of cultivated minds, if we take their own word for it, is always a conclusion either from arguments called rational, or from the appearances in nature."

In the first chapter of his "Abregé de l'Origine de Tous les Cultes," Charles Francis Dupuis (born 16th October, 1742, died 29th September, 1809) says: "The word God appears destined to express the idea of the universal and eternally active force which gives motion to everything in nature, following the laws of a constant and admirable harmony, which develops itself in the diverse forms taken by organised matter, which mingles in all, animates all, and which seems to be one in its infinitely varied modifications, and to belong only to itself. This is the active force which the Universe, or that regular assemblage of all bodies linked together by an eternal chain, and rolling with a perpetual movement in the womb of space for unlimited time, contains within itself. It was in this vast and marvellous whole that man, from the moment that he desires to reason on the causes of his existence and preservation, as well as on the various effects which were produced and destroyed around him, was obliged from the first to place the sovereignly-powerful cause which evolved all, and into the womb of which all re-enters, to again evolve by a succession of new generations, and under different forms. This force being that of the Universe itself, the Universe was regarded as God, or the supreme and universal cause of all the effects it produced, and of which humanity was part. Behold the great God, the first or rather the only God, who has manifested himself to man through the veil of the matter which he animates, and which constitutes the vast body of the Divinity. Such is the name of the sublime inscription of the temple of Sais: 'I am all that has been, all that is, and all that shall be; and no mortal has yet lifted the veil which covers me.'"

"Theism or Monotheism is the belief in a single personal agent as the sole cause of all things" (*Westminster*

Review, vol. xcvi., p 456). The Theist says that God is a person, infinite, eternal, omniscient, omnipotent, all-perfect, Creator and Ruler of the Universe. The formula is on the face of it self-contradictory, and the word "God" may be fairly said to be used by the Theist as the solution of every problem which his experience does not enable him to solve.

The Atheist does not say "There is no God," but he says, "I know not what you mean by God; I am without idea of God; the word 'God' is to me a sound conveying no clear or distinct affirmation. I do not deny God, because I cannot deny that of which I have no conception, and the conception of which, by its affirmer, is so imperfect that he is unable to define it to me."

"If, however, God is affirmed to represent an existence which is distinct from the existence of which I am a mode, and which it is alleged is not the *noumenon*, of which the word 'I' represents only a speciality of *phenomena*, then I deny 'God,' and affirm that it is impossible 'God' can be. That is, I affirm that there is one existence, and deny that there can be more than one."

William Rathbone Greg says ("Enigmas of Life," preface, p. 5): "The question, when stated with that perfect unreserve which alone befits it, lies in a small compass. Of actual knowledge we have simply nothing. Those who believe in a creative spirit and ruler of the universe, are forced to admit that they can adduce no proofs or arguments cogent enough to compel conviction from sincere minds constituted in another mould. There are facts, indications, corollaries, which seem to suggest the great inference almost irresistibly to our minds. There are other facts, indications, corollaries, which to other minds seem as irresistibly to negative that inference. Data admitted by both appear of different weight to each. The difficulties in the way of either conclusion are confessedly stupendous. The difficulty of conceiving the eternal pre-existence of a personal creator I perceive to be *immense;* the difficulty of conceiving the origin and evolution of the actual universe, independently of such personal creator, I should characterise as insuperable."

[Mr. Greg does not tell why it is necessary to try to imagine the *origin* of the actual universe, nor does he show us that it is even possible to imagine such origin with an admittedly difficult conception of a personal creator superadded.]

"The Positivist, the devotee of pure science, would simply reverse the adjectives. We can neither of us turn the minor into the major difficulty for the other without altering the constitution of his intelligence. He does not say 'there is no God;' he merely says 'I see no phenomena which irresistibly suggest one: I see many which negative the suggestion; and I have greater difficulty in conceiving all that the existence of such a being would involve than in the contrary assumption.' I do not say 'I know there is a God;' I only say that I observe and infer much that forces that conviction upon me; but I recognise that these observations and inferences would not entitle me to demand the same conviction from him."

The general outlines, and also the difficulties of the Theistic argument were fairly stated in an article in the *British Quarterly Review*, for July, 1871, p. 34, in reading which, however, it is necessary always to bear in mind that the writer is a Theist. He says: "We are limited to the well-known but precarious scheme of proofs *à priori* and *à posteriori*, and to the more accurate classification of Kant, the ontological, the cosmological, and the physico-theological proofs with his own argument from the moral faculty or practical reason."

"The terms *à priori* and *à posteriori* are misleading. Arguments called *à priori* are usually mixed, and involve elements strictly *à posteriori;* experiential facts are inlaid within them. And the proof *à posteriori* ascends (if it ascends high enough) by the aid of *à priori* principles. In its rise to the supersensible, it makes use of the noetic principle of the reason."

Dividing the Theistic theories into classes, the *British Quarterly Review* says: "The first class of theories are strictly *ontological* or onto-theological. They attempt to prove the objective existence of God from the subjective notion of necessary existence in the human mind, or from the assumed objectivity of space and time, which they interpret as the attributes of a necessary substance."

"The second are the *cosmological* or *cosmo-theological* proofs. They essay to prove the existence of a supreme self-existent cause, from the mere fact of the existence of the world by the application of the principle of causality. Starting with the postulate of any single existence whatsoever, the world, or anything in the world, and proceeding to argue backwards or upwards, the existence of one supreme cause is held to be 'a regressive inference' from the existence of these effects. As there cannot be, it is alleged, an infinite series of derived or dependent effects, we at length reach the infinite or uncaused cause. This has been termed the proof from contingency, as it rises from the contingent to the necessary; from the relative to the absolute. But the cosmological proof may have a threefold character, according as it is argued. 1, That the necessary is the antithesis of the contingent; or 2, That because some being now exists, some being must always have existed; or 3, That because we now exist, and have not caused ourselves, some cause adequate to produce us must also now exist."

"A third class of proofs are somewhat inaccurately termed physico-theological, a phrase equally descriptive of them and of these last mentioned. They are rather teleological or teleo-theological. The former proof started from any finite existence. It did not scrutinise its character, but rose from it to an absolute cause, by a direct mental leap or inference. This scrutinises the effect and [claims that it] finds traces of intelligence within it. It [alleges that it] detects the presence or the vestiges of mind in the particular effect it examines, viz., the phenomena of the world, and from them infers the existence of Deity. One branch of it is the argument from design, or adaptation in nature, the fitness of means to end, implying, it is said, an architect or designer. It may be called *Techno-Theology*, and is variously treated according as the technologist starts from human contrivance and reasons to nature, or starts from nature's products and reasons towards man. Another branch is the argument from the order of the universe, from the types or laws of nature, indicating, it is said, an orderer or law-giver, whose intelligence we thus discern. It is not in this case that the adjustment of means to ends proves the presence of a mind that has adjusted these. But the law itself, in its regularity and continuity, implies [it is contended] a mind behind it, an intelligence animating the otherwise soulless universe. It might be termed *nomo-theology* or *typo-theology*. Under the same general category may be placed the argument from animal instinct, which is distinct at once from the evidence of design, and that of law or typical order."

"The next class of arguments are based on the moral nature of man. They may be termed in general *ethico-theological;* and there are at least two main branches in this line of proof: 1. The argument from conscience, as a moral law pointing to another above it......It is [alleged to be] the moral echo within the soul of a voice louder and vaster without......and as evidence it is direct and intuitive, not inferential. 2. The argument of Kant, is indirect and inferential, based upon the present phenomena of our moral nature. The moral law declares that the evil is punishable, and to be punished; that virtue is rewardable, and to be rewarded; but in this life they are not so: therefore, said Kant, there must be a futurity in which the rectification will take place, and a moral arbiter by whom it will be affected."

"Finally, there is the argument which, when philosophically unfolded, is, says the *British Quarterly Review*, the only unassailable stronghold of Theism, that of intuition." This is called eso-theological, or esoterico-theological, thus making the following chart of Theistic theories to be examined by the Freethinker:—

I. Onto-Theological.

1. From necessary notion to reality.
   a. Anselm's proof.
   b. Descartes' first argument.
2. From space and time as attributes to their substance.

II. Cosmo-Theological.

1. Antithetic.
2. Causal.
3. Sufficient reason (Leibnitz).

III. Teleo-Theological.

1. Techno-theology.
2. Typo-theology.
3. (Animal instinct).

IV. Ethico-Theological.

1. Deonto-theological.
2. Indirect and inferential (Kant).

V. Eso-Theological.

1. The infinite (Fénélon, Cousin).
2. The world soul.
3. The instinct of worship.

The ontological argument is presented by St. Augustine in his various works, notably, in his "De Civitate Dei," City of God, and his "Confessions." St. Augustine was born 13th November, A.D. 354, at Tagaste, in Africa, and died at

Hippone, in Africa, on the 28th August, A.D. 430. A very weak notice of Augustine is given in Enfield's "History of Philosophy," book vi., chap. 3, and a summary of his position is given in Tenneman's "Manual of the History of Philosophy," sect. 232. Dr. J. Pye Smith gives a vivid picture of Augustine and his doctrines from a religious stand-point ("First Lines of Christian Theology," pp. 279 to 285). The best edition of his works was that made by the Benedictines, in the latter part of the 17th century. The translation of the Confessions used here is that of Arnault d'Andilly, republished at Paris in 1840 ("Choix d'Ouvrages Mystiques," par J. A. C. Buchon, book i.). Many portions of the Confessions are strongly Pantheistic. "By Le Clerc, Augustine is charged with being the first who advanced two doctrines which take away goodness and justice both from God and man; the one representing the Deity as dooming human beings to eternal torments for sins which they cannot avoid, and the other stirring up the civil magistrate to persecute those who differ from them in religion" (Gorton's "Biographical Dictionary").

Another advancer of the ontological argument is St. Anselm, born at Aosta, in Piedmont A.D. 1034, and died Archbishop of Canterbury, A.D. 1109. He has been called the second St. Augustine ("History of Modern Philosophy," by Victor Cousin, Lecture IX). His two last works, Monologium and Proslogium, contain his argument. In the first, "Monologue, or example of the manner in which one may account for his faith," Anselm supposes an ignorant man seeking truth by force of his reason only. "This mode, this plan, consists in drawing all theological truths from a single point, the essence of God, and the essence of God from the only ideal of beauty, of goodness, of grandeur, which all men possess, and which is the common measure of all that is beautiful. This ideal, this unity, must exist, for it is the necessary form of all that exists. Unity is anterior to plurality, and it is its root. This unity is God." One fatal objection to Anselm's Monologium is, that there is no such ideal of beauty, goodness, and grandeur common to all men. In his second work, Proslogium, Anselm supposes himself in the possession of the truth, and tries to demonstrate it. "The maddest Atheist has, in his thought, an idea of a sovereign good, above which he can conceive no other. This sovereign good cannot exist solely in the thought, for we might conceive a still greater. This we cannot do, therefore this sovereign good exists out of the thought, therefore God exists." This, again, falls under the objection that no one has such an idea of a sovereign good." Dr. J. P. Smith refers to Anselm ("First Lines of Christian Theology," p. 106), and thus states his argument: "We can form an idea of an absolutely perfect being; but we should not have the capacity for doing so if such a being did not exist." This involves two errors: first, that "an idea of an absolutely perfect being" can be formed; and, second, that every idea in the mind must have its actual counterpart existent. An insane person's idea, that he is followed by a yellow dog, with six tails and four heads, would, in this case, require the admission of the actuality of the abnormal dog. The truth is that every supposed extra-natural being is only a compound of parts of natural beings, severed from their appropriate belongings; man's imaginative faculties cannot so transcend his experience as to enable him to create new materials; they can only re-combine the old materials in new forms; and from the horns, hoofs, tails, shapes, of the animals around him, unicorns, devils, or dragons are moulded.

Saint Thomas Aquinas, arrayed in the same ranks, was born at Aquino, near Naples, in 1225, died in 1274, at Terracina, on the way to a general council at Lyons.

Descartes, also a maintainer of the ontological argument, was born in 1596, at La Haye, in Touraine; he died at Stockholm in 1650. The clearest and most accessible statement of his views is in Lewes's "Biographical History of Philosophy," vol. ii., p. 137. A somewhat different estimate of Descartes is given by Victor Cousin ("History of Modern Philosophy," Lecture II.). Treating on the application of the method of Descartes, Mr. Lewes says: "Interrogating his consciousness, he found that he had the idea of God; understanding by God a substance infinite, eternal immutable, independent, omniscient, omnipotent. This, to him, was as certain a truth as the truth of his own existence I exist: not only do I exist, but exist as a miserably imperfect finite being, subject to change, greatly ignorant, and in capable of creating anything. In this, my consciousness, I find by my finitude that I am not the all; by my imperfection, that I am not the perfect. Yet an infinite and perfect Being must exist, because infinity and perfection are implied as correlatives in my ideas of imperfection and finitude. God, therefore, exists; his existence is clearly proclaimed in my consciousness, and can no more be a matter of doubt, when fairly considered, than my own existence. The conception of an infinite being proves his real existence; for if there is not really such a being, I must have made the conception; but if I could make it, I could also unmake it, which evidently is not true; therefore, there must be, externally to myself, an archetype from which the conception was derived."

To this we reply, denying the conception, infinite is inconceivable, infinite is indefinite; to speak of idea of the infinite is to talk of idea of the indefinable, which is absurd (see Hobbes' "Leviathan," part i., chap. 3). "Whatever we imagine is finite. Therefore this is no idea or conception of anything we call infinite.........When we say anything is infinite, we signify only that we are not able to conceive, the ends and bounds of the thing named, having no conception of the thing but of our own inability."

"The ambiguity in this case," it has been remarked (Mill's "System of Logic," vol. ii., p. 447), "is the pronoun *I*, by which in one place is to be understood my *will;* in another, the laws of my nature. If the conception existing, as it does in my mind, had no original without, the conclusion would unquestionably follow that *I* had made it—that is, the laws of my nature must have spontaneously evolved it; but that my will made it would not follow. Now, when Descartes afterwards adds that I cannot unmake the conception, he means that I cannot get rid of it by an act of my will, which is true, but is not the proposition required. That what some of the laws of my nature have produced, other laws, or the same laws in other circumstances, might not subsequently efface, he would have found it difficult to establish" (Lewes's "History of Philosophy," vol. ii., p. 150).

"Descartes," writes the *British Quarterly Reviewer*, "was the most illustrious thinker who, at the dawn of modern philosophy, developed the scholastic Theism. While inaugurating a new method of experimental research, he nevertheless retained the most characteristic doctrine of mediæval ontology. He argues that necessary existence is as essential to the idea of an all-perfect being, as the equality of its three angles to the two right angles is essential to the idea of a triangle. But though he admits that his 'thought imposes no necessity on things,' he contradicts his own admission by adding, 'I cannot conceive God except as existing, and hence it follows that existence is inseparable from him.' In his 'Principles of Philosophy' we find the following argument: 'As the equality of its three angles to two right angles is necessarily comprised in the idea of the triangle, the mind is firmly persuaded that the three angles of a triangle are equal to two right angles; so from its perceiving necessary and eternal existence to be comprised in the idea which it has of an all-perfect being, it ought manifestly to conclude that this all-perfect being exists (part i., sec. 14). This argument is more formally expounded in his 'Reply to Objections to the Meditations,' thus: 'Proposition 1. The existence of God is known from the consideration of his nature alone—demonstration. To say that an attribute is contained in the nature, or in the concept of a thing, is the same as to say that this attribute is true of this thing, and that it may be affirmed to be in it. But necessary existence is contained in the nature or in the concept of God. Hence, it may be with truth affirmed, that necessary existence is in God, or that God exists.' A slight amount of thought will suffice to show that, in this elaborate array of argumentation, Descartes is the victim of a subtle fallacy. Our conception of necessary existence cannot include the fact of necessary existence, for one is an ideal concept of the mind, the other is a fact of a real existence. The one demands an object beyond the mind, the other does not. All that the Cartesian argument could prove, would be that the mental concept was necessary, not that the concept had a counterpart in the outer universe. It is, indeed, a necessary judgment that the three angles of a triangle are equal to two right angles, because this is an identical proposition; the subject and the predicate are the same, the one being only an expansion of the other. We cannot, therefore, destroy the predicate, and leave the subject intact. But it is otherwise when we affirm that any triangular object exists; we may then destroy the predicate existence, and yet leave the subject (the notion of the triangle) intact in the mind" (*British Quarterly Review*, No. cvii., p. 43).

Ralph Cudworth—born in Somerset 1617, died 1688, author of "The True Intellectual System of the Universe" —was a correspondent, and at one time an admirer, of Descartes (Tenneman's "Manual," p. 331; Cousin's "History of Modern Philosophy," p. 115; Buckle's "History of Civilisation," vol. iii., p. 348); and his writings are often referred to by those who rely on "innate ideas." "Aiming at a unification of science, philosophy, and religion, he found it in the conception of a 'plastic nature,' as immediate cause and guide of all existence. Such a plastic nature avoided, to his mind, the difficulties of Atheism on the one hand, and of continued creation and Divine interference on the other. Without it, things must proceed with utter fortuitousness, or 'God himself doth all immediately, and, as it were, with his own hands, form the body of every gnat and fly.' He posited, therefore, a plastic nature, which, while devoid of consciousness and reason, subserved the final end and ultimate good of all existence. This plastic nature 'doth never consult or deliberate;' it 'goes on in one constant, unrepenting tenor, from generation to generation;' it 'acts artificially, and for the sake of ends,' but itself 'understands not the ends which it acts for;' it resembles 'habits which do in like manner gradually evolve themselves in a long train or series of regular and artificial motions, readily prompting the doing of them, without comprehending that art and reason by which they are directed;' it corresponds to those 'natural instincts that are in animals, which, without knowledge, direct them to act regularly in order, both to their own good and the good of the universe.' 'The plastic nature in the formation of plants and animals seems to have no animal fancy, no express consciousness of what it doth;' it is parallel to those 'nocturnal volutations in sleep,' those movements of the heart and lungs, over which we exercise no conscious influence. 'Wherefore, the plastic nature, acting neither by knowledge nor by animal fancy, neither electively nor hormetically, must be concluded to act fatally, magically, and sympathetically.' But this plastic nature Cudworth conceives as simply the subordinate instrument of higher power. 'Perfect knowledge and understanding, without consciousness, is nonsense and impossibility. If there be *physis*, there must be *nous;* if there be a plastic nature, that acts regularly and artificially in order to ends, and according to the best wisdom, though itself not comprehending the reason of it, not being clearly conscious of what it doth, then there must of necessity be a perfect mind or deity upon which it depends'" (*Westminster Review*, No. xcvii., p. 144, comparing Cudworth with Hartmann).

Cudworth advanced the three following propositions, which he regarded as the fundamentals or essentials of true religion: "First, that all things in the world do not float without a head and governor; but that there is a God, an omnipotent understanding being presiding over all. Secondly, that this God, being essentially good and just, there is something in its own nature eternally just and unjust; and not by arbitrary will, law, and command only. And, lastly, that we are so far forth principals, or masters of our own actions, as to be accountable to justice for them, or to make us guilty and blameworthy for what we do amiss, and to deserve punishment accordingly." Cudworth was usually so fair in his treatment of his antagonists that many religious persons charged him with heresy, some even calling him Atheist. He says, in his "Intellectual System": "It does not follow, because God is incomprehensible to our finite and narrow understandings, that he is utterly inconceivable by them, so that they cannot frame any idea of them at all, and he may therefore be concluded to be a nonentity." But it does follow that, if the word God is incomprehensible, that then no one has a right to require another to accept the word God as representing some person whose existence is to be believed. "For," adds Cudworth, "it is certain that we cannot comprehend ourselves, and that we have not such an adequate and comprehensive knowledge of the essence of any substantial thing as that we can perfectly master and conquer it." In truth, all knowledge is relative; we have only the impressions the thing comprehended makes upon us, and we do not and cannot know it in itself. A table is a mode of substance; it is conditioned in thought by the characteristics, diversities of sensation, by which we are enabled to think it. The thing in itself (substance) we cannot ignore; but we do not comprehend, we know it only in its modes. Cudworth says we cannot comprehend ourselves; this is not exact; phenomenally, relatively, we can and do comprehend ourselves, but of God we have neither relative nor absolute knowledge. (See chapter on the Relativity of Human Knowledge, Mill's "Examination of Hamilton.") Cudworth goes on: "For even body itself, which the Atheists think themselves so well acquainted with, because they can feel it with their fingers—and which is the only substance that they acknowledge either in themselves or in the universe—hath such puzzling difficulties and entanglements in the speculation of it that they can never be able to extricate themselves from.........This is one badge of our creaturely state, that we have not a perfectly comprehensive knowledge, or such as is adequate and commensurate to the essences of things; from thence we ought to be led to this acknowledgment, that there is another perfect mind or understanding being above us in the universe, from which our imperfect minds were derived, and upon which they do depend."

This argument of Cudworth's involves the assumption that a perfectly wise, good, and powerful person could and would make a person incapable of properly comprehending facts.

"Wherefore," continues Cudworth, "if we can have no idea or conception of anything, whereof we have not a full and perfect comprehension, then can we not have an idea or conception of the nature of any substance. But though we do not comprehend all truth, as if our minds were above it, or master of it, and cannot penetrate into, and look quite through the nature of everything, yet may rational souls frame certain ideas and conceptions of whatsoever is in the orb of being proportionate to their own nature and sufficient for their purpose. And though we cannot fully comprehend the Deity, nor exhaust the infiniteness of its perfection, yet we may have an idea of a being absolutely perfect." If Cudworth means some imaginary *x*, from which we in turn exclude all imperfections, this does not help him to a proof of God; and if he means that we have an incomplete idea of some particular being, of whom we know something, but whom we do not entirely know, but of whom we know enough to say that he is absolutely perfect, then it is denied that we "may have" any such "idea of a being absolutely perfect."

"Whatsoever," says Cudworth, "is in its own nature absolutely inconceivable, is nothing; but not whatsoever is not fully incomprehensible by our imperfect understandings." Admitting, then, that "the Deity is more incomprehensible to us than anything else whatsoever," he goes on: "The incomprehensibility of the Deity is so far from being an argument against the reality of its existence as that it is most certain, on the contrary, that were there nothing incomprehensible to us, who are but contemptible pieces and small atoms of the universe; were there no other beings in the world but what our finite understandings could span or fathom, and incompass roundabout, look through and through, and have a commanding view of, and perfectly conquer and subdue under them, then there could be nothing absolutely and infinitely perfect—that is, no God."

On the topic of the creation Cudworth writes: "Because it is undeniably certain concerning ourselves, and all imperfect beings, that none of these can create any new substance, men are apt to measure all things by their own scantling, and to suppose it universally impossible for any power whatever thus to create. But since it is certain that imperfect beings can themselves produce some things out of nothing pre-existing, as new cogitations, new local motion, and new modifications of things corporeal, it is surely reasonable to think that an absolutely perfect being can do something more, that is, create new substances, or give them their whole being." Here Cudworth is inaccurate; "cogitations" are not "things;" "motion" is not a thing, and the word create is improperly used. New modification is not the equivalent in analogy for origination of substance, and throughout the whole of Cudworth's writing there is the fault common to writers in favour of Theism, that words are used with the most confusing disregard of their real value. He affirms "that it may well be thought as easy for God, or an omnipotent being, to make a whole world, matter and all, as it is for us to create a thought or move a finger, or for the sun to send out rays, or a candle light; or lastly, for an opaque body to produce an image of itself in a glass or water, or to project a shadow; all these imperfect things being but the energies, rays, images, or shadows of the Deity."

Henry More—born October 12th, 1614, died September, 1687—was educated in the same University with Cudworth, and maintained the same views. In his "Antidote to Atheism" Dr. More writes:—

"When I say that I will demonstrate that there is a God, I do not promise that I will always produce such arguments that the reader shall acknowledge so strong, as he shall be forced to confess that it is utterly unpossible that it should be otherwise; but they shall be such as shall deserve full assent, and win full assent, from any unprejudiced mind.

"For I conceive that we may give full assent to that which, notwithstanding, may possibly be otherwise; which I shall illustrate by several examples: Suppose two men got to the top of Mount Athos, and there viewing a stone in the form of an altar with ashes on it, and the footsteps of men on those ashes, or some words, if you will, as *Optimo Maximo*, or *To agnosto Theo*, or the like, written or scrawled out upon the ashes; and one of them should cry out, Assuredly here have been some men that have done this. But the other, more nice than wise, should reply, Nay, it may possibly be otherwise; for this stone may have naturally grown into this very shape, and the seeming ashes may be no ashes, that is, no remainders of any fuel burnt there; but some unexplicable and unperceptible motions of the air, or other particles of this fluid matter that is active everywhere, have wrought some parts of the matter into the form and nature of ashes, and have fridged and played about so, that they have also figured those intelligible characters in the same. But would not anybody deem it a piece of weakness, no less than dotage, for the other man one whit to recede from his former apprehension, but as fully as ever to agree with what he pronounced first, notwithstanding this bare possibility of being otherwise?

"So of anchors that have been digged up, either in plain fields or mountainous places, as also the Roman urns with ashes and inscriptions, as *Severianus Ful. Linus*, and the like, or Roman coins with the effigies and names of the Cæsars on them, or that which is more ordinary, the skulls of men in every churchyard, with the right figure, and all those necessary perforations for the passing of the vessels, besides those conspicuous hollows for the eyes and rows of teeth, the *os styloeides*, *ethoeides*, and what not. If a man will say of them, that the motions of the particles of the matter, or some hidden spermatic power, has gendered these, both anchors, urns, coins, and skulls, in the ground, he doth but pronounce that which human reason must admit is possible. Nor can any man ever so demonstrate that these coins, anchors, and urns were once the artifice of men, or that this or that skull was once a part of a living man, that he shall force an acknowledgment that it is impossible that it should be otherwise. But yet I do not think that any man, without doing manifest violence to his faculties, can at all suspend his assent, but freely and fully agree that this or that skull was once a part of a living man, and that these anchors, urns, and coins were certainly once made by human artifice, notwithstanding the possibility of being otherwise.

"And what I have said of assent is also true in dissent; for the mind of man, nor crazed nor prejudiced, will fully and irreconcilably disagree, by its own natural sagacity, where, notwithstanding, the thing that it doth thus resolvedly and undoubtedly reject, no wit of man can prove impossible to be true. As if we should make such a fiction as this—that Archimedes, with the same individual body that he had when the soldiers slew him, is now safely intent upon his geometrical figures under ground, at the centre of the earth, far from the noise and din of this world, that might disturb his meditations, or distract him in his curious delineations he makes with his rod upon the dust; which no man living can prove impossible. Yet if any man does not as irreconcilably dissent from such a fable as this, as from any falsehood imaginable, assuredly that man is next door to madness or dotage, or does enormous violence to the free use of his faculties."

Throughout this argument runs the fallacy, that because experience leads us to draw certain conclusions from certain appearances, therefore lack of experience should jump to conclusions from appearances different in kind: thus, because having seen men writing, we deduce the earlier presence of men from an inscription discovered, therefore, not having seen gods making worlds, we are to deduce the earlier presence of gods from worlds about us. It is a complete *non sequitur*. The last paragraph, relating to Archimedes, we leave to the refutation of those who believe that men are alive after they are dead.

Dr. Samuel Clarke—born at Norwich 1675, died 1729—is specially notable amongst the ontological advocates for his "Demonstration of the Being and Attributes of a God," in which Dugald Stewart thought that Dr. Clarke "soared into regions where he was lost in the clouds." William Gillespie (in the "Necessary Existence of God," p. 23) says that "the Doctor's demonstration is no more than a pretended one. It is wholly and evidently inconclusive." This criticism from a very earnest Theist cannot be altogether disregarded by those amongst the pious who vaunt Dr. Clarke's argument, which, taken from his Boyle lecture in 1704 on the Being and Attributes of God, is as follows:—

1. Something has existed from all eternity.

2. There has existed from eternity some one unchangeable and independent being.

3. That unchangeable and independent being, which has existed from eternity without any external cause of its existence, must be self-existent—that is, necessarily existing.

4. What the substance or essence of that being, which is self-existent, or necessarily existing, is, we have no idea, neither is it at all possible for us to comprehend it.

5. Though the substance or essence of the self-existent being is in itself absolutely incomprehensible to us, yet many of the essential attributes of his nature are strictly demonstrable, as well as his existence. Thus, in the first place, the self-existent being must of necessity be eternal.

6. The self-existent being must of necessity be infinite and omnipresent.

7. The self-existent being must of necessity be but one.

8. The self-existent and original cause of all things must be an intelligent being.

9. The self-existent and original cause of all things is not a necessary agent, but a being endued with liberty and choice.

10. The self-existent being, the supreme cause of all things, must of necessity have infinite power.

11. The supreme cause and author of all things must of necessity be infinitely wise.

12. The supreme cause and author of all things must of necessity be a being of infinite goodness, justice, and truth, and all other moral perfections, such as become the supreme governor and judge of the world.

A long examination of Dr. Clarke's argument will be found in the work by D'Holbach, known as Mirabaud's "System of Nature," vol. ii., chap. iv.

It will be noticed that having affirmed in No. 4 that we have no idea of the nature of the being alleged in No. 1, yet that in No. 5 Dr. Clarke uses the pronoun "his," converting the incomprehensible substance into a masculine person with a stroke of his pen. Nos. 6 and 7 are but one proposition, and they negate the "cause of all things" in No. 8, because if there be but "one" "infinite," there cannot be any "all things," unless in the No. 1 "something" is used in the absolute as "noumenon;" and in No 8 "all things" are used in the relative as "phenomena," in which case, they are only the "something" of No. 1 conditioned in the human mind. The added assumption that the cause "must be an intelligent being" has no meaning if by "intelligence" is to be understood the same of God as of man; and, if it is to be understood differently, then has no value until the different meaning is fixed. No. 9 opens up the whole freewill question, if "volition," used of

God, is to mean the same as volition used of man. But, used of God, liberty of choice negates No. 11. In choosing or selecting there is the weighing the advantages and disadvantages, and during the process of choosing, the moment of uncertainty as to which is best; but with the "infinitely wise" such "choice" would be impossible. There can be no choice where the knowledge has been always complete, and therefore the determination never undetermined.

The argument used by Dr. Clarke to support his second proposition is that "either there has always existed some one unchangeable and independent being, from which all other beings that are or ever were in the universe, have received their original; or else there has been an infinite succession of changeable and dependent beings produced from one another in endless progression without any original cause at all;" and Dr. Clark describes the latter hypothesis as "so very absurd." This argument assumes too much, for it assumes, without any proof, "beings" that have been originated, as well as the unoriginated being, whose existence is to be demonstrated; and it assumes, most carelessly, that the want of origin for an endless chain is a difficulty. If it be possible to conceive an endless chain, there is no room to talk of its beginning, nor can you pick it to pieces; nor would the rejection of the endless chain demonstrate "the one independent being."

One of the latest amongst the *à priori* advocates is William Gillespie, whose works have recently been widely circulated, though we think his line of argument a very weak one. The propositions in his "Argument *à Priori*" for the being and attributes of a Great First Cause are:—

"1. Infinity of extension is necessarily existing.

"2. Infinity of extension is necessarily indivisible.

"*Corollary.*—Infinity of extension is necessarily immovable.

"3. There is necessarily a being of infinity of extension.

"4. The being of infinity of extension is necessarily of unity and simplicity.

"*Sub-proposition.*—The material universe is finite in extension.

"5. There is necessarily but one being of infinity of expansion.

"*Part 2, Proposition* 1.—Infinity of duration is necessarily existing.

"2. Infinity of duration is necessarily indivisible.

"*Corollary.*—Infinity of duration is necessarily immovable.

"3. There is necessarily a being of infinity of duration.

"4. The being of infinity of duration is necessarily of unity and simplicity.

"*Sub-proposition.*—The material universe is finite in duration.

"*Corollary.*—Every succession of substances is finite in duration.

"5. There is necessarily but one being of infinity of duration.

"*Part* 3, *Proposition* 1.—There is necessarily a being of infinity of expansion and infinity of duration.

"2. The being of infinity of expansion and infinity of duration is necessarily of unity and simplicity.

"*Division* 2, *Part* 1.—The simple sole being of infinity of expansion and of duration is necessarily intelligent and all-knowing.

"*Part* 2.—The simple sole being of infinity of expansion and of duration, who is all-knowing, is necessarily all-powerful.

"*Part* 3.—The simple sole being of infinity of expansion and of duration, who is all-knowing and all-powerful, is necessarily entirely free.

"*Division* 3.—The simple sole being of infinity of expansion and of duration, who is all-knowing, all-powerful, and entirely free, is necessarily completely happy.

"*Sub-proposition.*—The simple sole being of infinity of expansion and of duration, who is all-knowing, all-powerful, entirely free, and completely happy, is necessarily perfectly good."

The foregoing argument seeks to prove too much. It affirms one existence (God) infinite in extent and duration, and another entirely different and distinct existence (the material universe) finite in extent and duration. It therefore seeks to substantiate everything, and something more. Infinite signifies nothing more than indefinite. When a person speaks of infinite extension he can only mean to refer to the extension of something to which he has been unable to set limits. The mind cannot conceive extension *per se*, either absolute or finite. It can only conceive something extended. It might be impossible mentally to define the extension of some substance. In such a case its extension would be indefinite; or, as Mr. Gillespie uses the word, infinite. No one can therefore possibly have any idea of infinity of extension. Yet it is upon the existence of such an idea, and on the impossibility of getting rid of it, that Mr. Gillespie grounds his first proposition. If the idea does not exist, the argument is destroyed at the first step. To this it has been replied: "The infinite and indefinite are not identical; the first refers to a positive attribute, the last simply indicates a negative deficiency—the want of a cognised boundary" (Debate between Iconoclast and W. H. Gillespie, p. 31). We rejoin that there is no such positive attribute. Attributes are of the conditioned.

Mr. Gillespie argues that it is utterly beyond the power of the human mind to conceive infinity of extension non-existent. It is utterly beyond the power of the human mind to conceive, in truth, infinity of extension at all, either existent or non-existent. Extension can only be conceived as quality of some mode of substance. It is possible to conceive various modes of substance extended. It is impossible in thought to either conceive or to limit the possible extension of substance. Mr. Gillespie having asserted that we cannot but believe that infinity of extension exists, proceeds to declare that it exists necessarily, and says, "everything, the existence of which we cannot but believe, is necessarily existing." Then, as we cannot but believe in the existence of the universe, or, to adopt Mr. Gillespie's phrase, the material universe, the material universe exists necessarily. If, by "anything necessarily existing," he means anything the essence of which involves existence, or the nature of which can only be considered as existent, then Mr. Gillespie, by demonstrating the necessary existence of the universe, refutes his own later argument, that God is its creator.

The whole of the propositions following the first fall if it falls. The second proposition is, that infinity of extension is necessarily indivisible. In dealing with this proposition, Mr. Gillespie talks of the *parts* of infinity of extension, and says that he means parts in the sense of partial consideration only. Now, not only is it denied that you can have any idea of infinity of extension, but it is also denied that infinity can be the subject of partial consideration. Mr. Gillespie's whole proof of this proposition is intended to affirm that the parts of infinity of extension are necessarily indivisible from each other. I have already denied the possibility of conceiving infinity in parts; and, indeed, if it were possible to conceive infinity in parts, then that infinity could not be indivisible, for Mr. Gillespie says that, by indivisible, he means indivisible, either really or mentally. Now, each part of anything conceived is, in the act of conceiving, mentally separated from, either other parts of, or from the remainder of, the whole of which it is part. It is clearly impossible to have a partial consideration of infinity, because the part considered must be mentally distinguished from the unconsidered remainder, and, in that case, you have, in thought, the part considered finite, and the residue certainly limited, at least, by the extent of the part under consideration.

The argument in favour of the corollary to the second proposition is, that the parts of infinity of extension are necessarily immovable amongst themselves; but if there be no such thing as infinity of extension—that is, if extension be only a quality of condition, and not therefore infinite; if infinite mean only indefiniteness or illimitability, and if infinity cannot have parts, this argument goes for very little. The argument, that the parts of infinity of extension are immovable, is refuted by Mr. Gillespie's sub-proposition (4), that the parts of the material universe are movable and divisible from each other. He urges that a part of the infinity of extension or of its substratum must penetrate the material universe and every atom of it. But, if infinity can have no parts, no part of it can penetrate the material universe. If infinity have parts (which is absurd), and if some part penetrate every atom of the material universe, and if the part so penetrating be immovable, how can the material universe be considered as movable, and yet as penetrated in every atom by immovability? If penetrated be a proper phrase, then, at the moment when the part of infinity was penetrating the material universe, the part of infinity so penetrating must have been in motion. There is either no penetration, or there is no immovability.

In his argument for proposition 5, Gillespie says that "any one who asserts that he can suppose two or more necessarily existing beings, each of infinity of expansion, is no more to be argued with than one who denies, Whatever is, is." Why is it more difficult to suppose this, than to suppose one being of infinity, and, in addition to this infinity, a material universe? If it be replied that you cannot conceive two distinct and different beings occupying the same point at the same moment, then it must be impossible to conceive the material universe and God existing together. Any argument which proves that two infinites cannot co-exist negates also the possibility of the co-existence of an infinite and the finite.

Having demonstrated to his own satisfaction an infinite substance, and also having assumed in addition a finite substance, and having called the first, infinite "being"—perhaps from a devout objection to speak of God as substance—Mr. Gillespie seeks to prove that the infinite being is intelligent. He says : " Intelligence either began to be, or it never began to be. That it never began to be is evident in this, that if it began to be, it must have had a cause, for whatever begins to be must have a cause. And the cause of intelligence must be of intelligence, for what is not of intelligence cannot make intelligence begin to be. Now, intelligence being before intelligence began to be, is a contradiction. And this absurdity following from the supposition, that intelligence began to be, it is proved that intelligence never began to be—to wit, is of infinity of duration." Mr. Gillespie does not say why " what is not of intelligence cannot make intelligence begin to be ;" but it is not unfair to suppose that he means that of things which have nothing in common one cannot be the cause of the other. Let us apply Mr. Gillespie's argument to the material universe, the existence of which is to him so certain that he has treated it as a self-evident proposition.

The material universe—that is, matter—either began to be, or it never began to be. That it never began to be is evident in this, that if it began to be, it must have had a cause, for whatever begins to be must have a cause. And the cause of matter must be of matter, for what is not of matter cannot make matter begin to be. Now, matter being before matter began to be, is a contradiction. And this absurdity following from the supposition that matter—*i.e.*, the material universe—began to be, it is proved that the material universe never began to be—to wit, is of indefinite duration.

This argument as to the eternity of matter is at least as logical as the argument for the eternity of intelligence. Mr. Gillespie might reply, that he affirms the material universe to be finite in duration, and that by the argument for his proposition, Part 2, he proves that the one infinite being (God) is the creator of matter. His words are, "As the material universe is finite in duration or began to be, it must have had a cause; for, whatever begins to be must have a cause. And this cause must be [Mr. Gillespie does not explain why], in one respect or other, the simple sole being of infinity of expansion and duration, who is all-knowing [the all-knowing or intelligence rests on the argument which has just been shown to be equally applicable to matter] inasmuch as what being, or cause independent of that being, could there be? And, therefore, that being made matter begin to be." Taking Mr. Gillespie's own argument, that which made matter begin to be, must be of matter, for what is not matter, cannot make matter begin to be; then Mr. Gillespie's infinite being (God) must be matter. Having as above argued that the being made matter, he proceeds, "and this being shown, it must be granted that the being *is*, necessarily, all-powerful." Nothing of the kind need be granted. If it were true that it was demonstrated that the infinite being (God) made matter, it would not prove him able to make anything else; it might show the being cause enough for that effect, but does not demonstrate him cause for all effects. So that if no better argument can be found to prove God all-powerful, his omnipotence remains unproved.

Mr. Gillespie's last proposition is that the being (God) is necessarily completely happy. In dealing with this proposition, Mr. Gillespie talks of unhappiness as existing in various kinds and degrees. But, to adopt his own style of argument, unhappiness either began to be, or it never began to be. That it never began to be is evident in this, that whatever began to be must have had a cause; for whatever begins to be must have a cause. And the cause of unhappiness must be of unhappiness, for what is not of unhappiness cannot make unhappiness begin to be. But unhappiness being before unhappiness began to be, is a contradiction; therefore unhappiness is of infinity of duration. But proposition 5, part 2, says there is but one being of infinity of duration. The one being of infinity of duration is therefore necessarily unhappy. Mr. Gillespie's arguments recoil on himself, and are destructive of his own affirmations.

In his argument for the sub-proposition, Mr. Gillespie says that God's motive, or one of his motives, to create, must be believed to have been a desire to make happiness, besides his own consummate happiness, begin to be. That is God, who is consummate happiness everywhere for ever, *desired* something. That is, he wanted more than then existed. This is, his happiness was not complete. That is, Mr.

Gillespie refutes himself. But what did infinite and eternal complete happiness desire? It desired (says Mr. Gillespie) to make more happiness—that is, to make more than an infinity of complete happiness.

The writer in the *British Quarterly Review*, in the article before quoted, says: "The ontological argument has always possessed a singular fascination for the speculative mind. It promises and would accomplish so much, if it were only valid. It would be so powerful, if it were only conclusive. But had demonstration been possible, the Theistic argument, like the proofs of mathematics, would have carried conviction to the majority of thinkers long ago. The historical failure is signal, whether in the form in which it was originally cast by Augustine, Anselm, and Aquinas, or in the more elaborate theory of Descartes, or as presented by the ponderous English mind of Cudworth, Henry More, and Dr. Samuel Clarke, it is altogether a *petitio principii*. Under all its modifications it reasons from the necessary notion of a God to his necessary existence; or from the necessary existence of space and time, which are assumed to be the properties or the attributes of a substance, to the necessary existence of that substance. A purely subjective necessity of the reason is carried from within and held conclusive in the realm of objective reality. But the very essence of the problem is the discovery of a valid pathway, by which to pass from the notions of the intellect to the realities of the universe beyond it; we may not, therefore, summarily identify the two, and at the outset take the existence of one as demonstrative of the other. In the affirmation of real existence, we pass from the notion that has entered the mind (or is innate) to the realm of objective being, which exists independently of us who affirm it; and how to pass warrantably from the ideal world within to the real world without is the very problem to be solved. To be valid at its starting point the ontological argument ought to prove that the notion of God is so fixed in the very root of our intelligent nature, that it cannot be dislodged from the mind; and this some thinkers, such as Clarke, have had the hardihood to affirm. To be valid as it proceeds, it ought to prove that the notion, thus necessary in thought, has a real counterpart in the realm of things, in order to vindicate the step it so quietly takes from the ideal notion to the world of real existence. It passes from thought to things, as it passes from logical premiss to conclusion

But to be logical it must rest contented with an ideal conclusion deduced from its ideal premiss. And thus, the only valid issue of the ontological argument is a system of absolute idealism, of which the theological corollary is Pantheism. But as this is not the Deity the argument essays to reach, it must be pronounced illogical throughout.

"Thus the ontological argument identifies the logical and the real. But the illicit procedure in which it indulges would be more apparent than it is to *à priori* theorists, if the object they imagine they have reached were visible in nature and apprehensible by the senses. To pass from the ideal to the real sphere by a transcendent act of thought, is seen at once to be unwarrantable in the case of sense-perception. In this case it is the presence of the object that alone warrants the transition, else we should have as much right to believe in the real existence of the hippogriff as in the reality of the horse. But when the object is invisible, and is, at the same time, the supreme being in the universe, the speculative thinker is more easily deceived. We must, therefore, in every instance ask him, where is the bridge from the notion to the reality? What is the plank thrown across the chasm which separates these two regions (to use an old philosophical phrase) 'by the whole diameter of being?' We can never, by any vault of logic, pass from the one to the other. We are imprisoned within the region of mere subjectivity in all *à priori* demonstration, and how to escape from it is, as we have said before, the very problem to be solved."

And he adds afterwards: "Suppose that a supreme existence were demonstrable, that bare entity is not the God of Theism, the infinite intelligence and personality of whose existence the human spirit desires some assurance, if it can be had. And a formal demonstration of a primitive source of existence is of no theological value. It is an absolute zero, inaccessible alike to the reason and to the heart, before which the human spirit freezes."

Pearson's "Prize Essay on Infidelity," p. 16, says: "The *à priori* mode of reasoning is the exclusive idol of many of the German logicians......But in their hands this kind of reasoning has completely failed. It conducts the mind to no firm resting-place; it bewilders instead of elucidating our notions of God, of man, and the universe. It gives us no divine personal existence, and leaves us floating in a region of mere vague abstractions. Such reasonings are either altogether vain, or are not really what they profess to be. In our country the name of Dr. Clarke is chiefly associated with the *à priori* argument. He, and many others, attached to it an immense importance. But however highly extolled in past times, and worthy to be admired as a specimen of intellect, it is now generally set aside as insufficient of itself to demonstrate the being and the attributes of God. Clarke himself found it necessary to stoop to the argument *à posteriori*, and thereby acknowledged the fallacy of attempting to reason exclusively *à priori*......The fate of Dr. Clarke's pretended demonstration, and the result, in so far as theology is concerned, of the transcendental reasoning of the continental philosophers, show the futility of attempting to rise up to the height of the great argument of the existence of God by the *à priori* method alone."

We now come to the design argument, popularised by Paley, Lord Brougham, and others (see Discussion between Robert Dale Owen and Origen Bacheler).

"Stated in brief compass," the design argument is as follows: "We see marks of adaptation, of purpose, or of foresight, in the objects which, as we learn from experience, proceed from the contrivance of man. We see [it is alleged] similar marks of design or adaptation in nature. We are, therefore, warranted in inferring a world designer; and from the indefinite number of these an infinite designer, and from their harmony his unity. Or thus, we see [it is alleged] the traces of wise and various purpose everywhere in nature. But nature could not of herself have fortuitously produced this arrangement. It could not have fallen into such harmony by accident. Therefore, the cause of this wise order cannot be a blind, unintelligent principle, but must be a free rational mind."

William Gillespie "Treatise on the Necessary Existence of Deity," writes that the design argument "can never make it appear that infinity belongs in any way to God." It "can only entitle us to infer the existence of a being of finite extension, for, by what rule in philosophy can we deduce from the existence of an object finite in extent (and nothing is plainer than that the marks of design which we can discover must be finite in their extent) the existence of a cause of infinity of extension? What, then, becomes of the omnipresence of the Deity, according to those who are content to rest satisfied from the reasoning of experience?......It will be vain to talk of the Deity being present by his energy, although he may not be present by his substance, to the whole universe. For, 'tis natural to ask not so much how it is proved that God is virtually present, though not substantially present, in every part of nature; as what can be meant by being everywhere present by mere energy?" This "reasoning can no more make out that the Deity is omnipresent by his virtue, than that he is omnipresent as to his substance......And, from the inaptitude of the reasoning under consideration to show that immensity, or omnipresence, belongs to God, it will be found to follow, directly and immediately, that his wisdom and power cannot be shown to be more than finite, and that he can never be proved to be a free agent.........Omnipresence (let it be only by energy) is absolutely necessary in a being of infinity of wisdom. And, therefore, 'the design argument' is unable to evince that the Deity is in possession of this attribute. It likewise plainly follows, from the inaptitude of this argument to show that God is omnipresent, that thereby we cannot prove infinity of power to belong to him. For, if the argument cannot make out that the being it discovers is everywhere present, how can it ever make out that he is everywhere powerful? By careful reflection, too, we may perceive that omnipotence of another kind than power, which can exert itself in all places, requires the existence of immensity." The design argument "can never evince that God is a free agent......If we cannot prove the immensity or omnipresence of the Deity, we can for that reason never show that he is omniscient, that he is omnipotent, that he is entirely free.......If the Deity cannot be proved to be of infinity in any given respect, it would be nothing less than absurd to suppose that he could be proved to be of infinity in any other respect." It "can do no more than prove that at the commencement of the phenomena which pass under its review, there existed a cause exactly sufficient to make the effects begin to be. That this caul existed from eternity, the reasonings from experience by no means show. Nay, for aught they make known, the designer himself may not have existed long before those marks of design which betoken his workmanship." This reasoning "cannot prove that the God whom it reveals has existed from all eternity; therefore, for anything it intimates, God may at some time cease to be, and the workmanship may have an existence when the workman hath fallen into annihilation.......Such reasonings can never assure us of the unity of the Deity." "Whether there be one God or not, the argument from experience doth by no means make clear. It discovers marks of design in the phenomena of nature, and infers the existence of at least one intelligent substance sufficient to produce them. Further, however, it advances not our knowledge. Whether the cause of the phenomena be one god or many gods, it pretends not to determine past all doubt.......But did this designer create the matter in which the design appeared? Of this the argument cannot convince us, for it does no more than infer a designing cause from certain appearances, in the same way we would infer, from finding some well-contrived machine in a desert, that a human being had left it there.......Now, because this reasoning cannot convince us of such a creation, it cannot convince us there is not a plurality of deities, or of the causes of things.......If we cannot prove the eternity of God, it is not possible we can prove the unity of God. To say that, for anything we know to the contrary, he may have existed from all eternity, being much the same as saying that, for anything we know to the contrary, there may be another god or many gods beside." (Prefatory Introduction.)

In the course of an examination of the hypotheses of Charles Darwin, in the *Fortnightly Review* for 1868, Mr. George Henry Lewes, dealing with the embryonic stages of animal life, and objecting to the hypothesis of a creative plan, asks: "What rational interpretation can be given to the succession of phases each embryo is forced to pass through? None of these phases have any adaptation to the future state of the animal, but are in positive contradiction to it, or are simply purposeless; many of them have no adaptation, even to its embryonic state. What does the fact imply? There is not a single known organism which is not developed out of simpler forms. Before it can attain the complex structure which distinguishes it, there must be an evolution of forms which distinguish the structures of organisms lower in the series. On the hypothesis of a plan which pre-arranged the organic world, nothing could be more unworthy of a supreme intelligence than this inability to construct an organism at once, without making several tentative efforts, undoing to-day what was so carefully done yesterday, and repeating for centuries the same tentatives and the same corrections in the same succession. Do not let us blink this consideration. There is a traditional phrase which is in vogue amongst anthropomorphists—a phrase which has become a sort of argument—'the great architect.' But if we are to admit the human point of view, a glance at the facts of embryology must produce very uncomfortable reflections. For what shall we say to an architect who was unable—or, being able, was obstinately unwilling—to erect a palace, except by first using his materials in the shape of a hut, then pulling them down and rebuilding them as a cottage, then adding storey to storey, and room to room, not with any reference to the ultimate purposes of a palace, but wholly with reference to the way in which houses were constructed in ancient times? Would there be a chorus of applause from the Institute of Architects, and favourable notices in newspapers of this profound wisdom? Yet this is the sort of succession on which organisms are constructed. The fact has long been familiar; how has it been reconciled with infinite wisdom?" (See *Quarterly Review*, vol. cxxvii., p. 143, where the reader will find a long and special pleading in favour of the design argument.)

Objecting to the validity of the design argument, which he regards as a signal failure, the writer in the *British Quarterly Review* says (July, 1871, p. 47): "1. The effects it examines, and from which it infers a cause, are finite, while the cause it assumes is infinite; but the infinity of the cause can be no valid inference from an indefinite number of finite effects. The indefinite is still the finite; and we can never perform the intellectual feat of educing the infinite from the finite by the multiplication of the latter. It has been said by an acute defender of the teleological argument that the number of designed phenomena (indefinitely vast) with which the universe is filled, is sufficient to suggest the infinity of the designing cause............The vastest range of design is of no greater validity than one attested instance of it, so far as proof is concerned. It is not accumulation, but relevancy, of data that we need. But (2), at the most, we only reach an artificer or protoplast, not a creator—one who arranged the phenomena of the world, not the originator of its substance—the arehitect of the cosmos, not the maker of the universe. Traces of mind [if] discoverable amid the phenomena of the world cast no light upon the fact of its creation, or the nature of its source. There is no analogy between a human artificer arranging a finite mechanism and a divine creator originating a world; nor is there a parallel between the order, the method, and the plan of nature, and what we see when we watch a mechanician working according to a plan, to produce a designed result. The only real parallel would be our perception by sense of a world lowly evolving from chaos, according to a plan previously oreseen. From the product you are at liberty to infer a producer only after having seen a similar product formerly produced. But the product which supplies the basis of this argument is unique and unparalleled; 'a singular effect,' in the language of Hume, whose reasoning on this point has never been successfully assailed. And the main difficulty which confronts the Theist, and which Theism essays to remove, is precisely that which the consideration of design does not touch—viz., the origin, and not the arrangement, of the universe. The teleological analogy is, therefore, worthless. There is no parallel, we repeat, between the process of manufacture and product of creation, between the act of a carpenter working with his tools to construct a cabinet and the evolution of life in nature. On the contrary, there are many marked and sharply-defined contrasts between them. In the latter case there is fixed and ordered regularity, no deviation from law; in the former, contingency enters, and often alters and mars, the work. Again, the artificer simply uses the materials which he finds lying to hand in nature. He *detaches* them from their natural connections. He arranges them in a special fashion. But in nature, in the successive evolution of her organisms, there is no detachment, no displacement, no interference, or isolation. All things are linked together. Every atom is dependent on every other atom, while the organisms seem to grow and develop 'after their kind' by some vital force, but by no manipulation similar to the architect's or builder's work. And yet, again, in the one case the purpose is comprehensible. The end is foreseen from the beginning. We know what the mechanician desires to effect; but in the other case we have no clue to the 'thought' of the architect. Who will presume to say that he has adequately followed the purposes of nature in the adjustment of her phenomena to one another? But (3) the only valid inference from the phenomena of design would be that of a phenomenal first cause. The inference of a personal divine agent or substance, from the observation of the mechanism of the universe, is invalid. What link connects the traces of mind which are [said to be] discernible in nature with an agent who produced them? There is no such like. And thus the divine personality remains unattested. The same may be said of the divine unity. Why should we rest in our inductive inference of one designer from the [alleged] phenomena of design, when these are [claimed to be] so varied and so complex? Or grant that in all we observe a subtle and pervading unity is found, and as a consequence all existing arrangements point to one designer, why may not that designer have been at some remote period himself designed? And so on *ad infinitum* (see on this 'Paley Refuted in his Own Words,' by George Jacob Holyoake; and, *per contrâ*, 'Theism,' by John Orr).

"But, in the second place, not only is the argument defective (admitting its validity as far as it goes), even partial validity cannot be conceded to it. The phenomena of design not only limit us to a finite designer, not only fail to lead us to the originator of the world, or to a personal first cause, but they confine us within the network of observed designs, and do not warrant faith in a being detached from, or independent of, these designs, and therefore able to modify them with a boundless reserve of power. These designs only suggest mechanical agency working in fixed forms according to prescribed law. In other words, the phenomena of the universe, which distantly resemble the operations of man, do not in the least suggest an agent exterior to themselves. We are not intellectually constrained to ascribe the arrangement of means to ends in nature to anything supra-mundane." Why may not the phenomena of the universe be the mere endless evolution of the universe itself? "But if the inference from design is valid at all, it must be valid everywhere; all the phenomena of the world must yield it equally. No part of the universe is better made than any other part. Every phenomenon is adjusted to every other phenomenon nearly, or remotely, as means to ends. Therefore, if the few phenomena, which our teleologists single out from the many, are a valid index to the character of the source whence they have proceeded, everything that exists must find its counterpart in the divine nature. If we are at liberty to infer an Archetype above, from the traces of mind beneath, must not the phenomena of moral evil and sin be on the same principle carried upwards by analogy? a procedure which would destroy the notion of Deity which the teleologists advocate. If we are at liberty to conclude that a few phenomena, which seem to us designed, proceed from and find their counterpart in God, reason must be shown why we should select a few and pass over other phenomena of the universe. In other words, if the constructor of the universe designed one result from the agency which he has established, must he not have designed all the results that actually emerge? and if the character of the architect be legitimately deduced from one or a few designs, must we not take all the phenomena which exist to help out our idea of his character? Look, then, at these phenomena as a whole. Consider the elaborate contrivances for inflicting pain, and the apparatus so exquisitely adjusted to produce a wholesale carnage of the animal tribes. They have existed from the very dawn of geologic time. The whole world teems with the proofs of such intended carnage. Every organism has parasites which prey upon it; and not only do the superior tribes feed upon the inferior (the less yielding to the greater), but the inferior prey at the very same time no less remorselessly upon the superior. If, therefore, the inference of benevolence be valid, the inference of malevolence is at least equally valid: and as equal and opposite the one notion destroys the other" (*British Quarterly Review*, No. cvii., p. 52).

Victor Cousin, in his 25th Lecture ("History of Modern Philosophy," pp. 418 to 426), examining Locke's "Essay on the Human Understanding," takes occasion to sum up, from a Theistic point of view, the various arguments for the existence of God; but all his points having been already touched on here, it is unnecessary to do more than to refer the student to him.

We come now to the fourth division of our subject (see page 121). Sir William Hamilton says ("Discussions on Philosophy," p. 623): "The only valid arguments for the existence of a God and for the immortality of the human soul rest on the ground of man's moral nature." It is with a phase of this argument that Kant's name is especially associated. Immanuel Kant was born at Königsberg, 22nd April, 1724, died 12th February, 1804. Unquestionably one of the greatest thinkers of the eighteenth century, Kant is very differently judged by opposing readers. His words are difficult to comprehend, partly because of his special terminology, and partly because his style is extremely involved. Kant was a Theist, but his notions of future life seem occasionally to savour of the doctrine of metempsychosis. Victor Cousin says that, "after having commenced by a little idealism, Kant ends in Scepticism" ("History of Modern Philosophy," vol. i., p. 132); and it is affirmed that, questioned towards the close of his life as to his ideas on a future state, the Prussian philosopher responded, "I have no notion of a future state" ("Biographie Universelle," vol. vii., p. 92). But see on this "Life and Works of Kant," by A. G. Henderson, p. liii., introduction to Victor Cousin's "Lectures on the Philosophy of Kant." De Quincey rather recklessly declares of Kant that "he exulted in the prospect of our absolute and ultimate annihilation; that he planted his glory in the grave, and was ambitious of rotting for ever."

Before stating the ethico-theological argument, it will be well to show how Kant deals with the first and second divisions of the Theistic evidences ("Philosophy of Kant," by Victor Cousin, translated by A. G. Henderson, p. 120):

"Speculative reason has but three species of arguments to demonstrate the existence of God; Kant calls them *physico-theological*, *cosmological*, and *ontological*.

"The two first set out from experience; in the *physico-theological* proof we examine the order and beauty of the world, and establish the existence of God as an explanation of this order and beauty." [We have already fully stated the objections both to the "order and beauty" assumed, and the conclusion sought to be deduced from this alleged order and beauty, and in restating, in Cousin's words, the three classes of arguments, we need only ask the reader to bear this in mind.] "In the *cosmological* proof we take no account of the harmony revealed to us by experience; it is sufficient that this experience should attest any contingent existence to enable us to pass from this contingent existence to that of an existence absolutely necessary. Finally, in the third proof, the *ontological*, we throw aside all experience, and conclude from the *idea* of perfect being to its existence.

"Kant begins by discussing the *ontological* proof, because, according to him, the two others rest upon this one.

"This proof is no other than that of St. Anselm. It was introduced into modern philosophy by Descartes, and the last form under which it appears was given to it by Leibnitz. It is under this form that Kant considers it, and undertakes to refute it; perfect being contains all reality, and it is admitted that such a being is possible—that is to say, that its existence implies no contradiction. Now, all reality supposes existence. There is therefore a thing possible, in the concept of which is comprised existence. If this thing be denied, the possibility of its existence is also denied, which is contradictory to the preceding. You see here Leibnitz's argument, viz., God is, if he is possible, since his possibility—that is to say, his very essence—carries with it his existence; and thus to admit it as possible, and not, at the same time, to admit it as existing, is a contradiction. Kant attacks this argument in the following manner:—First, we must carefully distinguish between logical necessity, or that species of necessity which connects together an attribute with its subject, with the real necessity of things, and guard ourselves from concluding the second from the first. When I say a triangle is a figure which has three angles, I indicate a necessary relation in such a way that, the subject once given, the attribute is inevitably linked with it. But, although it is contradictory to suppose a triangle after suppressing in thought the three angles, it involves no contradiction to suppress both one and the other, both subject and predicate. In like manner, though it is a contradiction to deny omnipotence when we suppose God, it is no contradiction to deny both; here all disappears, attribute and subject, and there is no longer any possible contradiction. If it be said that there is such a subject which cannot be suppressed, and should therefore remain, the answer is, that this is reaffirming an absolutely necessary subject, and is begging the question.

"Kant insists that there is no contradiction in the negation of God's existence. When we say of such and such a thing, whose existence we regard as possible, that such a thing exists, what species of proposition is employed? Do we employ an analytical or a synthetical proposition? If, in affirming the existence of anything, an analytical proposition be employed, we add nothing to the idea we have of it, and we consequently affirm this existence only because it is already in the idea which we have already of the thing itself, which is but a repetition. It proves nothing in reference to the *real* existence, for it is not already given as existent. On the other hand, is the proposition which affirms the existence of any certain thing synthetical? In that case there is no contradiction in suppressing the predicate of existence; for analytical propositions are the only ones in which, according to Kant, any contradiction is implied by a denial of the predicate, the subject being once given. It is by this means that we recognise such propositions. It is thus a contradiction to suppose a triangle, if in thought we suppress the three angles—to suppose God, if we deny omnipotence; because these propositions, a triangle is a figure which has three angles, God is omnipotent, are analytical propositions. But if the proposition which affirms the existence of God be synthetical, how can it involve any contradiction to suppose the non-existence of God? The contradiction would only be possible on the supposition that the proposition is analytical, and this can only be on the condition of its proving nothing.

"Again, how can we conclude, from the mere conception of a perfect being, that it exists, so long as the existence itself is not an attribute, a predicate which determines the idea of the subject? Now, existence cannot be regarded as an attribute, whose idea, added to that which we have of the subject, developes it, completes it, determines it. When I say God is all powerful, the attribute all-powerful determines the idea of God; but when I conceive God as simply possible or real, the idea of him rests the same in both cases. Here it is certain that the real involves nothing more than the possible; if it were otherwise, the idea which we have of anything would not be complete until we had conceived it as possible. It follows that if I conceive a being as perfect, I may perplex myself as much as I please by trying to evolve from the idea the real existence. The question of existence always remains, and it is not from the conception of the object, conceived as possible, that we can draw the concept of its reality. We are, therefore, obliged to quit the concept of an object if we would accord to it any real existence. This conclusion, if just, upsets the ontological argument, since this argument pretends to conclude from the idea of a perfect being, conceived as possible, its reality. 'Thus,' says Kant, 'Leibnitz is far from having done what he intended, though he may have arrived at the knowledge *à priori* of the possibility of the existence of an ideal being so elevated. In this celebrated ontological proof for the existence of a supreme being, all labour is in vain; and a man no more augments his knowledge by ideas than a merchant augments his fortune by adding a few cyphers to the sum which expresses his capital.'

"But though the argument which has just been examined

may prove nothing, and may not establish the real existence of God, may we not hope to succeed by adopting a different mode of argument? No, according to Kant; and here reappears the difficulty, insoluble according to him, which the transcendental dialectic opposes to the validity of human knowledge. As the existence of God, or of the perfect being, is placed beyond the conditions of experience, we have no right either to deny or affirm it; to suppose it, is to make a supposition which may be useful, perhaps necessary to the development and perfection of intelligence, but which can in no other manner be justified, at least under the actual conditions of human existence."

Again (page 130): "The argument which Kant calls *cosmological* is that which Leibnitz has named *à contingentiâ mundi.* Kant thus presents it: 'If anything whatever exists, then there must exist an absolutely necessary being; now, something does exist, as, for example, myself, therefore an absolutely necessary being exists. The minor contains an experimental fact, and the major concludes from an experimental fact in general to the existence of a necessary being. The proof thus sets out from experience, and is not, therefore, *à priori* or ontological.

"Kant makes necessary being a sort of monstrosity. 'The absolute necessity,' he says, 'which we seem to consider so indispensable a thing as the last support of all things, is the veritable gulf of human reason. Eternity itself, however sublime and however terrible, as depicted by Haller, turns the brain less, for it but measures the durat on of things, and does not attempt to sustain them. We can neither banish the thought, nor can we support it, that a being, which we represent to ourselves as the highest of all possible beings, might say to himself, 'I am from all eternity; out of me nothing exists but as I will. *But whence am I, then?* Here we are lost.'"

Dr. John Pye Smith says ("First Lines of Christian Theology," p. 170):

"It is one of the fundamental principles of the moral philosophy of Kant that we cannot but perceive a *connection,* constant and inseparable, between virtue and happiness; that this connection is totally *independent* of ourselves—we did not make it, it has a manifest existence (though debilitated and confined) under the most unfavourable circumstances, and we cannot abrogate it; and that, therefore, it is *communicated by God,* the Being of Supreme

Perfection, and to whom moral goodness must be necessarily and always agreeable."

"The sovereign good," says Kant ("Philosophy of Kant," p. liv.), "is not possible in the world unless we admit a Supreme Being, endowed with a causality conformable to moral intention. Now, a being which is capable of acting according to the representation of certain laws is an intelligence (a rational being), and the causality of such a being, as determined by this representation, is a will. Therefore, the supreme cause of nature, as a condition of the sovereign good, is a being who is the cause of nature, as intelligence and will (consequently the author of nature)—that is to say, *God.*" This assumed "sovereign good" exists only in the imagination of Kant. We can only measure the goodness of any given act by its tendency to happiness. If a "supreme being" be assumed as "cause of nature," cause of "sovereign good," then no state should exist, which is not within those words. The existence of any "guilt" or "misery" is conclusive against a supreme cause sufficient for universal "sovereign good."

In a dialogue between a preceptor and scholar, Kant says (p. lxi.):

"P. Has reason any ground for believing it *as real*, any such supreme power, dealing out happiness and misery according to desert and guilt, having sway over the whole physical system, and governing the world with the most unerring wisdom—in other words, that God exists?

"S. Yes; for we discover in those works of nature that we can judge of, marks of wisdom so vast and profound that we can account for it only by ascribing it to the unsearchable will of a Creator, from whom we deem ourselves entitled to expect an equally admirable adjustment of the moral order of the world—that is, a harmony between virtue and happiness—and that we may hereafter hope to become partakers of this happiness, provided we do not, by a neglect of our duty, render ourselves unworthy of it." This is no more than saying that to account for uncomprehended phenomena we invent "the unsearchable will;" these words really meaning nothing whatever.

"The thinking subject," says Kant (p. 90), "is the object of psychology, the union of all phenomena (the world) is the object of cosmology; and that which contains the supreme condition of the possibility of all that can be thought, the being of all beings, is the object of theology.

Thus, the pure reason furnishes the ideas of a transcendental science of the soul *(rational psychology)*, a transcendental science of the world *(rational cosmology)*, and, lastly, a transcendental science of God *(transcendental theology)*."

"Let us add," says Victor Cousin (p. 177), "that Kant's God, or, at least, the God of his metaphysic, is not the God of humanity. What, indeed, is he? A pure ideal, at the summit of human knowledge, which allows the mind to raise it to the highest possible unity, but which can have no legitimate value. Is it this ideal, destitute of reality; is it this hypothetical object of a regulative idea, which all men look up to as the cause and primitive substance of all things, the Being of Beings, and the Father of the human race?"

Victor Cousin is right in his objection to Kant's God as "destitute of reality;" but the same objection is, we submit, equally potent against M. Cousin's "Being of Beings and Father of the human race." There is surely no more reality in the one "ideal" than in the other. There is no legitimate value in the phrase "Father of the human race," and we maintain that the words, if submitted to analysis, contain no truth. Kant presents us with an unsatisfactory array of subtle word-play; and it is sometimes difficult to imagine that he was earnestly enlisted on either side, so much do his reasonings tell for and against both positions. This is remarkably illustrated in his four antimonies.

The four antinomies of Kant are ("Philosophy of Kant," p. 106):—First, the *thesis* is: "The universe has had a beginning in time, and has a boundary in space." To establish this thesis, Kant shows that the contrary supposition is inadmissible, and that it is impossible to regard the universe as not having a beginning. In fact, if it never had a beginning, it follows that every moment is in eternity—in other words, that at each instant the successive state of things in the universe form an infinite series. Now, the characteristic of an infinite series is this, that it can never be completed by a successive synthesis. Consequently, this infinite series of successive states is impossible. Therefore, we have a right to conclude that the world has had a beginning. In the same manner, it may be established that space is limited, by showing the impossibility of its being unlimited. If the world fills space entirely, we can only conceive it as an infinite number of parts. If this composition (of parts), which can only be successive, requires a time proportioned to it, viz., an infinite time, it supposes an infinite time already passed, and we thus admit the hypothesis that has already been rejected; therefore, the world is limited in space.

"Such are the arguments in favour of the thesis. Those in favour of the antithesis, that *the world has not had a beginning in time, and that it has no limits in space*, are as conclusive. To establish the thesis, Kant has previously shown the impossibility of admitting the antithesis; now, in order to establish the antithesis, he shows the impossibility of admitting the thesis. If the world has had a beginning, the time which preceded its existence must have been void. Now in such a time nothing can begin to be, because existence in such a case must be as unconditional as non-existence; and we are driven to the supposition of things either passing from nothing to existence of themselves, or by the action of a foreign cause. On the other hand, if the world be limited in space, there is an empty space which limits it, which empty space is impossible. In fact, space, as we have seen, is simply the form of external intuition; its existence vanishes the moment it is considered independently of objects; consequently, though there may exist a relation amongst things in space, there cannot exist a relation of things to space, which it would be necessary to admit, under the supposition that the world is limited. It is, therefore, infinite.

"Second Antinomy.—*Thesis:* 'Every compound substance is made up of simple parts; and everything in the universe is either simple or composed of simple elements.' If we suppose that compound substances are not composed of simple elements, these substances once decomposed, there would exist neither compound nor simple—there would, in fact, be nothing; and, consequently, the existence of substance itself might be denied, which is absurd. It follows that all substances are simple, and that compound bodies must be composed of simple parts, which demonstrates the thesis. But here is the antithesis: 'No compound thing is made up of simple parts, and nowhere do any such parts exist.' Suppose a compound body to be composed of simple parts, all such parts, like the compound body itself, must exist in space. Now, space itself, not being composed of simple parts, everything which occupies a space must have elements external to each other, and must consequently be compound. The simple would, therefore, be compound, which is a contradiction. Besides, we can have no intuition of an ultimate uncomposed object; a simple substance is, therefore, but an idea, to which, in the sensible world, nothing corresponds. It may, therefore, be affirmed that no simple bodies exist in the world.

"Third Antinomy.—*Thesis:* 'Everything that happens in the world cannot depend upon natural laws alone; we must admit the action of a free cause.' If there be only physical and natural laws, every event succeeds some anterior state. But this anterior state must have had a beginning, and, therefore, it supposes a state anterior to itself, and we arrive at a series of successive states, each engendering the other; so that we can never arrive at a commencement, and thus the series remains without any absolute condition. Now, it is a law that nothing happens without an efficient cause; it is, therefore, a contradiction to admit only the causality of nature; we must also admit an absolute and primitive causality, producing a series of phenomena by its absolute spontaneity—that is to say, a free cause. *Antithesis*. 'There is no such thing as liberty; everything in the world submits blindly to the laws of nature.' In any given moment, a cause is operative only on condition of its being itself previously uncaused. Now, either these two states of action and inertia are related to each other, or they are not. If one engenders the other, it may be asked, whence comes the first in its turn? and in this infinite series of causes, which we are obliged to acknowledge, the liberty of the agent disappears. If, on the contrary, these two states are independent of each other, then an effect may take place without a cause, which is absurd. Therefore, everything in the world is governed by the fatality of natural laws.

"Fourth Antinomy.—*Thesis:* 'A necessary condition for the existence of the world is, that there should exist at the same time, whether in the world as making part of it, or out of the world as its cause, a necessarily existent being.' The sensible world, considered as an assemblage of phenomena, contains at the same time a series of changes. Now every change, every contingent phenomenon, implies an anterior condition; and reason obliges us to ascend from condition to condition until we arrive at something which does not depend upon any other—that is to say, something necessary. But this necessary being belongs himself to the sensible world, otherwise he would not exist in time, and could not in any sense be said to be the cause of a series of events. There is, therefore, in the world something absolutely necessary, which is either the totality of the phenomena or simply a part of them. *Antithesis:* 'There is nowhere, neither in the world nor out of it, as its cause an absolutely necessary being.' Suppose that the world should either be itself, or contain in itself, a necessary being; there is then in the series of changes a beginning absolutely necessary, which is freed from the law of causality, or the series itself is without any beginning; and although all the parts are contingent, the union is necessary, which is contradictory. And, again, we cannot suppose a being placed *out* of the world, whose action takes place in time, who is himself consequently in time—that is to say, *in* the world. There is, then, nowhere a necessary being."

As there is very much difference of opinion as to Kant, and as Victor Cousin is charged with "having flagrantly misunderstood him on certain points," the reader is referred to the splendid summary by Mr. G. H. Lewes, in his "Biographical History of Philosophy" (vol. ii., ninth epoch), from which the scope of this work allows only a limited quotation:

"From Spinoza to Kant," writes Mr. Lewes (Lewes's "Biographical History of Philosophy." vol. ii., pp. 441-445), "the great question we have seen to be this: Have we any ideas which can be accepted as objective truths, and which, removed from the possible illusions of the senses and the understanding, may be made the basis of a philosophy revealing the realities of existence?

"This question, variously answered, resolved itself into the more definite question: Have we any ideas independent of experience?

"It had become evident that, before we could determine the objective value of our knowledge, we were bound to investigate the nature and conditions of the knowing faculties. Ontology thus was, for a time, superseded by psychology. Locke, Hume, the Sensational School, the Scotch School, and Gall, all these proclaim experience the foundation of knowledge; and yet, inasmuch as experience led irresistibly to scepticism, this was a dilemma which seemed only to be avoided by seeking refuge in common sense, *i.e.*, a denial of philosophy. Kant declined this refuge. He said it was the notable invention of modern times, whereby the emptiest noodle could place himself on a level with the profoundest thinker ('*Prolegomena: Vorrede,*' werke iii.,

170). He saw two conceptions of the world to be logically tenable: Materialism and Scepticism. He rejected both, and strove to reconcile what was true in both with what was true in the *à priori* doctrine. He called his system a *Criticism*. His object was to examine into the nature of this experience which led into scepticism. While men were agreed that experience was the source of all knowledge, Kant asked himself, What is this experience? what are its elements?

"The problem he set himself to solve was but a new aspect of the problem of Locke's *Essay*. On this deep and intricate question of human knowledge two opposite parties had been formed—the one declaring that all our knowledge was given in experience, and that all the materials were derived from sensation, and reflection upon those materials; the other declaring that these only furnished a portion of our knowledge. This second part maintained that there were elements of knowledge which not only were never derived from sensation, but which absolutely *transcended* all sensation; such, for instance, is the idea of substance. Experience only informs us of *qualities*. To these qualities we add a substratum, which we call substance; and this idea of a substratum, which, we are *compelled* to add, Locke himself confesses we never gained through any sensation of matter. Other ideas, such as causality, infinity, eternity, &c., are also independent of experience; *ergo*, said this school, antecedent to it.

"In the course of inquiry, the untenableness of the theory of innate ideas has become apparent. Descartes himself, when closely pressed by his adversaries, gave it up. Still, the fact of our possessing ideas apparently *not* derivable from experience remained, and this fact was to be explained. To explain it, Leibnitz asserted that, although all knowledge *begins with* sensation, it is not all *derived from* sensation—the mind furnishes its quota; and what it furnishes has the character of universality, necessity, consequently of truth, stamped on it. This doctrine, slightly modified, is popularly known as the doctrine of 'original instincts,' of 'fundamental laws of belief.'

"Kant also recognised the fact insisted on by the adversaries of the Sensational School; and this fact he set himself carefully to examine. His first object was, therefore, a criticism of the operations of the mind.

"Kant considered that his conception of a purely critical

philosophy was entirely original. No one before him had thought of thus subjecting reason itself to a thoroughly critical investigation, in order to reach answers to such questions as: Are *à priori* synthetic judgments possible? Is a science of metaphysics possible? And here may be noted an illustration of what was said at the opening of this section respecting Kant's originality. Certainly, no one had isolated the *à priori* elements of knowledge from those given in experience, as Kant isolated them, to build a system thereon; nevertheless the whole tendency of speculative development, since Hobbes, has been, as we have seen, towards the investigation of the grounds of certitude, *i.e.*, towards a criticism of the knowing faculties.

"On interrogating his consciousness, Kant found that neither of the two ordinary explanations would account for the phenomena; certain ideas, such as time, space, causality, &c., could not be resolved into experience alone; nor, on the other hand, although *à priori*, could they be supposed absolutely *independent* of experience, being, as it were, only the *forms* (necessary conditions) of our experience.

"There are not *two* sources of knowledge, said he: on the one side external objects, and on the other human understanding. Knowledge has but *one* source, and that is the *union* of object and subject; it is the function of two co-efficients. Thus, water is the union of oxygen and hydrogen; but you cannot say that water has two causes, oxygen and hydrogen. These are its conditions *(Bedingungen)*, its co-efficients; it has only one cause, namely, the union of the two.

"In this conception the existence of the two distinct factors is assumed. 'That all our knowledge begins with experience,' he says, 'there can be no doubt. For how is it possible that the faculty of cognition should be awakened into exercise otherwise than by means of objects which affect our senses, and partly of themselves produce representations *(Vorstellungen)*, partly rouse our powers of understanding into activity, to compare, to connect, or to separate these, and so to convert the raw material of our sensuous impressions into a knowledge of objects which is called experience? In respect of time, therefore, no knowledge of ours is antecedent to experience, but begins with it. But although all our knowledge begins with experience, it by no means follows that it arises out of experience. For, on the contrary, it is quite possible that our empirical knowledge

(Erfahrungserkenntniss) is a compound of that which we receive through impressions, and that which the faculty of cognition supplies from itself (sensuous impressions giving merely the *occasion*), an addition which we cannot distinguish from the original element given by sense, till long practice has made us attentive to and skilful in separating it. It is, therefore, a question which requires close investigation, and is not to be answered at first sight: Whether there exists a knowledge altogether independent of experience, and even of all sensuous impressions?' "

Mr. Lewes says of Kant (Lewes's "Biographical History of Philosophy," vol. ii., pp. 461-462):

"His object was to give a theory of all the pure elements, *à priori*, which enter into knowledge as distinguished from the *à posteriori* elements. He advances four fundamental propositions :

"1. That experience does not furnish the whole of our knowledge.

"2. That what it does furnish has the character of contingency and variability.

"3. That the mind also furnishes an element, which element is an inseparable condition of all knowledge; without it knowledge could not be.

"4. That this element has the character of universality and necessity.

"5. And that the principle of all certitude is precisely this universality and necessity.

"He set himself to examine the nature of the mind, and to trace the distinctive characters of each element of knowledge, *i.e.*, the objective and the subjective. Instead of saying, with the Sensational School, all our knowledge is derived from the senses, Kant said, *Half* of our knowledge is derived from the senses, and the half which has another origin, is *indissolubly bound up with the former half.* Thus, instead of saying with the Cartesians, that, besides the ideas acquired through the sense, we have also certain ideas, which are innate and irrespective of sense, Kant said *all* our ideas have a double origin, and this two-fold co-operation of object and subject is *indispensable* to all knowledge."

"*First Result* (Lewes's "Biographical History of Philosophy," vol. ii., pp. 471-473).—A knowledge of things *per se (Dinge an sich)* is impossible, so long as knowledge remains composed as at present. Consequently ontology, as a science, is impossible. But it may be asked, if we never knew noumena *(Dinge an sich)*, how do we know that they exist? The answer is simple: Their existence is a necessary postulate. Although we can only know the appearances of things, we are forced to conclude that the things exist. Thus, in the case of a rainbow, we discover that it is only the appearance of certain drops of water. These drops of water, again, although owing their shape, colour, &c., to our sensibility, nevertheless exist. They do not exist *as* drops of water, because drops of water are but phenomena; but there is an unknown something which, when affecting our sensibility, appears to us as drops of water. Of this unknown something we can affirm nothing, except that it necessarily exists because it affects us. We are conscious of being affected; we are conscious also that that which affects us must be something different from ourselves. This the law of causation reveals to us. A phenomenon, inasmuch as it is an appearance, pre-supposes a noumenon—a thing *which appears;* but this noumenon, which is a necessary postulate, is only a negation to us. It can never be positively known; it can only be known under the conditions of sense and understanding—*ergo*, as a phenomenon.

"*Second Result.*—The existence of an external world is a necessary postulate; but its existence is only logically affirmed. From the foregoing, it appears that we are unable to know anything respecting things *per se;* consequently, we can never predicate of our knowledge that it has objective truth. But our knowledge being purely subjective and relative, can we have no certainty? are we to embrace scepticism? No.

"*Third Result.*—Our knowledge, though relative, is *certain.* We have ideas independent of experience, and these ideas have the character of universality and necessity. Here we see the effect of confusing cognitions with conditions of cognition. It is not ideas that are independent of experience, but organic conditions on which ideas depend. Although we are not entitled to conclude that our subjective knowledge is completely true as an expression of an objective fact, yet we are forced to conclude that within its own sphere it is true.

"*Fourth Result.*—The veracity of consciousness is established.

"*Fifth Result.*—With the veracity of consciousness is

established the certainty of morals. It is here we see the importance of Kant's analysis of the mind. Those who reproach him with having ended, like Hume, in scepticism, can only have attended to his *Critique of the Pure Reason*, which certainly does, as we said before, furnish a scientific basis for scepticism. It proves that our knowledge is relative; that we cannot assume things external to us to be as we conceive them; in a word, that ontology is impossible.

"So far Kant goes with Hume. This is the goal they both attain; this is the limit they agree to set to the powers of the mind. But the different views they took of the nature of mind led to the difference we before noted respecting the certainty of knowledge. Kant having shown that consciousness, as far as it extended, was veracious, and having shown that in consciousness certain elements were given which were not derived from experience, but which were necessarily *true;* it followed that whatever was found in consciousness, independent of experience, was to be trusted without dispute.

"If in consciousness I find the ideas of God and Virtue. I cannot escape believing in God and Virtue. This belief of mine is, I admit, practical, not theoretical; it is founded on a *certainty*, not on a *demonstration;* it is an ultimate fact, from which I cannot escape—it is not a conclusion deduced by reason.

[The answer simply is, that you do not find in consciousness the ideas of "God" and "virtue," except as artificial results, each of the words varying in their significance in different individuals (see page 118); the word "God" generally being the equivalent for all uninvestigated cause, and the word "virtue" sometimes being the exact equivalent in the mind of one person for conduct for which the word "vice" is the equivalent in the mind of another.]

"The attempt to demonstrate the existence of God is an impossible attempt. Reason is utterly incompetent to the task. The attempt to penetrate the essence of things—to know things *per se*—to know noumena—is also an impossible attempt. And yet, that God exists, that the world exists, are irresistible convictions.

[Here the difficulty is, that "world" is used for the substance of all phenomena, and "God" is a sign of three letters, with no meaning attached.]

"There is another certitude, therefore, besides that

derived from demonstration, and this is moral certitude, which is grounded upon belief. I cannot say, 'It is morally certain that God exists;' but I must say, 'I am morally certain that God exists.'"

"After having shown (Lewes's 'Biographical History of Philosophy,' vol. ii., pp. 486-487), as he conceives, the vanity of all theology based on the intellect and Speculative Reason, Kant professes to restore what he had apparently destroyed, by means of the moral or Practical Reason. Relying upon this, he reintroduces to us the theological doctrine, that the world is governed by a Personal God, a righteous Judge, who awards to men after death the lot which they deserve; appropriate misery to the bad, and appropriate bliss to the good.

"But if the principles employed in the critique of the Speculative Reason are correct, how can judgments obtained by means of the Practical Reason possess any absolute truth? It is urged that they have a character of necessity or universality, and that judgments having this character should be regarded as absolutely true. If the critique is correct, it has been shown that the character in question may arise simply from the fact that our minds are constituted in a particular way; and that it does not authorise us to believe that other beings think or judge in like manner. If this be the case, the judgments in question, however useful they may be for the regulation of our conduct, cannot authorise us to affirm the existence of an unseen noumenon, wholly beyond the field of experience, and to affirm that this noumenon governs the universe according to our idea of justice.

"Further, it is evident that when Kant, in his moral theology, affirms God to exist, to be a righteous Governor of the Universe, rewarding the good and punishing the bad, he sets quite at nought the principle laid down in his critique; that categories and conceptions have no valid application, except to phenomena and to objects of experience. For it is uniformly assumed by Kant that God is a noumenon, not a phenomenon, and that he does not lie within the field of possible experience. Were this otherwise, all Kant's critique of rational theology would fall to the ground. If, then, we can legitimately predicate of God existence, goodness, righteousness, power, and the attributes of a moral governor, we can legitimately make application of categories and conceptions to a noumenon, and that, too, not merely problematically, but assertorically."

To again use the acute Theistic writer in the *British Quarterly* (p 74): "The Kantian argument is more intricate and much less satisfactory than the common evidence from the phenomena of conscience itself. It is founded on the moral law, with its 'categorical imperative,' asserting that certain actions are right and others wrong, in a world in which the right is often defrauded of its legitimate awards, and the wrong is temporarily successful. This, however, says Kant, points to a future, in which the irregularity will be redressed, and, *therefore*, to a Supreme Moral Power, able to effect it. The argument is altogether inferential. It is circuitous, its conclusion being, in a sense, an appendix to the doctrine of immortality, and it has only a secondary connection with the data of the moral law itself."

We do not feel sure that we have either fairly stated Kant's position, or efficiently replied to so much as we have stated. In condensing within the limits of this Text-Book the views of a writer so involved in his expressions as is Immanuel Kant, we may have failed both in exposition and answer, but have the consolation that we, at any rate, place before our readers the sources of completer knowledge.

We now arrive at the last division of the Theistic arguments, quoting here again the able anonymous writer to whose thoughts we have been so much indebted, and to whom specially we are now to attempt some reply (*British Quarterly Review*, No. CVII., p. 54).

The "evidence of intuition" is urged by the writer as "of greatest value," although he fairly states some of the arguments against it—viz., "that it is at best only valid for the individual who may happen to feel its force; that it is not a universal endowment (as it should be, if trustworthy), but often altogether wanting; and that it can never yield us certainty, because its root is a subjective feeling or conviction, which cannot be verified by external test. These charges," says the Theistic writer, "cannot be ignored or lightly passed over. And for the Theist merely to proclaim, as an ultimate fact, that the human soul has an intuition of God, that we are endowed with a faculty of apprehension of which the correlative object is divine, will carry no conviction to the Atheist. Suppose he replies: 'This intuition may be valid evidence for you, but I have no such irrepressible instinct; I see no evidence in favour of innate ideas in the soul, or of a substance underneath the phenomena of nature of which we can have any adequate knowledge;' we may close the argument by simple re-ass rtion, and vindicate our procedure on the ground that, in the region of first principles, there can be no farther proof. [But, if the "argument" be thus closed, it is because the alleged intuition is only asserted, is not proved, and there is really no proof at all; see page 114.] We may also affirm that the instinct, being a sacred endowment, and delicate in proportion to the stupendous nature of the object it attests, it may, like every other function of the human spirit, collapse from mere disuse. [But, at least, then, this delicate sacred endowment should be found clear and complete in the child. Is it so found? and what is meant by a sacred intuition collapsing by disuse?] But if we are to succeed in even suggesting a doubt in the mind of our opponent as to the accuracy of his analysis, we must verify one primary belief, and exhibit its credentials so far as that is possible."

To the anticipated answer, that the Atheist has no such intuition, the answer is, that the mind starts with "gifts in embryo. They are not full-formed powers, so much as the capacities and potentialities of mental life. [But a capacity to think is not a thought, and may never be exercised.] Their growth to maturity is most gradual, and the difference between their adult and their rudimentary phases is as wide as the interval between a mature organisation and the egg from which it springs. It is, therefore," he contends, "no evidence against the reality or the trustworthiness of the intuition to which we appeal, that its manifestations are not uniform, or that it sometimes seems absent in the abnormal states of consciousness, or among the ruder civilisations of the world." An "intuition," which sometimes "seems absent," and the "manifestations" of which differ in the same individual at different stages, is, we submit, scarcely a very reliable witness.

Mrs. Besant, in her "True Basis of Morality," has sharply attacked the intuition theory, and we avail ourselves here of the argument she states:—"One fatal defect promptly disposes of the claims of intuition as a safe and reliable basis. Intuition, to be of any real value, must be fairly universal in its testimony: but it turns out to be as variable as the various nations of the earth. It depends on race civilisation, on custom, on habit; intuition does not speak *one* language, it speaks in many tongues; it varies its dictates according to the use of the people. To say that intuition is God's voice in the soul of man, and then to exalt one set of intuitions as the rule for the world, is simply to juggle with words, and to set up a new *authority* on the pedestal whence the old has been taken down. If one intuition be pronounced to speak justly, then all other intuitions, speaking at variance with it, must be held to be false; and the reason and judgment of one man will choose differently from the reason and judgment of his neighbour; and so there will be many divine voices contradicting each other, a result not consonant either with reason or with reverence. Besides, if intuition deceives our fellow creatures on all sides, are we wise, or even safe, in trusting it in our own cases? Is there any particular reason why *our* intuition should be *the* intuition? The real truth is, that what is called intuition is only the result of transmitted tendencies; it is a conveniently vague word under which to group certain phenomena of the mind, which are governed by laws at present very imperfectly known to us. Instinct and intuition only denote the tendency to do certain actions, or to think certain thoughts, and this tendency, which may be easily nullified or modified by changed conditions, arises from our ancestors having done these actions for generation after generation, until the doing became a habit, the predisposition to which is transmitted from parent to child. Instinct is the accumulated experience of the race impressed upon the yet unborn creature, and, unless checked, moulding many of its habits before any personal thought or experience comes in. And so intuition represents the result of the cumulated experience of the race, transmitted to the individual."

"We admit," the Theistic writer says (p. 55), "that it is difficult for the uninitiated to trace any affinity between its normal and its abnormal manifestations, when it is modified by circumstances to any extent. We farther admit that, while never entirely absent, it may sometimes seem to slumber, not only in stray individuals, but in a race or an era, and be transmitted from generation to generation in a latent state. It may hibernate, and then awake as from the sleep of years, arising against the will of its possessor, and refusing to be silenced. Almost any phenomenon may call it forth, and no single phenomenon can quench it. It is the spontaneous utterance of the soul in presence of the object whose existence it attests, and as such it is necessarily prior to any act of reflection upon its character, validity, or significance. Reflex thought, which is the product of experience, cannot in any case originate an intuition, or account for those phenomena which we may call by that name, supposing them to be delusive. Nothing in us, from the simplest instinct to the loftiest intuition, could in any sense create the object it attests, or after which it seeks and feels. And all our ultimate principles, irreducible by analysis, simply attest and assert.

"The very existence of the intuition of which we now speak is itself a revelation, because pointing to a Revealer within or behind itself. And, however crude in its elementary forms, it manifests itself in its highest and purest state at once as an act of intelligence and of faith. [On page 114 we have already quoted from Mr. George H. Lewes on intuition. We not only deny the possibility of intuition, independent of or preceding experience, but we urge that the writer, in saying that "any phenomenon may call it forth," really admits that what he calls intuition is a judgment on events.] It proclaims a supreme existence without and beyond the mind, which it apprehends in the act of revealing itself."

But the nature of the proclamation depends on the inherited thought-ability and predisposition, and on the conditions of thought-activity; and the "proclamation" varies with each individual variation. The acute writer seems to overlook that he alleges "God" revealing himself directly to the individual in the intuition, and yet speaks of abnormal manifestations of this revelation, and concedes that the revelation may seem to slumber in a race or an era. To ourselves—denying, as we do, the possibility of intuition, except as explained on page 114—the writer's own candid admissions are fatal to his case. Seeking to describe in some degree the character of the intuition to which he appeals as evidence, he says (p. 57): "It is one thing to create or evolve (even unconsciously) a mental image of ourselves, which we vainly attempt to magnify to infinity, and thereafter worship the image that our minds have framed; it is another to discern for a moment an august Presence *other than the human*, through a break in the clouds which usually veil him from our eyes. And it is to the inward recognition of this self-revealing object that the Theist makes appeal. What he discerns is at least not a 'form of his mind's own throwing;' while his knowledge is due not to the penetration of his own finite spirit, but to the condescension of the infinite."

This is an emotional declaration, not a reasonable argument; no reply can be given to it, for it advances no plea capable of analysis for the existence of God.

"Our knowledge," says the writer, p. 58, "of the object which intuition discloses is at first, in all cases, necessarily unreflective. In the presence of that object, the mind does not double back upon itself, to scrutinise the origin and test the accuracy of the report that has reached it. And thus the truth which it apprehends is at first only presumptive. It remains to be afterwards tested by reflection, that no allusion be mistaken for reality. What, then, are the tests of our intuitions? There are sundry elements in every intuition on which we do not here enlarge, as they are necessary features rather than criteria, characteristics rather than tests. Two of them may be merely stated: 1st., Every intuition is ultimate, and carries its own evidence within itself; it cannot appeal to any higher witness beyond itself: and, 2nd., The fact or facts which it proclaims, while irreducible by analysis, must be incapable of any other explanation."

Here there is no fact proclaimed, the words "supreme existence," "august presence," are not the counters for expressing concepts of fact; they are only fine sounds which avoid instead of proclaiming, which hide instead of making clear.

"The following seem sufficient criteria of their validity and trustworthiness: 1st. The persistence with which they appear and reappear after experimental reflection upon them, the obstinacy with which they reassert themselves when silenced, the tenacity with which they cling to us: 2nd. Their historical permanence; the confirmation of ages and of generations. The hold they have upon the general mind of the race is the sign of some 'root of endurance' planted firmly in the soil of human nature. If 'deep in the general heart of men, their power survives,' we may accept them as true, or interpret them as a phase of some deeper yet kindred truth, of which they are the popular distortion. [Unlike Schelling, who contended for an intellectual intuition not common to all men, but the endowment only of a few of the privileged (George H. Lewes' "History of Philosophy," vol. ii., p. 521), the Theistic writer we are quoting contends for an intuition "common to all," but he fails to furnish an atom of evidence either of the existence or of the "historical permanence" of any such intuition.] 3rd. The interior harmony which they exhibit with each other, and with the rest of our psychological nature; each of the intuitions being in harmony with the entire circle, and with the whole realm of knowledge If any alleged intuition should come into collision with any other and disturb it, there would be good reason for suspecting its genuineness; and in that case the lower and less authenticated must always yield to the higher and better attested. But if the critical intellect carrying our intuition (if we may so speak in a figure) round the circle of our nature, and in turn placing it in juxtaposition with the rest, finds that no collision ensues, we may safely conclude that the witness of that intuition is true. [No clear intuitions have even been alleged by the writer; it is, therefore, impossible to plead harmony between them. The Theistic writer even admits that the special intuition, which is his whole evidence, is on its first use "crude, dim, and inarticulate." Dim and inarticulate intuitions can hardly be expected to come into collision with each other.] 4th. If the results of its action and influence are such as to elevate and etherealise our nature, its validity may be assumed. This is no test by itself, for an erroneous belief might for a time even elevate the mind that held it, as the intellectual life evoked by many of the erroneous theories and exploded hypotheses of the past has been great. But no error could do so permanently. No illusion could survive as an educative and elevating power over humanity; and no alleged instinct could sustain its claim, and vindicate its presumptive title, if it could not stand the test we mention. [The answer here is that the "Theistic faith" has not been found "permanently educative and elevating." Its moral leverage is not denied, but is affirmed to have been injurious. Education and elevation have been in degree proportionate to the emancipation of the mind from Theistic faith.] A theoretic error is seen to be such when we attempt to reduce it to practice; as a hidden crack or fissure in a metal becomes visible when a strain is applied, or the folly of an ideal Utopia is seen in the actual life of a mixed commonwealth. Many of those scientific guesses which have served as good provisional hypotheses, have been abandoned in the actual working of them out; and so the flaw that lurks within an alleged intuition (if there be a flaw), will become apparent when we try to apply it in actual life, and take it as a regulative principle in action. Thus, take the belief n the divine existence, attested, as we affirm, by intuition, and apply it in the act of worship or adoration. Does that belief (which fulfils the conditions of our previous tests, for it appears everywhere and clings tenaciously to man, and comes into collision with no other normal tendency of our nature, or defrauds any instinct of its due) does it elevate the nature of him who holds it? The reply of history is conclusive, and its attestation is abundantly clear. The power of the Theistic faith over the rest of human nature is such that it has quickened the other faculties into a more vigorous life. Its moral leverage has been vast, while it has sharpened the æsthetic sense to some of its more delicate perceptions, and in some instances brought a new accession of intellectual power."

Though we have stated the tests and criteria of the argument sought to be maintained in favour of intuition so fully that we believe the Theistic writer will be satisfied with our fairness, it will be seen that we utterly deny that any intuition has been shown to exist coming within those tests. Every fact alleged to be evidenced by intuition can be reduced and explained by analysis, unless the alleged fact be so vaguely stated that it is utterly useless and impracticable to attempt its examination.

The Theistic writer adds (p. 59):—"It is not only essential to the validity of the Theistic intuition that the human mind has a positive though imperfect knowledge of the infinite, but the assertion of this is involved in the very intuition itself. If we had no positive knowledge of the source it seeks to reach, the instinct, benumbed as by an intellectual frost, and unable to rise, would be fatally paralysed; or if it could move along its finite area, it would wander helplessly, feeling after its object, 'if haply it might find it.' And it will be found that all who deny the validity of our intuition, either limit us to the knowledge of phenomena, or, while admitting that we have a certain knowledge of finite substance, adopt the cold theory of nescience."

"Comte, Lewes, Mill, Mr. Bain, Herbert Spencer, and the majority of our best scientific guides (however they differ in its detail) agree in the common postulate that all that man can know, and intelligibly reason about, are phenomena, and the laws of these phenomena, 'that which doth appear.'"

On this the reader is especially referred to the chapter on "The Relativity of Human Knowledge," by J. S. Mill, in his Examination of Sir W. Hamilton.

"With us," says the *British Quarterly Review* writer (p. 62,) "the relativity of knowledge is a first principle in philosophy. But to affirm it, is merely to assert that all that is known occupies a fixed rela ion to the knower. It is to affirm nothing as to the character or contents of his knowledge. As regards the objects known, we further maintain that they are apprehended only in their differences and contrasts. We know self only in its contrast with w at is not self, a particular portion of matter only in its relation to other portions which surround and transcend it. So also, and for the same reason, with the finite and infinite. The one is not a po-itive notion, and the other negative; the one clear, and the other obscure. Both are equally clear, both sharply defined, so far as they are given us in relation. If the one notion suffers, the other suffers with it. In short, if we discharge any notion from all relation with its opposite or contrary, it ceases to be a notion at all. The finite, if we take it alone, is as inconceivable as the infinite, if we take it alone; phenomena by themselves are as incogitable as substance by itself, and the relative as a notion cut off from the absolute which antithetically bounds it, is not more intelligible than the absolute as an essence absolved from all relations. And thus the entire fabric of our knowledge being founded on contrasts, and arising out of differences, involving in its every datum another element hidden in the background, may be said to be a vast double chain of relatives mutually complementary. It looks ever in two directions, without and within, above and beneath, before and after.

"We main ain, therefore, that we have positive knowledge of the infini e. Whosoever says that the infinite cannot be known contradicts himself. For he must possess a notion of it before he can deny that he has a positive knowledge of it, before he can predict aught regarding it. And so he says he cannot know what he says, though in another fashion, that he does know. It could never have come within the horizon of hypothetical knowledge, never have become the subject of discussion, unless positively (though inadequately) known; and thus the infinite stands as the antithetic background of the finite."

If by taking the finite "alone" is meant thinking any

phenomena as entirely sole and utterly out of relation to ourselves or any other phenomenon or phenomena, then undoubtedly "the finite if we take it alone is inconceivable;" but if it is meant that an ounce of lead taken alone is as inconceivable as an illimitable number of undefined quantities of undescribed material, then we deny the writer's position. Positive knowledge of the indefinable is a contradiction in terms.

" But," answers the *British Quarterly Review* writer (p. 64), " it is objected that as human knowledge is always finite, we can never have a positive apprehension of an infinite object; that as the subject of knowledge is necessarily finite, its object must be the same. Let us sift this objection.

" I may know an object in itself as related to me the knower, or I may know it in its relation to other objects also known to me the knower. But in both and all cases, knowledge is limited by the power of the knower; therefore, it is always finite knowledge. But it may be finite knowledge of an infinite object, incomplete knowledge of a complete object, partial knowledge of a transcendent object. The boundary or fence may be within the faculty of the knower, while the object he imperfectly grasps may not only be infinite, but be known to transcend his faculties in the very act of conscious knowledge. For example, I may know that a line is infinite, while I have only a finite knowledge of the points along which that line extends. And similarly my knowledge of the Infinite Mind is partial and incomplete, but it is clear and defined. It is a definite knowledge of an indefinite obj ct. We may have a partial knowledge not only of a part, but of the whole. Thus I have a partial knowledge of a circle, because I know only a few of its properties; but it is not to a part of the circle that my partial knowledge extends, but to the whole which I know in part. In like manner, as the Infinite Object has no parts, it is not of a portion of his being that we possess a partial knowledge, but of the whole. We know him as we know the circle, inadequately yet directly, immediately, though in part."

Here again we have a trick of words. I cannot kno more of a line than my knowledge " of the points along which that line extends." I may believe there is a beyond; I do not know it, because each point known is an addition to my finite line. Then there is no fair transition in thought from the line finite to the line infinite. The first is thinkable, the second is unthinkable, for one point of the line, being always in reach of the thinker, the line cannot accurately be termed infinite; the knowledge of the thinker limits it in one part, and a limitation of the infinite is, again, a contradiction in terms. Still less can this be urged as evidence of "knowledge of infinite mind," for the last two words are meaningless.

"Again," argues the writer in the *British Quarterly Review* (p. 64), "it is said that to know the infinite is to know the sum of all reality, and as that would include the universe and its source together, it must necessarily include, on the one hand, the knower along with his knowledge, and on the other, all the possibilities of existence. The possibility of our knowing the Infinite Being as distinct from the universe is denied, since infinite existence is said to be co-extensive with the whole universe of things. But that the source of the universe must necessarily exhaust existence, and contain within himself all actual being, is a mere theoreti assumption. The presence of the finite does not limit the infinite, as if the area of the latter were contracted by so much of the former as exists within it. For the relation of the infinite being to the finite is not similar to the relation between infinite space and a segment of it. It is true that so much of finite space is so much cut out of the whole area of infinite space—though, if the remainder is infinite, the portion removed will not really limit it. [First, space is only conceivable as the area of extension of some object, or the measure of distance between two or more objects, or as the area beyond some object. Infinite space is unthinkable, except as the area of extension of some unmeasured object. We cannot, except by a misuse of words, speak of cutting "so much" "out of the *whole* area of infinite space." The word "whole" is definite. The word "infinite" is the equivalent for inability to define.] But as our intuition of the infinite has no resemblance to our knowledge of space, we believe that the relations which their respective objects sustain have no affinity with each other. The intuition of God is a purely spiritual revelation, informing us not of the quantity, but of the quality, of the Supreme Being in the universe. And to affirm that the finite spirit of man standing in a fixed relation to the infinite spirit of God limits it, by virtue of that relation, is covertly to introduce a partial concept into a region to which it is utterly foreign, and which it has no right to enter." But if spiritual knowledge of

God deals with his quality only, and not with his quantity, why should a word be employed to describe him which is usable of quantity only and not of quality? To speak of a spirit as "infinite" does not tell us anything of its quality; it might be good, bad, or indifferent, loving or hating, holy or wicked, and yet, if boundless, would rightly be described as infinite. But, however admirable the quality, the spirit is not infinite unless boundless, not only in our ignorance of its bounds, but in reality. To employ the term *infinite* as though it were an equivalent of *perfect*, is a loose use of words which destroys all accuracy of thought.

"Similarly," continues the Theistic writer of the above *Review*, "with the action of the infinite and absolute *cause*. The creative energy of that cause is not inconsistent with its changelessness. To say so, is to introduce a quantitative notion into a sphere when quality is alone to be considered. A cause in action is the force which determines the changes which occur in time. But the *primum mobile*, the first cause, need not be itself changed by the forth-putting of its causal power.

"We therefore maintain, in opposition to the teachers of nescience, that a positive knowledge of the infinite is competent to man, because involved in his very consciousness of the finite. And when psychologically analysed, this intuition explains and vindicates itself."

Our answer is, that man has no conception whatever, either innate or acquired, of "infinite God." Thus Sir William Hamilton (in his "Discussions on Philosophy" page 12) says: "The unconditioned is incognisable and inconceivable, its notion being only the negative of the conditioned, which last can alone be positively known or conceived......The unconditionally unlimited, or the infinite, cannot possibly be construed to the mind."

Mansel says: "To be conscious, we must be conscious of something; and that something can only be known, as that which it is, by being distinguished from that which it is not. But distinction is necessarily limitation; for, if one object is to be distinguished from another, it must possess some form of existence which the other has not, or it must not possess some form which the other has......A consciousness of the Infinite as such thus necessarily involves a self-contradiction; for it implies the recognition, by limitation and difference, of that which can only be given as unlimited and indifferent. That a man can be conscious of the infinite is thus a supposition which, in the very terms in which it is expressed, annihilates itself. Consciousness is essentially a limitation; for it is the determination of the mind to one actual out of many possible modifications. But the infinite, if it is to be conceived at all, must be conceived as potentially everything and actually nothing; for, if there is anything in general which it cannot become, it is thereby limited; and, if there is anything in particular which it actually is, it is thereby excluded from being any other thing. But, again, it must also be conceived as actually everything and potentially nothing; for an unrealised potentiality is likewise a limitation. If the infinite can be that which it is not, it is by that very possibility marked out as incomplete, and capable of a higher perfection. If it is actually everything, it possesses no characteristic feature by which it can be distinguished from anything else, and discerned as an object of consciousness. This contradiction, which is utterly inexplicable on the supposition that the infinite is a positive object of human thought, is at once accounted for when it is regarded as [or rather admitted to be] the mere negation of thought. If all thought is limitation—if whatever we conceive is, by the very act of conception, regarded as finite—the *infinite*, from a human point of view, is merely a name for the absence of those conditions under which thought is possible. To speak of a *conception of the infinite* is, therefore, at once to affirm those conditions and to deny them. The contradiction which we discover in such a conception is only that which we have ourselves placed there, by tacitly assuming the conceivability of the inconceivable. The condition of consciousness is distinction, and the condition of distinction is limitation. We can have no consciousness of Being in general which is not some Being in particular: a thing, in consciousness, is one thing out of many. In assuming the possibility of an infinite object of consciousness, I assume, therefore, that it is at the same time limited and unlimited—actually something, without which it could not be an object of consciousness, and actually nothing, without which it could not be infinite" (Bampton Lectures, by Dean Mansel, pp. 71—73).

The whole of the foregoing division of Theistic argument is based on the fallacy of innate ideas. Locke, in his "Essay on Understanding," took plain stand against this fallacy. "If it shall be demanded," he says, "when a man begins to have any ideas? I think the true answer is, when he first has any sensation." Lewes, in his "Problems of Life and Mind," vol. i. p. 236, says: "Neither observation nor reflection warrants the supposition that the infant......has on entering the world innate ideas......What is innate or connate, is the structure which will react under stimulus in certain definite ways, and these reactions will depend on the degree of development which the structure has acquired ......all perception, consequently all conception, is the product of the reaction of the organism stimulated by the cosmos, which is saying in other words that all our knowledge had its origin in experience—the registration of such reactions. And this is further confirmed by the fact that on the one hand the development of the organism has its prescribed course, any interference with the series of successive stages causing another form of structure to result, while, on the other hand, any interference with the normal course of experience will correspondingly affect the result; so that even results, which have the fixed character of instincts, may be frustrated by an interruption of the prescribed course of evolution."

Leaving the pure Theistic argument, we take another phase of the pleading for religion.

Joseph Butler, Bishop of Durham, born 1692, died 1752, in his famous "Analogy of Religion," has some points which here require notice, rather from the reputation of the writer than for the real merit of his arguments. It must not be forgotten that Butler's "Analogy" is only available in the hands of the orthodox, and for use against persons already believing in a God, for he takes it "for proved that there is an intelligent author of nature and natural governor of the world" (Introduction, p. xxviii.).

Chapter 1 of Part I. of the "Analogy of Religion" treats of a future life, and professes to argue from the analogy of nature. Bishop Butler never says what he means by the word *nature*, and he sometimes uses it in senses inconsistent with the fashion which he gives to it at other times. By nature, as before explained (see page 112), we mean the totality of existence, including in this all actual and past phenomena, all possible phenomena, and all that is or has been necessary for the happening of phenomena. Bishop Butler says, section 1, that "we find it to be a general law of nature" that human beings "should exist in degrees of life, in one period of their being greatly different from those appointed them in another," and adds, "therefore that we are to exist hereafter in a state as different (suppose from our present) as this is from our former, is but according to the analogy of nature." Here "law of nature" is not defined, but, most clearly, it is not meant to signify merely "observed order of event," which is the definition we should give to it, for Bishop Butler uses the word "appointed," which, read by the light of his assumption "that there is an intelligent author of nature and natural governor," would make "law of nature" equivalent to a commandment issued to nature by this author and governor. The argument fails; the analogy is rather that, as the human being commences, grows, arrives at his prime, decays and finishes, so the death or finish will be the end, as the generation was the beginning To make any analogy, Bishop Butler ought to show the individual life before the body began, as a ground for presuming the individual life continuing after the body had finished.

In section 2 of the same chapter the Bishop writes: "We know that we are endowed with capacities of action, of happiness, and misery Now that we have these powers and capacities before death is a presumption that we shall retain them through and after death; indeed a probability of it abundantly sufficient to act upon, unless there be some positive reason to think that death is the destruction of those living powers." This argument would be quite as valid if it ran: "that we have these powers and capacities after birth is a presumption that we possessed them before birth." The words "living powers," in this argument, are loosely substituted for "capacities of action," and two paragraphs later these living powers get changed into "living agents." Giving the Bishop credit for sincerity of intention, these changes of phraseology are most unfortunate, as they obscure the argument and confuse the reader. A bucket has a capacity for holding water; knocking out the bottom of the bucket finishes the capacity; no such capacity belongs to the bottomless pail, and no sane person would think of arguing that the holding capacity was a holding power, or holding agent, enduring after the pail had been knocked to pieces.

The Bishop says that "destruction of living powers is a manner of expression unavoidably ambiguous;" but that it is used in the sense of "the destruction of a living being, so as that the same living being shall be incapable of ever perceiving or acting again at all."

To prevent as far as possible the misapprehension likely

to arise from the repetition of undefined words, we deny any "living powers" other than "life;" and, excluding vegetable life, define life to mean the total normal organic functional activity of each animal—varying in different animals, and varying in the same animal at different dates between its generation and death. The separate individual life commences with the birth, and death is the cessation of life. Dr. Maudsley ("Body and Mind," p. 162), after arguing that vitality is not a special principle but a result, which will be ultimately explainable by operation of so-called molecular forces, says:—"It is desirable to examine into that which is generally deemed to constitute the specialty of life. Now it is certain, when we consider the vast range of vitality, from the simple life of a molecule or cell to the complex life of man, that valid objections may be made to any definition of life. If it be wide enough to comprise all forms, it will be too vague to have any value; if narrow enough to be exact, it will exclude the most lowly forms. The problem is, to investigate the conditions of the manifestation of life. A great fault in many attempted definitions has been the description of life as a resistance or complete contrast to the rest of nature, which was supposed to be continually striving to destroy it. But the elements of organic matter are not different from those of the inorganic, whence they are derived, and to which they return; and the chemical and mechanical forces of these elements cannot be suspended or removed within the organism. What is special is the manner of composition of the elements; there is a concurrence of manifold substances, and they are combined or grouped together in a very complex way. Such union or grouping is, however, only a further advance upon, and by no means a contrast to, the kind of combination which is met with in inorganic bodies. Life is not a contrast to non-living nature, but a further development of it. The more knowledge advances, the more plainly is it shown that there are physical and chemical processes upon which life depends. Heat is produced by combustion in the organism, as it is in the fire; starch is converted into sugar there, as it is in the chemical laboratory; urea, which is so constant a product of the body's chemistry, can be formed artificially by the chemist; and the process of excitation in a nerve, on the closure of a constant stream, appears to be analogous to the process of electrolysis, in which hydrogen is given off at the negative pole. The peculiarity of life is the complexity of combina tion in so small a space, the intimate operation of many simultaneously acting forces in the microcosm of the organic cell."

An anonymous writer says: "Life is that state of an organised body in which all the organs concerned perform their individual and collective functions. Health is that state of an organised body in which *all* the organs perform their individual and collective functions, and perform them well. Disease is that state of an organised body in which one or more of the organs fail to perform their functions, or to perform them well. Death is that state of an organised body in which all the organs of life cease to perform the functions of life" ("Biology *versus* Theology," No. 6).

Unfortunately, Bishop Butler not only refrains from any definition, but uses the words "living powers" and "living agents," without regard to accuracy. With him "living agent" is repeated, without any proof, as if it were an identifiable spiritual entity. On this point Dr. Maudsley well puts it: "The burden of proving that the *Deus ex machinâ* of a spiritual entity intervenes somewhere, and where it intervenes, clearly lies upon those who make the assertion, or who need the hypothesis. They are not justified in arbitrarily fabricating an hypothesis entirely inconsistent with experience of the orderly development of nature, which even postulates a domain of nature that human senses cannot take any cognisance of, and in then calling upon those who reject their assumption to disprove it" ("Body and Mind," p. 162).

A confusion more complete, arising from the loose use of words, is even found in the same section (2) of Butler's "Analogy," when the Bishop, arguing for the presumption of continuance, says: "It seems our only reason for believing that any one substance now existing will continue to exist a moment longer—the self-existent substance only excepted." This assumes, without any proof, that there are several substances, and that there is one substance distinguishable from the others as "the self-existent." Probably the Bishop used the words, "any one substance," relatively, of phenomena, but he says nothing to that effect; and his "self-existent substance" is either the "intelligent author of nature," or exists besides nature and its author.

The apprehension of death, as the end of living, "must arise," we are told, "either from the reason of the thing, or from the analogy of nature."

"But," says Bishop Butler, "we cannot argue, from the reason of the thing, that death is the destruction of living agents, because we know not at all what death is in itself, but only some of its effects, such as the dissolution of flesh, skin, and bones; and these effects do in nowise appear to imply the destruction of a living agent." A billiard ball rolls, a man lives; break the billiard ball perfectly in half, neither of the halves will roll; knock off the man's head, he cannot live. Just as there is no "rolling agent" other than the striker and his cue, so there is no living agent other than the food and necessary sustenance for the living man. As an argument from analogy, Bishop Butler's is worthless.

The Bishop further urges that "sleep, or a swoon, shows us that not only these (living) powers exist when they are not exercised, as the passive power of motion does in inanimate matter, but shows also that they exist when there is no present capacity of exercising them; or that the capacity of exercising them for the present, as well as the actual exercise of them, may be suspended, and yet the powers themselves remain undestroyed." Life is not suspended in sleep; and the analogy here is utterly wanting. In a perfect swoon there is no consciousness, but there is not suspended vitality; the person in the swoon continues to live, although the activity of some of the functions is suspended.

"Nor," says the Bishop, "can we find anything through the whole analogy of nature to afford us even the slightest presumption that animals ever lose their *living powers;* much less, if it were possible, that they lose them by death; for we have no faculties wherewith to trace any beyond or through it, so as to see what becomes of them." If for the two words italicised the word "life" be substituted, as it ought properly to be, for no living powers have been shown other than life, then the utter nonsense of the Bishop's position becomes apparent. Go into a slaughter-house, and watch the butcher. Is there no presumption that the oxen, calves, and sheep he slaughters lose their lives? Oh! answers Bishop Butler, death "destroys the sensible proof which we had before their death of their being possessed of living powers, but does not appear to afford the least reason to believe that they are then, or by that event, deprived of them. And our knowing that they were possessed of these powers up to the very period to which we have faculties capable of tracing them is itself a probability of their retaining them beyond it."

"All presumption," says the Bishop, "of death's being the destruction of living beings must go upon the supposition that they are compounded, and so discerptible. But, since consciousness is a single and indivisible power, it should seem that the subject in which it resides must be so too." "Consciousness" is used by Bishop Butler as identical with "perception;" and "perceptive power" is used at meaning "the power of consciousness;" and "the subject in which it resides" is termed "the conscious being." In truth, consciousness is a varying quantity, being the sum of our remembered perceptions, and of our thinkings on such perceptions. On this question of consciousness Lewes says ("Biog. Hist. of Philosophy," vol. i., p. 369): "Perception is nothing more than a state of the percipient—*i.e*, a state of consciousness. This state may be occasioned by some external cause, and may be as complex as the cause is complex; but it is still nothing more than a state of consciousness—an effect produced by an adequate cause. Of every change in our sensation we are conscious, and in time we learn to give definite names and forms to the causes of these changes. But in the fact of consciousness there is nothing beyond consciousness. In our perceptions we are conscious only of the changes which have taken place within us: we can never transcend the sphere of our own consciousness; we can never go out of ourselves, and become aware of the objects which caused these changes. All we can do is to identify certain external appearances with certain internal changes—*e.g.*, to identify the appearance we name 'fire' with certain sensations we have known to follow our being placed near it. Turn the fact of consciousness how we will, we can see nothing in it but the change of a sentient being operated by some external cause. Consciousness is no mirror of the world; it gives no faithful reflection of things as they are *per se*; it only gives a faithful report of its own modification as excited by external things."

Having thus affirmed "a single and indivisible power," and asserted that "it is as easy to conceive that we may exist out of bodies as in them," Bishop Butler goes on:— "We see by experience, that men may lose their limbs, their organs of sense, and even the greatest part of their bodies, and yet remain the same living agents. And persons can trace up the existence of themselves to a time when the bulk of their bodies was extremely small, in comparison with what it is in mature age; and we cannot but think that they might then have lost a considerable part of that small body, and yet have remained the same living agents, as they may now lose great part of their present body and remain so." First, it is not true that the "life" continues, or has continued, the same. "Life" is increased with the growth from babyhood, and is diminished by every diminution of body. Although it may be difficult to estimate the change in thinking-ability consequent on the loss of "any organ of sense," yet, as percepti e ability is certainly the foundation of all consciousness, injury must necessarily result to consciousness from loss of organs of perception. It is not true that men lose their spines, their heads, or their hearts, and continue to live at all; yet Bishop Butler goes on to say, "We have already, several times over, lost a great part, or perhaps the whole, of our body, according to certain common established laws of nature, yet we remain the same living agents; when we shall lose as great a part, or the whole, by another common established law of nature, death, why may we not also remain the same." It will, of course, be replied that the Bishop does not mean a total sudden loss, but a gradual change. In truth, with his usual looseness of expression, the Bishop applies "lose" to a limb, meaning that the limb is totally and suddenly lost, while in the same sentence the word "lose" only expresses extremely slow and almost imperceptible change in the whole body. Dr. Maudsley says ("Body and Mind," page 127.): "When we are told that every part of the body is in a constant state of change, that within a certain period every particle of it is renewed, and yet that amidst these changes a man feels that he remains essentially the same, we perceive nothing inconsistent with the idea of the action of a material organ; for it is not absurd to suppose that in the brain the new series of particles take the pattern of those which they replace, as they do in other organs and tissues which are continually changing their substance yet preserve their identity. Even the scar of a wound on the finger is not often effaced, but grows as the body grows; why, then, assume the necessity of an immaterial principle to prevent the impression of an idea from being lost?"

In the second chapter Bishop Butler nominally deals with the government of God by rewards and punishments;

and he maintains that "the whole analogy of nature, the whole present course of things, most fully shows that there is nothing incredible in the general doctrine of religion, that God will reward and punish men for their actions hereafter; nothing incredible, I mean, arising out of the notion of rewarding and punishing, for the whole course of nature is a present instance of His exercising that government over us, which implies in it rewarding and punishing."

The argument on the Bishop's assumption "that there is an intelligent author of nature and natural governor of the world" is only maintainable by ignoring a whole series of contradictions. Punishment is only justifiable as a deterrent from future vicious conduct; but, according to the Bishop, the punishment is to come when there is no longer any possibility of continued vicious conduct. The punishment is not for "the government of the world," but is simply vengeance for past conduct. If God is "governor," either all acts result from his government, or there are some which occur in spite of it. In the last case he is not omnipotent, and in the first case the act is not one that ought to be punished. The Bishop strives to meet this and similar objections by urging (Part I., cap. 7) that analogy "makes it credible that his (God's) moral government must be a scheme quite beyond our comprehension." But, surely, the utter incomprehensibility of a scheme ought not to be urged as a ground for its acceptance. See on the question of punishment Emile de Girardin's "Droit de Punir," and Jeremy Bentham's works especially.

The theory of government by rewards and punishments is very vaguely stated by Bishop Butler. "Pain," as the "consequence" of certain actions, seems to be regarded by the Bishop as arranged by God; but pain may be incurred in doing a good action. A courageous man breaks his collar bone in rescuing some people from that which, without his interference, would have been almost certain death. According to the theory of Bishop Butler, the pain of the broken collar bone is a punishment knowingly inflicted by the intelligent author of nature on the brave rescuer. In chapter 6 the Bishop treats of "necessity as influencing practice," and as this seems inseparable from the problem of punishment, we here give, with slight modification, two extracts from John Stuart Mill—one on Freewill, the other on Punishment—first remarking that Necessitarianism and Fatalism are no co-equivalent terms. The Fatalist says what is, is, and must be, could not have been otherwise, and cannot be altered. The Necessitarian says what is, is, and must have resulted from such and such conditions; but the conditions might have been varied, and the results would then have been different:—

"What experience makes known is the fact of an invariable sequence be ween every event and some special combination of antecedent conditions—in such sort that, whereever and whenever that union of antecedents exists, the event does not fail to occur. Any *must* in the case, any necessity, other than the unconditional universality of the fact we know nothing of.

"Now, the so-called Necessitarians demand the application of the same rule of judgment to our volitions. They maintain that there is the same evidence for it. They affirm, as a truth of experience, that volitions do, in point of fact, follow determinate antecedents with the same uniformity, and (when we have sufficient knowledge of the circumstances) with the same certainty as other effects follow their causes" ("Examination of Sir W. Hamilton," p. 561).

"The feeling of liability to punishment is of two kinds. It may mean expectation that, if we act in a certain manner, punishment will actually be inflic ed upon us by our fellow-creatures or by a Supreme Power. Or it may only mean, knowing that we shall deserve that infliction.

"The first of these cannot, in any correct meaning of the term, be designated as a consciousness. If we believe that we shall be punished for doing wrong, it is because the belief has been taught to us by our parents and tutors, or by our religion, or is generally held by those who surround us, or because we have ourselves come to the conclusion by reasoning, or from the experience of life. This is not consciousness. And, by whatever name it is called, its evidence is not dependent on any theory of the spontaneousness of volition. The punishment of guilt in another world is believed with undoubting conviction by Turkish Fatalists and by professed Christians, who are not only Necessitarians, but believe that the majority of mankind were divinely predestined from all eternity to sin, and to be punished for sinning. It is not, therefore, the belief that we shall be *made* accountable, which can be deemed to require or presuppose the freewill hypothesis; it is the belief that we ought so to be; that we are justly accountable; that guilt deserves punishment" (p. 571).

"The real question is one of justice—the legitimacy of retribution or punishment. On the theory of necessity, we are told, a man cannot help acting as he does; and it cannot be just that he should be punished for what he cannot help. Not if the expectation of punishment enables him to help it, and is the only means by which he can be enabled to help it?

"To say that he cannot help it is true or false, according to the qualification with which the assertion is accompanied. Supposing him to be of a vicious disposition, he cannot help doing the criminal act, if he is allowed to believe that he will be able to commit it unpunished. If, on the contrary, the impression is strong on his mind that a heavy punishment will follow, he can, and in most cases does, help it.

"The question deemed to be so puzzling is, how punishment can be justified, if men's actions are determined by motives, among which motives punishment is one. A more difficult question would be, how it can be justified if they are not so determined? Punishment proceeds on the assumption that the will is governed by motives. If punishment had no power of acting on the will, it would be illegitimate, however natural might be the inclination to inflict it. Just so far as the will is supposed free—that is, capable of acting *against* motives—punishment is disappointed of its object and deprived of its justification.

"There are two ends which, on the Necessitarian theory, are sufficient to justify punishment: the benefit of the offender himself, and the protection of others. The first justifies it, because to benefit a person cannot be to do him an injury. To punish him for his own good, provided the inflictor has any proper title to constitute himself a judge, is no more unjust than to administer medicine. As far, indeed, as respects the criminal himself, the theory of punishment is that, by counterbalancing the influence of present temptations or acquired bad habits, it restores the mind to that normal preponderance of the love of right which many moralists and theologians consider to constitute the true definition of our freedom. In its other aspect, punishment is a precaution taken by society in self-defence. To make this just, the only condition required is, that the end which society is attempting to enforce by punishment should be a just one. Used as a means of aggression by society on the just rights of the individual, punishment is unjust. Used to protect the just rights of others against unjust aggression by the offender, it is just. If it is possible to have just rights (which is the same thing as to have rights at all), it cannot be unjust to defend them. Freewill or no freewill, it is just to punish so far as is necessary for this purpose, as it is just to put a wild beast to death (without unnecessary suffering) for the same object" (p. 578).

A writer in the *Westminster Review* for April, 1876, p. 459, says:—"Punishment, as a human institution, is warranted by our very helplessness, by the inability in which we are of producing, otherwise than through the infliction of suffering, that mental change in an offender which alone can render him compatible with the existence of his fellow creatures. But what ground shall we assign for punishment when we suppose it inflicted by a Deity? Granting all the previous difficulties solved, putting aside the question of the origin of evil, putting aside the hypothesis of a creator, still more so of an omnipotent creator, and considering the Deity simply as a ruler, what reason would he have for instituting suffering? Does he institute it in his own defence, or solely in the interest of transgressors? On either supposition the end might be secured by better means. The infliction of punishment is regarded as a defect, even by our poor human educators; their business is to govern by developing the sympathies, by moral suasion, by the influence of high example, and in proportion as they fail in this, they give the measure of their incapacity. How much more, then, must severity be discreditable to a Deity? If our penal legislators find that it is possible to reform criminals, even when taken at maturity, if the progress of our civilisation has been marked by a progressive mildness in our codes, and if the duration of each penalty is being made, as far as possible, dependent on the offender's own behaviour, must we not expect a policy benigner still from God, who has the moulding of his charges from their earliest hour, and who can act directly on their minds? If, with such an expectation, we turn to Christianity, our disappointment will indeed be great. Not one of God's punishments is educational; all have the character of wanton ferocity. They are neither made to depend on the offender's subsequent behaviour, nor do they exhibit any proportionality to the transgression; the code of providence is infinitely worse than Draco's, since even death is not allowed to put an end to the transgressor's sufferings. Adam, having sinned once is punished for ever; and as the punishment is maximum, whatever subsequent disobedience Adam may commit, he cannot deserve worse than eternal damnation. We might at least imagine that if this first infliction is not intended as a check on Adam's conduct, it is intended as a check on his descendants. Not at all, the maximum penalty is pronounced for Adam's sin on his descendants also! We shall pursue no further; the exposition of such a scheme as this is an outrage on the reader's understanding."

In chapter 3 Bishop Butler says:—"When we speak of God's natural government of the world, it implies government of the very same kind with that which a master exercises over his servant, or a civil magistrate over his subjects." Surely there is no analogy here, the master does not create his servant, the civil magistrate is neither omniscient nor omnipotent. The subject may rebel to overthrow the civil governor; the servant may escape from the control of the master. Does Bishop Butler mean that any similar contingencies are conceivable of God and his creatures? But adds Bishop Butler:—"This alone does not appear, at first sight, to determine anything certainly concerning the moral character of the author of nature, considered in this relation of governor, does not ascertain his government to be moral, or to prove that he is the righteous judge of the world. Moral government consists, not barely in rewarding and punishing men for their actions, which the most tyrannical person may do; but in rewarding the righteous and punishing the wicked; in rendering to men according to their actions, considered as good or evil. And the perfection of moral government consists in doing this, with regard to all intelligent creatures, in an exact proportion to their personal merits or demerits.'

One answer alone is needed to this, viz., that in no sense can the award of "eternal torment" be considered as "in an exact proportion to the offence for which it is the punishment."

INDEX TO SECTION II. OF PART I.

WORKS QUOTED.

SUBJECTS.

PART II.—CHRISTIANITY.

BY

ANNIE BESANT.

SECTION 1.—Its Evidences Unreliable.

SECTION 2.—Its Origin Pagan.

SECTION 3.—Its Morality Fallible.

SECTION 4.—Its History.

IN Section 1 the Evidences of Christianity are examined, the value of the external evidences brought forward in its favor is weighed, and the internal evidences as contained in its own documents investigated; a special reply is thus offered to the case presented by Paley. The worth of the "Messianic prophecies" is also tested, and the possibility of miracles denied. The opening deals with the alleged testimonies of Roman writers and of Josephus; challenges the value of the early patristic authorities; and seeks to prove that, before A.D. 180 at the earliest, no trace of Four Gospels is discoverable.

7th Edition. December, 1892

CATALOGUE OF WORKS

INCLUDING MANY OF

THE PUBLICATIONS

OF

THE LATE FREETHOUGHT PUBLISHING COMPANY,

PUBLISHED BY

A. & H. BRADLAUGH BONNER,

63 FLEET STREET, LONDON, E.C.

Sold also by R. Forder, 28 Stonecutter St., London, E.C.

Orders of 1s. and upwards, post free.

The Works of Charles Bradlaugh.

THEOLOGICAL.

Doubts in Dialogue. Discussions between Orthodox and Heterodox. Demy 8vo, boards, 1s.

Genesis: its authorship and authenticity. Crown 8vo, cloth gilt, 5s. ("*International Library of Science and Freethought*," *see also page* 13.)

The Freethinker's Text-Book. Section 1. "The Story of the Origin of Man, as told by the Bible and by Science." Section 2. "What is Religion?" "How has it Grown?" "God and Soul." Crown 8vo, cloth, 2s. 6d.

Theological Essays. Bound in 2 vols., cloth, uniform.

Vol. I contains: Heresy, its Morality and Utility; Is there a God?; Has Man a Soul?; Were Adam and Eve our first Parents?; Who was Jesus?; What did Jesus Teach?; The Atonement; Life of Abraham; Life of Jacob; Life of Moses; Life of David; Life of Jonah; The Twelve Apostles; When were our Gospels Written?; Plea for Atheism. 3s.

Vol. II contains: Humanity's Gain from Unbelief; Notes on Christian Evidences (In Reply to the Oxford House Papers); Mr. Gladstone's Reply to Colonel Ingersoll on Christianity; Supernatural and Rational Morality; A Few Words about the Devil; Has Man a Soul? (Debate with Rev. W. M. Westerby); Secularism Unphilosophical, Unsocial, and Immoral (Debate with Rev. Dr. McCann); A Cardinal's Broken Oath. 3s.

Debates in Theology, between Charles Bradlaugh and others. Bound in 2 vols, cloth, uniform.

Vol. I contains the debates with Revs. Dr. Baylee, A. J. Harrison, J. Lightfoot, R. A. Armstrong, and the Peterborough Controversy. Price 3s.

Vol. II contains the debates with Revs. M. Gibson, W. M. Westerby, and Dr. McCann, and Notes on Christian Evidences. Price 3s. 6d.

Debates—All Verbatim Reports.

God, Man, and the Bible. Three nights' discussion with the Rev. Dr. Baylee. (Liverpool, 1860.) 6d.

What does Christian Theism Teach? Two nights' Public debate with the Rev. A. J. Harrison. (London, 1872.) 6d.

Does the Church of England Teach Eternal Torment? Written debate with the Rev. J. Lightfoot. (1875.) 6d.

Is it Reasonable to Worship God? Two nights' debate with the Rev. R. A. Armstrong. (Nottingham, 1878.) 1s.

Christianity in Relation to Freethought, Scepticism, and Faith. Three Discourses by the Bishop of Peterborough, with special replies by Charles Bradlaugh. (1871.) 6d.

BRADLAUGH, CHARLES (*continued*)—

Has Man a Soul? Two nights' debate with the Rev. W. M. WESTERBY. (Burnley, 1879.) 1s.

Secularism Unphilosophical, Unsocial, and Immoral. Three nights' debate with the Rev. Dr. MCCANN. (London, 1881.) 1s.

Has Humanity Gained from Unbelief? Two nights' debate with Rev. MARSDEN GIBSON, M.A. (Newcastle, 1889.) Together with the pamphlet of same Title. 1s.

Notes on Christian Evidences. In reply to the Oxford House Papers, with rejoinders by Rev. E. S. Talbot, M.A., Rev. Francis Paget, D.D., W. Lock, M.A., T. B. Strong, B.A., Rev. V. S. S. Coles, M.A., 6d.

PAMPHLETS (Theological)—	*s.*	*d.*
Humanity's Gain from Unbelief	0	2
When were our Gospels Written?	0	6
The Laws relating to Blasphemy and Heresy	0	6
Heresy; its Morality and Utility. A Plea and a Justification	0	9
Supernatural and Rational Morality	0	1
The Christian's Creed. A Reproduction of Mr. Bradlaugh's first pamphlet. In cover	0	2
Mr. Gladstone's Reply to Col. Ingersoll on Christianity..	0	1
Were Adam and Eve our First Parents? (New Edition)..	0	1
A Few Words about the Devil	0	1
A Plea for Atheism	0	3
Has Man a Soul?	0	2
Is there a God? New ed.	0	1
Who was Jesus Christ?	0	1
What did Jesus Teach?	0	1
The Twelve Apostles	0	1
The Atonement	0	1
The New Life of David	0	2
The New Life of Jacob	0	1
The New Life of Abraham	0	1
The New Life of Moses	0	1
The New Life of Jonah	0	1

LABOR QUESTIONS AND SOCIALISM.

Labor and Law. Dealing with the Eight Hours' Movement and other Questions affecting Labor and Legislation. With Two fine Portraits taken in 1883 and 1890, and a Memoir by J. M. Robertson, 282 pp., demy 8vo (*uniform with "Speeches" and "House of Brunswick"*), 5s.

The Eight Hours' Movement. One night's debate with H. M. Hyndman. 6d.

The Eight Hours' Movement..	0	2
Parliament and the Poor: What the Legislature can do; what it ought to do	0	2
The Employers' Liability Bill: A Letter to Thomas Burt, M.P.	0	3

BRADLAUGH, CHARLES (*continued*)—	s.	d.
Capital and Labor. New edition	0	2
Labor's Prayer	0	1

Socialism. Containing the written Debates with Annie Besant and E. Belfort Bax, and "Socialism: its fallacies and dangers". In paper cover, 1s.

Will Socialism benefit the English People? One night's debate with H. M. Hyndman. 3d.

Socialism: For and Against. Written debate with Mrs. Besant. 4d.

Will Socialism benefit the English People? Written debate with E. Belfort Bax, 6d.

Socialism: its fallacies and dangers	0	2
Some Objections to Socialism	0	1

POLITICAL.

Impeachment of the House of Brunswick.—Tenth edition, partly revised and increased from notes left by Mr. Bradlaugh) Demy 8vo, boards (*uniform with "Doubts in Dialogue"*), 2s.; Cloth (*uniform with "Labor and Law" and "Speeches"*), 2s. 6d.

Political Essays. Bound in 3 books.

Series I contains: Impeachment of the House of Brunswick; Real Representation of the People; John Churchill, Duke of Marlborough; Mr. Gladstone or Lord Salisbury; Five Dead Men whom I knew when living; Cromwell and Washington; The Land, the People, and the Coming Struggle. Cloth, 2s. 6d.

Series II contains: Taxation; The Channel Tunnel; The Radical Programme; Compulsory Land Cultivation. In paper cover, 1s.

Series III contains: Parliament and the Poor: What the Legislature can do, What it Ought to do; The Employers' Liability Bill (An Open Letter to Mr. Thomas Burt, M.P.); Capital and Labor; Civil Lists and Grants to the Royal Family; Letter to Lord Randolph Churchill, M.P., Chancellor of the Exchequer; What Freemasonry is, What it has been, and What it Ought to be; A Cardinal's Broken Oath. In paper cover, 1s.

PAMPHLETS (Political)—	s.	d.
How are we to Abolish the Lords? 2nd edition ..	0	1
Poverty, and its Effects on the Political Condition of the People. New edition, revised and partly re-written ..	0	1
Why do Men Starve?	0	1
The Real Representation of the People	0	2
Taxation: how it originated, how it is spent, and who bears it. 2nd Edition	0	6
England's Balance Sheet	0	1
Compulsory Land Cultivation	0	3
Letter to Lord Randolph Churchill, M.P., Chancellor of the Exchequer. 16 pp.	0	1

BRADLAUGH, CHARLES (*continued*)—

	s.	d.
Mr. Gladstone or Lord Salisbury: which? An appeal to the Electors. 12 pp.	0	1
The Land, the People, and the Coming Struggle.. ..	0	2
Royal Grants	0	1
The Radical Programme. 2nd Edition	0	2
The True Story of my Parliamentary Struggle. Containing a Verbatim Report of the proceedings before the Select Committee of the House of Commons; Mr. Bradlaugh's Three Speeches at the Bar of the House, etc., etc. ..	0	6
May the House of Commons Commit Treason?	0	½
Northampton and the House of Commons. Correspondence between Charles Bradlaugh, M.P., and the Right Hon. Sir Stafford Northcote, M.P.	0	2
John Churchill, Duke of Marlborough: "Mob, Scum, and Dregs"	0	2
A Cardinal's Broken Oath	0	1

MISCELLANEOUS.

Collected Speeches. With portrait specially executed by Messrs. Elliot and Fry (in Sept., 1890). 216 pp., demy 8vo (*uniform with "Labor and Law" and "House of Brunswick"*), 5s.

Autobiography. Reprinted, with portrait. 36 pp., in cover, 4d.

Anthropology. Four Lectures, in cover, 4d.

Hints to Emigrants. Notes of Employment, wages, cost of living, etc., personally made during three journeys in the United States of America. (Pubd. at 1s.) **Reduced to 4d.**

	s.	d.
The Channel Tunnel: ought the Democracy to support or oppose it?	0	2
What Freemasonry is, what it has been, and what it ought to be	0	2
Five Dead men whom I knew when living. Sketches of Robert Owen, Joseph Mazzini, John Stuart Mill, Charles Sumner, and Ledru Rollin	0	4
Cromwell and Washington: a Contrast	0	6

The Queen against Bradlaugh and Besant. Verbatim Report of the Trial of Mr. Bradlaugh and Mrs. Besant for publishing Dr. Knowlton's pamphlet "Fruits of Philosophy: an Essay on the Population Question". With Portraits and Autographs of the two Defendants. Second Edition, with Appendix, containing the Judgments of Lords Justices Bramwell, Brett, and Cotton. Cloth, 5s.

Biography of C. Bradlaugh, by Adolph S. Headingley; with Appendix by W. Mawer. With photograph. The fullest and best biography of Mr. Bradlaugh yet published. **Reduced price 1s. 6d.**

Bradlaugh, Charles, Portraits of—

Taken by Messrs. Elliott and Fry, September, 1890.

	s.	d.
Cabinets (Full face, Profile, or Half length), with signature, each	2	0
(The three for 5s.)		
Carte-de-visite	1	0
Large Photo. (date about 1882), $23\frac{1}{2}$ by $18\frac{1}{2}$	4	0
Large Litho portrait	0	6

Atheistic Platform, The.—Part I, 96 pp. in cover, 6d. Contains: "What is the Use of Prayer?", by Annie Besant; "Mind considered as a Bodily Function", by Alice Bradlaugh; "The Gospel of Evolution", by Edward Aveling, D.Sc.; "England's Balance Sheet", by Charles Bradlaugh; "The Story of the Soudan", by Annie Besant; "Nature and the Gods", by A. B. Moss, 6d.

Part II, 96 pp., in cover, 6d. Contains: "Some Objections to Socialism", by Charles Bradlaugh; "Is Darwinism Atheistic?", by C. C. Cattell; "The Myth of the Resurrection", by Annie Besant; "Does Royalty Pay?", by George Standring; "The Curse of Capital", by E. B. Aveling; "Why should Atheists be Persecuted?", by Annie Besant, 6d.

Parts I and II bound together, in paper cover, 1s.

Aveling, Edward B., D.Sc., Fell. of Univ. Coll., London—

The Student's Darwin. A condensation of Darwin's works, 5s. ("*International Library of Science and Freethought,*" *see also page* 13.)

General Biology. A text-book for students and classes. Cloth. (2s.) **Reduced to 1s. 6d.**

Biological Discoveries and Problems, 1s.

Physiological Tables (2s.), **Reduced to 1s.** } Invaluable
Botanical Tables, 1s. } to students.

The Value of this Earthly Life (In reply to W. H. Mallock), 1s.

Aveling, Edward, and Eleanor Marx—

The Woman Question. 16 pp., crown 8vo, 2d.

"B.V." (*See* "*Thomson*" *page* 10)—

Ball, W. P.—

The Ten Commandments, 1d.

Religion in Schools, 2d.

Bellamy, Edward—

Looking Backward from A.D. 2000. Cloth, American edition, (3s.) [Sold in America at 6s.] **Reduced to 2s.**

Bradlaugh, Alice—

Mind considered as a Bodily Function, 16 pp., 1d.

Bradlaugh Bonner, Hypatia—

Life of Charles Bradlaugh (See *National Reformer*, p. 1).

Princess Vera, and other Stories. Contains:—Princess Vera; A Day's Adventures; How the World was Made; Tommy and I; A Children's Picnic. Attractively bound 1 0

	s.	d.
The Chemistry of Home (four lectures)	0	4
The Slave Struggle in America (four lectures)	0	4

Buechner, Prof. Ludwig, M.D.—

Mind in Animals. Translated, with the author's consent, by Annie Besant, 5s. ("*International Library of Science and Freethought*," *see also page* 13.)

The Influence of Heredity on Free Will. Translated from the German by Annie Besant. 2d.

Cooper, Robert—

The Holy Scriptures Analysed. With Life of Cooper written by C. Bradlaugh. 6d.

Eadon, Sam., M.A., M.D., Ph.D.—

The Plain Truth about the Land Question. 20 pp., demy 8vo, 2d.

Garrison, Prof. H. D.—

The Absence of Design in Nature, 2d.

Haeckel, Ernst—

The Pedigree of Man, and other Essays (illustrated with 80 woodcuts), translated from the German, with the author's consent, by Edward B. Aveling, D.Sc. 6s. ("*International Library of Science and Freethought*," *see also page* 13.)

Headingley, A. S.—

Biography of Charles Bradlaugh. With Appendix by W. Mawer (revised and enlarged), and photograph. The best account of Mr. Bradlaugh in existence. **Reduced to 1s. 6d.**

Hume, David—

The Natural History of Religion. Complete and Unexpurgated Edition. With the original Notes, and an Introduction by J. M. Robertson. Cloth, 1s.

On Miracles (The famous Essay). Edited by J. M. Wheeler. 3d.

Hunter, W. A.., M.A., LL.D., M.P.—

The Past and Present of the Heresy Laws. 3d.

"Indian Officer, An"—

The True Source of Christianity; or, a Voice from the Ganges. (Originally pubd. at 5s.) Paper, 1s.; cloth, 1s. 6d.

Ingersoll, Col. Robert G.—

	s.	d.
Orations: On the Gods, Thomas Paine, Humboldt, Heretics and Heresies, The Arraignment of the Church.		
In 1 vol., cloth, limp	1	6
Oration on the Gods	0	6
Do. Thomas Paine	0	3
Do. Humboldt	0	2
Heretics and Heresies	0	4
Arraignment of the Church	0	2
The Liberty of Man, Woman and Child	0	6
Orations, Popular Edition, 16 pages:		
Take a Road of Your Own. New edition	0	1
Divine Vivisection, or Hell	0	1
The Christian Religion	0	1

	s.	d.
The Ghosts (2 Parts, 32 pp.)	0	2
Thomas Paine the Republican	0	1
Is all of the Bible inspired? (2 Parts, 32 pp.) ..	0	2
The Mistakes of Moses (40 pp., in cover)	0	3
Saviors of the World	0	1
How Man makes Gods	0	1
Law, not God	0	1
What Must I Do to be Saved? (2 Parts, 32 pp.) ..	0	2
The Spirit of the Age	0	1
Human Liberty; or, Intellectual Development (2 Parts)	0	2
Which Way?	0	1
Series I: Take a Road of your own; Divine Vivisection, or Hell; The Christian Religion; The Ghosts; Thomas Paine, the Republican. In paper cover ..	0	6
Series II: Is all of the Bible Inspired? Mistakes of Moses; Saviors of the World; How Man Makes Gods; Law, not God. In paper cover	0	6
Series III: What Must I do to be Saved? The Spirit of the Age; Human Liberty, or Intellectual Development; Which Way? In paper cover ·	0	6

L'Estrange, Thos.—
The First Seven Alleged Persecutions, A.D. 64 to A.D. 235. 6d.
The Eucharist, 6d.

Levy, J. Hyam—
Wealthy and Wise. A Lecture introductory to the Study of Political Economy. (6d.) **Reduced to 3d.**

Major, A.—
A Few Objections to Spiritualism, whether it be true or false, 2d.

Mawer, W.—
Reasons why Blasphemy Prosecutions should be abolished. 2d.
The Latest Constitutional Struggle; a Diary of the Northampton Struggle, 2d.

Mitchell, Logan—
Religion in the Heavens; or, Mythology Unveiled. A Series of Lectures. Cloth, 2s. 6d.

Mr. Asgill's Defence upon his Expulsion from the House of Commons of Great Britain in 1707. With an Introduction; The Parliamentary Oath in Queen Anne's Reign; and a P.S. from Southey's Doctor. 3d. P. ½d. (*Leek "Bijou" Edition.*)

Northampton's Voice on the Royal Grants. Speeches by Messrs. Labouchere and Bradlaugh in the Debate in the House of Commons. 40 pp., demy 8vo, 1d.

Paine, Thomas—
Common Sense. With Introduction by C. Bradlaugh. 6d.

Perot, J. M. A.—
Man and God. Cloth, gilt (4s.). **Reduced to 2s. 6d.** (*Uniform with "International Library of Science and Freethought".*)

Robertson, John M. (Editor, *National Reformer*)—

Essays in History and Politics. Comprising: The Perversion of Scotland; Royalism; Toryism and Barbarism; Socialism and Malthusianism; Over-population. Crown 8vo. Neatly bound in limp cloth, 1s. 6d.

Discourses on Life and Letters. Comprising lectures delivered at South Place Institute on The Pleasures of Malignity, Culture and Action, Equality, Emotion in History, and The Religion of Shakspere; also "The Upshot of Hamlet, by Arthur Gigadibs". Demy 8vo. Neatly bound in limp cloth, 1s. 6d.

Christ and Krishna. Reprinted from the *National Reformer* with many important Additions and Corrections, and with an analytical table of contents and a copious index. 2s. paper, 2s. 6d. cloth.

	s.	d.
The Perversion of Scotland (Sins of the Scotch Church). Cloth	0	9
Thomas Paine. An Investigation. 40 pp., in paper cover	0	4
Royalism	0	4
The Upshot of Hamlet	0	6
Socialism and Malthusianism	0	2
Toryism and Barbarism	0	2
Practical Radicalism. 16 pp. in cover	0	1

"Scotulus"—

Blunders of Faith, 2d. (*National Reformer*, Sept.-Oct, 1891.)

Soury, Jules—

Jesus and the Gospels, and The Religion of Israel, 4s. ("*International Library of Science and Freethought*," *see also page* 13.)

Symes, Jos.—

	s.	d.
Christianity essentially a Persecuting Religion	0	2
Christianity and Slavery	0	2
Christianity at the Bar of Science	0	3
Hospitals and Dispensaries not of Christian Origin ..	0	1
Universal Despair	0	2
Philosophic Atheism	0	4
Man's Place in Nature	0	4
The Methodist Conference and Eternal Punishment ..	0	3
Debate on Atheism with Mr. St. Clair	1	0
Debate and eight essays, bound, cloth, neat	3	0

Thomson, James ("B. V.")—

Poems, Essays, and Fragments. Edited, with Preface by J. M. Robertson. With portrait of Thomson, now first published. Cloth, 6s.

Thursday Lectures at the Hall of Science (Complete edition)—

Containing: Anthropology (Charles Bradlaugh); Electricity, and The Physiology of Home (Mrs. A. Besant); Chemistry of Home, and The Slave Struggle in America (Mrs. H. Bradlaugh Bonner); The Plays of Shakspere, and Macbeth (Dr. E. B. Aveling). Cloth, 2s.

Volney, C. F.—

The Ruins of Empires. The celebrated Deistic work. With Plates of Ancient Zodiac. Cloth, 2s.

A SELECTION
FROM THE
PUBLICATIONS of the late THOMAS SCOTT.

Bound in cloth, **2s. 6d.** *per vol. P.* 4½*d. The* 7 *vols. together for* 18*s.* 6*d., post free.*

Vol. 1.

SIXTEEN SIXPENNY TRACTS by Messrs. J. Muir, D.C.L., Ed. Maitland, Thos. Scott; Revs. T. P. Kirkman, M.A., F.R.S., Dr. Sam. Hinds (Bp.), R. R. Suffield, J. W. Lake, etc.

On Church Pedigrees. How to complete the Reformation. A reply to the question, "Shall I seek Ordination in the Church of England?" Modern Protestantism. Is Death the End of all Things for Man? The Vatican Decrees, and the "Expostulation". Notes on Bishop Magee's "Pleadings for Christ." The Dean of Ripon on the Physical Resurrection of Jesus. The Athanasian Creed. The Advantages, Mental, and Moral, of a Faith Unchangeable, Certain, and Complete. Orthodoxy from the Hebrew Point of View (two parts). Religious and Moral Sentiments, Freely translated from Indian Writers. Additional Moral and Religious Passages, metrically rendered from the Sanskrit, with exact prose translations.

Vol. 2.

SIXTEEN SIXPENNY TRACTS by Annie Besant, Prof. F. W. Newman, W. Jevons, Diderot, A. D. Graham, J. Robertson, W. D. Conway, Rev. G. Wheelwright, etc.

On the Atonement. Criticism the Restoration of Christianity. On Eternal Torture. Remarks on Paley's Evidences. On this and the Other World. Cruelty and Christianity. The Book of Common Prayer, examined in the light of the present age (two parts). On the Relations of Theism to Pantheism, and on the Galla Religion. The Voysey case from an Heretical Standpoint. A Philosophical Conversation. Intellectual Liberty. Three Letters on the Voysey Judgment and the Christian Evidence Society's Lectures. Sacred History as a branch of Elementary Education.

Vol. 3.

TWENTY TRACTS, published at 7s. 9d., by Rev. Jas. Cranbrook, Ed. Maitland, W. H. Domville, Prof. Orelli, etc.

On the Hindrances to Progress in Theology; Human Depravity; The Tendencies of Modern Religious Thought; On Responsibility; God's Method of Government; Positive Religion, its basis and characteristics, Parts I, II, and III; On the Formation of Religious Opinions; On the Existence of Evil; Rights and

Duties of Parents; Primitive Church History; The Opinions of Prof. David S. Strauss; An Examination of some Recent Writings about Immortality; The Church and its Reform; Greece; How to Complete the Reformation; The Utilization of the Church Establishment; Dr. Carpenter at Sion College, or the View of Miracles taken by Men of Science; Irenæus, a leaf of primitive church history corrected and re-written.

Vol. 4 out of print.)

Vol. 5.

SIXTEEN PAMPHLETS, published at 8s. 4d., by Annie Besant, Prof. F. W. Newman, Chas. Bray, Matt. Macfie, Dr. Kuenen, etc.

The Religious Faculty: its relation to the other faculties and its perils. The Church and its Reform. On Prayer. Which Things are an Allegory. On Inspiration. Toleration. Against Hero-making. An Interior. A Neglected View of Education. On the Mediation and Salvation of Ecclesiastical Christianity. Reign of Law in Mind as in Matter (two parts). The "Confounded" Convert. Euthanasia. Christianity in a New Light. Three Notices of the Speaker's Commentary. Remarks on Paley's Evidences.

Tracts by Prof. Newman, Rev. E. M. Geldart, Rev. T. P. Kirkman and Dr. G. G. Zerffi.—Pub. at 8s. Viz.: Ancient Sacrifice; On the Relations of Theism to Pantheism, and on the Galla Religion; On this and the other World; the Controversy about Prayer; The Two Theisms; Anthropomorphism; The True Temptation of Jesus; Divergence of Calvinism from Pauline Doctrine; Ancient Hero Making in Religion; Religious Weakness of Protestantism; The Living God; Clerical Intemperance; Church Cursing and Atheism; On Church Pedigrees; On the Infidelity of Orthodoxy; Immanual Kant in his Relation to Modern History; Ethics and Aæsthetics; The Spontaneous Dissolution of Ancient Creeds.

Christian Myths and Legends.—Fifteen Tracts, pub. at 7s. By Dupuis, J. P. Hopps, J. S. Stuart Glennie, W. Jevons, A. Bernstein, W. G. Clarke, Dr. Hinds, Rev. F. Hare, etc.

Viz.: Christianity, a form of the great Solar Myth; The Serpent in Mythology; Origin of the Legends of Abraham, Isaac, and Jacob; Christ and Osiris; The Twelve Apostles; The Book of Common Prayer; Thirty-Nine Articles; Dr. Farrar's Life of Christ; A Review of a Pamphlet entitled: The Present Dangers of the Church of England; The Difficulties and Discouragements which attend the Study of the Scriptures; The Questions of Method as affecting Religious Thought; A Reply to the Question "Shall I seek Ordination in the Church of England?" The Dean of Ripon on the Physical Resurrection of Jesus.

The Pentateuch and the Book of Joshua.—In the Face of the Science and Moral Sense of our Age. By a Physician. Pub. in Parts at 6s. 6d.

CONTENTS:

POEMS.

ESSAYS.

FRAGMENTS.

LONDON:
A. AND H. BRADLAUGH BONNER,
63 FLEET STREET, E.C.

London: Printed by A. BONNER, 34 Bouverie Street and 63 Fleet Street, E.C.—December, 1892. (25x4810.)

1194696R0

Printed in Germany by
Amazon Distribution
GmbH, Leipzig